Communication in Pharmacy Practice

Communication in Pharmacy Practice

Special Issue Editors

Sofia Kälvemark Sporrong
Susanne Kaae

MDPI • Basel • Beijing • Wuhan • Barcelona • Belgrade

MDPI

Special Issue Editors

Sofia Kälvemark Sporrong
University of Copenhagen
Denmark

Susanne Kaae
University of Copenhagen
Denmark

Editorial Office
MDPI
St. Alban-Anlage 66
4052 Basel, Switzerland

This is a reprint of articles from the Special Issue published online in the open access journal *Pharmacy* (ISSN 2226-4787) from 2017 to 2018 (available at: https://www.mdpi.com/journal/pharmacy/special_issues/Communication_Pharmacy_Practice)

For citation purposes, cite each article independently as indicated on the article page online and as indicated below:

LastName, A.A.; LastName, B.B.; LastName, C.C. Article Title. *Journal Name* **Year**, *Article Number*, Page Range.

ISBN 978-3-03897-576-2 (Pbk)
ISBN 978-3-03897-577-9 (PDF)

Contents

About the Special Issue Editors

Sofia Kälvemark Sporrong is a social scientist by training, which included communication science. She has for many years worked in different positions within the field of pharmacy and for the last 11 years as associate professor in social pharmacy (in Sweden and Denmark). Much of Sofia Kälvemark Sporrong's research deals with pharmacy practice and the role of pharmacists and pharmacies, with focus onprofessional ethics and communication.

Susanne Kaae is a trained pharmacist and worked for six years as a community pharmacist before joining academia. Her special research interests include pharmacy practice, i.e., the implementation of cognitive services in general and in relation to at-the-counter communication. Susanne Kaae has published several articles in the area and has been in charge of teaching activities for pharmacy students and staff in pharmacy communication along with being the principal investigator of several pharmacy projects engaged in investigating pharmacy communication.

Using a consistent approach to patient-centered care specific to pharmacy is advocated to assist pharmacists in fulfilling their professional responsibilities to a patient. The Pharmacists Patient Care Process (PPCP), supported by 13 national pharmacy organizations and the Accreditation Council for Pharmacy Education, is a model to optimize patient health and medication outcomes [32,33].

3. Pharmacists and Patient-Centered Communication

A patient-centered approach to communication is to acknowledge the whole person, their personality, life history, and social structure in order to develop a shared understanding of the problem, the goals of treatment, and the barriers to that treatment and wellness. With the practice of pharmacy expanding beyond the traditional medication dispensing roles, pharmacists must become competent in patient-centered communication. Expectations for professional communication in the 2016 Accreditation Council for Pharmacy Education (ACPE) guidelines for the Doctor of Pharmacy degree are found in Standard 3 (Approach to Practice and Care) and Appendix 1 [33]. There are many published articles on patient-centered communication in healthcare, but relatively few are specific to pharmacy. While the majority of publications are oriented towards physicians, three excellent examples with applicability to pharmacy practice are detailed below.

The Calgary-Cambridge guide was developed for use in medical education to teach and assess patient-centered communication [34,35]. It is widely used in over 60% of medical schools in the U.K. and is the second most-used guide in North America for teaching and assessing professional communication [36]. The guide's framework corresponds to the structured process of a medical interview (initiating the session, gathering information, physical examination, explanation and planning, and closing the session) and consists of 71 communication skills and behaviors [36,37]. Although lengthy, the authors of the guide meant for it to be comprehensive but modifiable depending upon the nature of the medical encounter. In a recent study, the applicability of the Calgary-Cambridge guide to assess pharmacist–patient communication was analyzed. Eleven pharmacists representing a variety of settings (e.g., community, primary care, and hospital) were observed and recorded during a total of 18 patient consultations. It was noted that many of the communication skills on the Calgary-Cambridge guide were represented during the pharmacist-led consultations and highlighted areas in which pharmacists may need more training [38].

The Four Habits Model is another framework for patient-centered communication also designed for physicians. It contains 23 clinician communication behaviors organized into four "habits": invest in the beginning, elicit the patient's perspective, demonstrate empathy, and invest in the end [39–41]. This model provides explicit examples of how to create rapport, elicit patient concerns and ideas, explore the illness experience, and convey empathy and can be helpful to other health care professionals wishing to improve their communication skills. The Four Habits Model was used as a foundation for the development of the Patient-Centered Communication Tools (PaCT) to measure pharmacy students' communication skills [42].

The PaCT includes 23 clinical communication skills categorized into five "tools" (establish a connection, explore and integrate the patient's perspective, demonstrate interest and empathy, collaborate and educate, and communicate with finesse). Each individual communication skill is scored using a five-point Likert scale (unsatisfactory, needs improvement, adequate, capable, and proficient). When comparing the PaCT and the Four Habits Model on the same performance, scores were significantly correlated. According to the authors, the instrument demonstrated significant face, content, construct, and test–retest validity [42].

4. Best Practices

Pharmacists provide patient care with varied responsibilities in a variety of practice settings. Pharmacist's clinical expertise and access to patients, particularly in the retail setting, place them in a unique position to improve health outcomes of individual patients and populations alike. In many cases, retail pharmacies are the primary point of health care access in rural communities [43].

Preface to "Communication in Pharmacy Practice"

Communication is a crucial part of pharmacy practice. It is through high quality communication that patients' needs can be assessed and information, education, and advice given, in this way ensuring a rational use of medicine. In addition, effective inter-professional communication with other health care professionals is central for positive health outcomes of patient treatments. Communication is a complex area, dealing not only with the transmission of content, but also intrapersonal relationships, social processes, etc. Through research in pharmacy practice communication we can help develop skills, tools, and processes to make patient encounters and other encounters as good as possible. This book provides an insight into the research being conducted in the field right now and thus helps to highlight specific areas in pharmacy communication that need attention in order to move further.

Sofia Kälvemark Sporrong, Susanne Kaae
Special Issue Editors

pharmacy

Editorial

Trends in Pharmacy Practice Communication Research

Sofia Kälvemark Sporrong and Susanne Kaae *

Department of Pharmacy, Faculty of Health and Medical Sciences, University of Copenhagen,
2100 Copenhagen, Denmark; sofia.sporrong@sund.ku.dk
* Correspondence: susanne.kaae@sund.ku.dk

Received: 30 November 2018; Accepted: 4 December 2018; Published: 5 December 2018

Communication is a crucial aspect of pharmacy practice—in community pharmacies and in other health care settings. The communicative role of pharmacists and other pharmacy staff is an important part of, e.g., dispensing, pharmaceutical care, and other counselling services provided to patients. It is through appropriate communication that patients' needs can be assessed and information, education, and advice can be given, in this way working towards a rational use of medicine. In addition, effective inter-professional communication with other health care professionals is central to health outcomes of patient treatments.

Communication is a highly complex area, dealing with not only the transmission of content but also interpersonal relationships, social processes, etc. Barriers and facilitators to communication are numerous, including psychological, socio-economic, cognitive, and environmental factors. Research in pharmacy practice communication can enable the development of the skills, tools, and processes to make patient encounters and other interactions as optimal as possible.

The Special Issue 'Communication in Pharmacy Practice' was thus launched to help improve communication practices by increasing our knowledge on different aspects of communication in pharmacy practice. From the articles we have received for this Special Issue, it is clear that pharmacy communication is a subject that is investigated globally and from many perspectives. The overall pharmacy communicational themes investigated and discussed include the following: Communication between health care professionals and elements of communication between pharmacists and patients, in the context of both prescription and OTC medicines; and factors impacting these types of communication. A central focus in this Special Issue is the specific need to further develop direct, face-to-face communication between pharmacy staff and patients/consumers.

With regard to communication between pharmacists and patients, the need to focus counselling on the patient's perspective is emphasized by several authors. When patients are involved in their own care and understand their plan of care, they are better able to manage their conditions. Naughton writes [1]:

> *Only when pharmacists have a holistic understanding of an individual patient, including their experience of illness and medication, can they effectively assess appropriateness, safety, efficacy, and adherence to medications and develop realistic treatment plans.*

This is supported by Hawes, who discusses how pharmacists' exploration of cultural aspects, including health and illness beliefs of the patient along with the patient's attitudes and practices, should be the basis for counselling. In her article about patient education on oral anticoagulation, she concludes that *"the teaching should be tailored to each patient"* [2].

As part of this patient-centred approach, Olufemi-Yusuf et al. explored patients' perceptions of asthma, asthma treatment, and pharmacist roles in order to optimize the design of patient-centred interventions in pharmacy care and improve care for asthma patients [3].

Other authors also investigated aspects influencing pharmacy staff-patient communication such as perception of roles, organizational aspects including the need for sufficient time, privacy, and use of adequate registration systems, and the importance of education for pharmacy staff [4–6].

Some specific technologies to develop patient–pharmacist communication are presented in this issue, e.g., pictograms, automated phone calls, and the use of videos to communicate information on inhaler techniques [7–9]. For example, Kanji et al. studied pictograms as a technique for pharmacy communication in the presence of language barriers and identified several challenges in patients' understanding of the pictograms [7].

> These signs [pictograms] on their own might not be enough to guarantee appropriate patient information and the expected medication usage.

A study on inhaler instruction videos found that, in addition to watching videos, participants asked for feedback from health care professionals to check their inhalation technique. Hence, it seems that technologies used on their own appear often to be of limited support for patients [9].

One basis for improving pharmacist–patient communication is to determine how the communication between the pharmacists and other health care professionals is conducted. The study by De Bock et al. investigating the implementation of medication reviews across hospital and community pharmacy sections found that discharge notes from hospital to community pharmacists facilitated pharmaceutical care counselling in the community pharmacy [10]. Noss et al. also highlighted the importance of adequate inter-professional communication for the monitoring or use of alternative therapy agents to avoid drug–drug interactions [11].

There are many challenges to communication in pharmacy practice, and many are highlighted in this Special Issue on pharmacy communication. Some appropriate and sustainable solutions are described, but in many cases, these seem to remain on a theoretical level. Seubert et al. tried to overcome this gap by developing specific tools for community pharmacies to overcome identified challenges at the pharmacy counter [12]. The tools were based on the existing literature and other types of empirical material; however, they still need to be implemented in practice.

Many relevant pharmacy practice communicational aspects have now been added to our knowledge, but even more research is needed. This is especially true for research dealing with how to overcome identified communication challenges in practice to ultimately help patients achieve better treatment outcomes.

Funding: This research received no external funding.

Conflicts of Interest: The authors declare no conflict of interest.

References

1. Naughton, C. Patient-Centered Communication. *Pharmacy* **2018**, *6*, 18. [CrossRef] [PubMed]
2. Hawes, E.M. Patient Education on Oral Anticoagulation. *Pharmacy* **2018**, *6*, 34. [CrossRef] [PubMed]
3. Olufemi-Yusuf, D.T.; Gabriel, S.B.; Makhinova, T.; Guirguis, L.M. "Being in Control of My Asthma Myself" Patient Experience of Asthma Management: A Qualitative Interpretive Description. *Pharmacy* **2018**, *6*, 121. [CrossRef] [PubMed]
4. Seubert, L.J.; Whitelaw, K.; Boeni, F.; Hattingh, L.; Watson, M.C.; Clifford, R.M. Barriers and Facilitators for Information Exchange during Over-The-Counter Consultations in Community Pharmacy: A Focus Group Study. *Pharmacy* **2017**, *5*, 65. [CrossRef] [PubMed]
5. Akazawa, M.; Mikami, A.; Tamura, Y.; Yanagi, N.; Yamamura, S.; Ogata, H. Establishing a Pharmacy-Based Patient Registry System: A Pilot Study for Evaluating Pharmacist Intervention for Patients with Long-Term Medication Use. *Pharmacy* **2018**, *6*, 12. [CrossRef] [PubMed]
6. Chinwong, S.; Chinwong, D. A National Survey of Community Pharmacists on Smoking Cessation Services in Thailand. *Pharmacy* **2018**, *6*, 101. [CrossRef] [PubMed]

7. Kanji, L.; Xu, S.; Cavaco, A. Assessing the Understanding of Pharmaceutical Pictograms among Cultural Minorities: The Example of Hindu Individuals Communicating in European Portuguese. *Pharmacy* **2018**, *6*, 22. [CrossRef]

8. Bones, M.; Nunlee, M. Uncertainty and Motivation to Seek Information from Pharmacy Automated Communications. *Pharmacy* **2018**, *6*, 47. [CrossRef] [PubMed]

9. Von Schantz, S.; Katajavuori, N.; Juppo, A.M. The Use of Video Instructions in Patient Education Promoting Correct Technique for Dry Powder Inhalers: An Investigation on Inhaler-Naive Individuals. *Pharmacy* **2018**, *6*, 106. [CrossRef] [PubMed]

10. De Bock, L.; Tommelein, E.; Baekelandt, H.; Maes, W.; Boussery, K.; Somers, A. The Introduction of a Full Medication Review Process in a Local Hospital: Successes and Barriers of a Pilot Project in the Geriatric Ward. *Pharmacy* **2018**, *6*, 21. [CrossRef] [PubMed]

11. Noss, K.; Aguero, S.M.; Reinaker, T. Assessment of Prescribing and Monitoring Habits for Patients Taking an Antiarrhythmic and Concomitant QTc-Prolonging Antibiotic. *Pharmacy* **2017**, *5*, 61. [CrossRef] [PubMed]

12. Seubert, L.J.; Whitelaw, K.; Hattingh, L.; Watson, M.C.; Clifford, R.M. Development of a Theory-Based Intervention to Enhance Information Exchange during Over-The-Counter Consultations in Community Pharmacy. *Pharmacy* **2018**, *6*, 117. [CrossRef] [PubMed]

pharmacy

MDPI

Concept Paper
Patient-Centered Communication

Cynthia A. Naughton

School of Pharmacy, College of Health Professions, North Dakota State University Fargo, ND 58108, USA;
Cynthia.Naughton@ndsu.edu; Tel.: +1-701-231-8487

Received: 2 January 2018; Accepted: 9 February 2018; Published: 13 February 2018

Abstract: As the population ages, morbidity and mortality associated with chronic disease will increase. Some patient-centered improvements have been made in health care services, but optimal health has not been fully realized. Only when pharmacists have a holistic understanding of an individual patient, including their experience of illness and medication, can they effectively assess appropriateness, safety, efficacy, and adherence to medications and develop realistic treatment plans. When patients are involved in their care, they are better able to manage complex chronic conditions by understanding and adhering to their plan of care. Pharmacists can enable patients to participate fully using patient-centered communication. There are relatively few published articles on patient-centered communication specific to pharmacists, but the Calgary-Cambridge guide and Four Habits model have applicability to pharmacy practice. The Patient-Centered Communication Tools (PaCT), created for use in pharmacy education and loosely based on the Four Habits model, can assist pharmacists in developing their patient-centered communication skills. Lastly, best practices for patient-centered communication in pharmacy practice are described.

Keywords: patient-centered communication; Calgary-Cambridge guide; four habits model; Patient-Centered Communication Tools (PaCT); communication models; pharmacists

1. Introduction

In 2007, the Institute for Healthcare Improvement launched its Triple Aim to focus on improving the patient's experience of care, achieving better health outcomes, and reducing the per capita cost of health care [1]. A key reason for establishing the Triple Aim was that health care costs in the United States were skyrocketing without any apparent improvement in the overall health of its citizens [2]. A decade later, the United States continues to spend more on health care with poorer health care outcomes compared to 10 other developed countries [3]. Chronic disease claims 86% of the total annual expenditures for healthcare in the U.S. and accounts for seven of the top ten causes of death in American adults [4,5]. As the population ages, the burden of chronic disease morbidity and mortality will increase unless a more holistic approach to health is adopted.

Health, as defined by the World Health Organization, is "a state of complete physical, mental, and social well-being and not merely the absence of disease or infirmary" [6]. There are many factors that influence the state of a person's health. Generally known as Determinants of Health, these factors can be grouped into five major categories (Table 1): (1) clinical health care; (2) genetic vulnerability; (3) socio-economic characteristics; (4) environmental and physical influences; and (5) individual health behaviors such as tobacco use, diet and exercise, and alcohol and drug use [7]. Only the first two determinates, clinical health care and genetic vulnerability, have a direct biological connection to our health. Socio-economic characteristics such as educational level, employment, income, marital status, and ethnicity along with environmental and physical influences such as place of residence, quality of air and water, buildings, spaces, and transportation are often referred to as the Social Determinants of Health. In short, the Social Determinants of Health are the conditions in which people are born, grow, live, work, and age [8]. The relative contribution of each health determinant towards overall health varies depending upon the disease, population, and geographical region. Typically, health care services and genetics only account for 10–20% of a person's health, whereas the largest contribution comes from the Social Determinants of Health as well as individual health behavior [9,10]. Therefore, rather than investing more dollars into healthcare services, factors that play a greater role in health are deserving of attention [11,12].

Table 1. Determinants of Health.

Determinants of Health [7]
clinical health care services
genetic vulnerability
socio-economic characteristics
physical environment
individual health behavior

Fortunately, modern medicine is moving away from a purely biomedical model of care with an emphasis on disease and its associated biological components (signs, symptoms, and laboratory tests) to a biopsychosocial model. The biopsychosocial model of care is a holistic framework to describe and explain how illness is the result of the interplay of biological, psychological, and social factors plus individual health-related behaviors (Figure 1) [13]. Recognizing, understanding, and responding to all factors that affect health requires the healthcare provider to integrate the biological aspects of the disease with the psychological and social aspects of the patient. The goal of this model is to develop a patient-centered care plan that is realistic in order to achieve the best possible health outcomes.

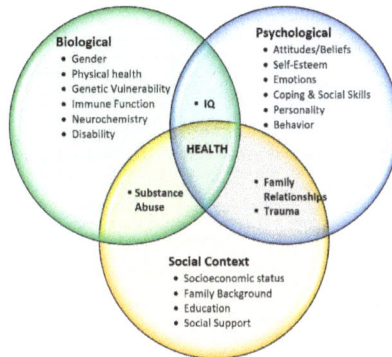

Figure 1. Biopsychosocial Model of Disease and Illness.

Another major improvement made in health care services delivery was the adoption of patient-centered care. The Institute of Medicine defines patient-centered care as *"a partnership among practitioners, patients, and their families ensures that decisions respect patients' wants, needs, and preferences, and that patients have the education and support they need to make decisions and participate in their own care, as well as participate in quality improvement efforts"* [14]. The term patient- and family-centered care acknowledges the importance of families on the health of patients of all ages in all settings of care as well as being essential allies for quality and safety [15]. In recent years, person-centered care has emerged as a new term that encompasses the entirety of a person's needs and preferences (biopsychosocial) beyond just the pathophysiology of the disease (biomedical) [16]. While the practice of pharmacy employs medications as its primary means of health care intervention, the professional and ethical responsibility of pharmacists are clearly more holistic. Pharmacists, in their Code of Ethics, promise to place the "well-being of the patient at the center and consider their stated needs as well as those defined by science" [17].

When patients are more involved in their care, they are better able to manage complex chronic conditions by understanding and incorporating their plan of care, are more likely to feel comfortable communicating their concerns and seeking appropriate assistance, have reduced anxiety and stress, and have shorter lengths of stay [18]. Patients involved in their own care also have a safer care experience [19]. Therefore, all healthcare providers have a professional and ethical responsibility to encourage patients to express their concerns. The effectiveness of patient-provider communication is not always optimal, however. For instance, early studies on patient recall of medical information showed that 40–80% of medical information provided by healthcare practitioners is forgotten immediately and nearly half of what is remembered is remembered incorrectly [20]. It is not surprising then that patient adherence to treatment recommendations for chronic disease varies between 37 and 87%, and only 50% of all prescription drugs are taken as prescribed [21,22]. To enable patients to participate fully in their care, healthcare professionals need to facilitate optimal information exchange using patient-centered communication.

2. Patient-Centered Communication

The core concepts of patient-centered communication include "(1) eliciting and understanding patient perspectives (e.g., concerns, ideas, expectations, needs, feelings, and functioning), (2) understanding the patient within his or her unique psychosocial and cultural contexts, and (3) reaching a shared understanding of patient problems and the treatments that are concordant with patient values" [23]. Although health care providers acknowledge that patients should play a more participative role to ensure they are informed about their care, several barriers to communication exist.

The first barrier to patient-centered communication is a perceived lack of time. Practitioners may feel they lack enough time to listen, explain, and negotiate with the patient. Sometimes patients are not able to fully articulate their initial concerns before being interrupted by the provider. In a study involving physicians and agenda-setting with patients, patients were interrupted after an average of 23.1 s [24]. Studies show, however, that patients rarely take more than 2–3 min to share their whole story when asked open-ended questions and are not interrupted [25,26]. Shared decision-making also takes time but on average only an additional 10% of the entire duration, i.e., 2 min for a 20 min encounter [27].

The second barrier relates to negotiating evidence-based treatment plans with patients. Evidence found in the literature to support treatment is often "disease-oriented" with reference to lab values, plaque size, or blood pressure; all of which are markers for disease outcomes rather than actual outcomes. Most patients have no frame of reference for the impact of those numbers. "Patient-Oriented Evidence that Matters" (POEMs); on the other hand, refer to outcomes that patients care about and can relate to [28]. Examples of POEMs include outcomes related to morbidity (symptoms), daily functioning, mortality, cost, and quality of life as defined by the patient [29]. Another consideration is that evidence-based medicine corresponds to population data and may not reflect the needs and preferences of individual patients. Rather than the rule, evidence-based medicine should only be a guide used along with provider expertise and the patient's goals, values, and preferences [30].

Finally, provider attitude can be a barrier to effective patient-centered communication. Traditionally, pharmacists have been educated as drug experts and have been taught about the pharmacologic and pharmacotherapeutic properties of a drug to meet a patient's medication-related needs and promote medication compliance [31]. Scientific drug knowledge is clearly important, but a patient-centered approach requires knowledge of the patient and their individual experience of illness and medication. Only after incorporating a holistic understanding of the patient's beliefs, attitudes, and behaviors towards health can pharmacists assess the appropriateness of indication, effectiveness, safety, and adherence to medications. In other words, "the pharmacist must maintain a high level of humility about their scientific knowledge so that the knowledge of the patient can be recognized" [31].

Regardless of practice setting, patient-centered communication such as openness, active listening, and plain speaking are three general skills in which all pharmacists should become competent.

4.1. Openness

Openness is demonstrated by making oneself available, not only with time but also by the manner in which the patient and their perspectives are acknowledged [31]. A curt greeting and appearing rushed or inconvenienced communicates to patients that their time and concerns are not important. Rather, identifying a patient by name in a warm greeting, offering a smile, being attentive, and maintaining friendly eye contact goes a long way in establishing rapport and building a relationship.

4.2. Active Listening

Attentive body language (e.g., open posture, eye contact, and interested expression), eliciting verbal (e.g., "uh-huh" and "I see") and nonverbal (e.g., nodding) encouragement, paraphrasing to confirm understanding, and keeping questions to a minimum demonstrates to the patient a genuine interest in them on the part of the pharmacist. Questions designed to collect patient perspectives should be open-ended questions using the words "what" or "how" instead of those that can be answered with "yes" or "no." Asking open-ended questions provide critical insight into the patient's experience of illness, yield critical information to promote medical adherence, and facilitate shared decision making.

4.3. Speaking Plainly

Health literacy is the degree to which individuals have the capacity to obtain, process, and understand basic health information needed to make appropriate health decisions [44]. Only 12% of adults have proficient health literacy according to the National Assessment of Adult Literacy. In other words, 9 out of 10 adults may lack the skills needed to manage their health and prevent disease. It is helpful to consider all patients as having low heath literacy and use appropriate communication techniques that ensure understanding. At a minimum, slow down and speak in plain, non-medical language! Allow time for patients and families to ask questions by asking "What questions do you have?" instead of "Do you have any questions?" Check the understanding of a patient by asking them to restate it in their own words, not just repeat it, to ensure the message is understood.

Best practices of patient-centered communication in medical encounters have been gleaned from empiric evidence and patient satisfaction data [45]. The best practices are organized into six functions with corresponding communication skills for each function. Although the framework is geared towards the physician–patient relationship, many of the communication concepts are transferrable to patient encounters involving pharmacists (Table 2).

Table 2. Best practices for Pharmacist Provided Patient-Centered Communication [a].

Goal	Pharmacist Responsibility	Communication Skills
Foster the Relationship	Build rapport Appear open Demonstrate respect Demonstrate caring and commitment Acknowledge feelings and emotions	Greet patient warmly and appropriately Maintain eye contact Show interest Listen actively Express empathy
Gather Information	Determine purpose of encounter Discover biomedical perspective (disease) Understand patient perspective (illness)	Ask open-ended questions Allow patient to complete responses Clarify and summarize information Explore impact of illness on patient
Provide Information	Identify patient informational needs Share information Overcome health literacy barriers	Speak plainly and avoid jargon Use "Patient-Oriented Evidence that Matters" (POEMs) Encourage questions Check for understanding
Share Decision-Making	Identify patient goals Outline collaborative treatment plan	Explore patient preferences Identify barriers to treatment choices Negotiate agreement
Enable Treatment Success	Assess the patient's capacity for self-management Arrange for needed support Advocate for and assist patient with health system	Summarize treatment plan Elicit patient understanding Discuss follow-up

[a] Adapted from King A, Hoppe RB. Best practice for patient-centered communication: A narrative review. JGME. 2013;5(3):385–393.

5. Conclusions

Pharmacists have a professional and ethical responsibility to consider the needs and situation of the patient holistically, in the psychological and social realms as well as the biological realm. Pharmacists can employ practical strategies to foster patient-centered communication that engages patients to participate in their care and facilitates in the development of a trusting pharmacist–patient relationship, leading to a shared understanding of the entire problem, the goals of treatment, and the barriers to wellness. Only then can a realistic plan of care be developed and followed, and in turn increase the likelihood of improved health outcomes.

Conflicts of Interest: The author declare no conflict of interest.

References

1. Institute for Healthcare Improvement. Triple Aim for Populations. Available online: http://www.ihi.org/Topics/TripleAim/Pages/Overview.aspx (accessed on 31 December 2017).
2. Institute for Healthcare Improvement. The IHI Triple Aim. Available online: http://www.ihi.org/Engage/Initiatives/TripleAim/Pages/default.aspxReference (accessed on 31 December 2017).
3. Commonwealth Fund. Mirror, Mirror 2017: International Comparison Reflects Flaws and Opportunities for Better U.S. Health Care. Available online: http://www.commonwealthfund.org/~/media/files/publications/fund-report/2017/jul/schneider_mirror_mirror_2017.pdf (accessed on 31 December 2017).
4. CDC. Chronic Disease Overview. Available online: https://www.cdc.gov/chronicdisease/overview/index.htm (accessed on 31 December 2017).
5. CDC. Health, United States. 2015. Available online: https://www.cdc.gov/nchs/data/hus/hus15.pdf#019 (accessed on 31 December 2017).
6. World Health Organization. Constitution of the World Health Organization. 1946. Available online: http://www.who.int/governance/eb/who_constitution_en.pdf (accessed on 31 December 2017).
7. McGinnis, J.M.; Foege, W.H. Actual causes of death in the United States. *JAMA* **1993**, *270*, 2207–2212. [CrossRef] [PubMed]
8. World Health Organization. What Are the Social Determinants of Health? Available online: http://www.who.int/social_determinants/sch_definition/en/ (accessed on 31 December 2017).

9. Gnadinger, T. Health Policy Brief: The Relative Contribution of Multiple Determinants to Health Outcomes. *Health Aff.* **2014**. [CrossRef]

10. Remington, P.; Catlin, B.; Gennuso, K. The County Health Rankings: Rationale and Methods. *Popul. Health Metr.* **2015**, *13*. [CrossRef] [PubMed]

11. Tarlov, A.R. Public policy frameworks for improving population health. *Ann. N. Y. Acad. Sci.* **1999**, *896*, 291–293. [CrossRef]

12. Adler, N.E.; Cutler, D.M.; Fielding, J.E.; Galea, S.; Glymour, M.M.; Koh, H.K.; Satcher, D. *Addressing Social Determinants of Health and Health Disparities*; Discussion Paper; Vital Directions for Health and Health Care Series; National Academy of Medicine: Washington, DC, USA, 2016. Available online: https://nam.edu/wp-content/uploads/2016/09/Addressing-Social-Determinants-of-Health-and-Health-Disparities.pdf (accessed on 31 December 2017).

13. Inerney, S.J.M. Introducing the biopsychosocial model for good medicine and good doctors. *Br. Med. J.* **2018**, *324*, 1533.

14. Committee on Quality of Health Care in America. *Crossing the Quality Chasm: A New Health System for the 21st Century*; Institute of Medicine, National Academy Press: Washington, DC, USA, 2001.

15. Institute for Patient- and Family-Centered Care. Available online: http://www.ipfcc.org/about/pfcc.html (accessed on 31 December 2017).

16. Goodwin, C. Person-centered care: A definition and essential elements. *J. Am. Geriatr. Soc.* **2016**, *64*, 15–18.

17. American Pharmacists Association. Code of Ethics for Pharmacists. Available online: http://www.pharmacist.com/code-ethics (accessed on 12 February 2018).

18. Bergeson, S.C.; Dean, J.D. A systems approach to patient-centered care. *J. Am. Med. Assoc.* **2006**, *296*, 2848–2851. [CrossRef] [PubMed]

19. Doyle, C.; Lennox, L.; Bell, D. A systematic review of evidence on the links between patient experience and clinical safety and effectiveness. *BMJ Open* **2013**, *3*, 1–18. [CrossRef] [PubMed]

20. McGuire, L.C. Remembering what the doctor said: Organization and adults' memory for medical information. *Exp. Aging Res.* **1996**, *22*, 403–428. [CrossRef] [PubMed]

21. Cantrell, C.R.; Priest, J.L.; Cook, C.L.; Fincham, J.; Burch, S.P. Adherence to treatment guidelines and therapeutic regimens: A U.S. claims-based benchmark of a commercial population. *Popul. Health Manag.* **2011**, *14*, 33–41. [CrossRef] [PubMed]

22. Brown, M.T.; Russell, J.K. Medication adherence: WHO cares? *Mayo Clin. Proc.* **2011**, *86*, 304–314. [CrossRef] [PubMed]

23. Epstein, R.M.; Street, R.L., Jr. *Patient-Centered Communication in Cancer Care: Promoting Healing and Reducing Suffering*; National Cancer Institute/National Institutes of Health Publication: Bethesda, MD, USA, 2007; Publication 07-6225. Available online: https://healthcaredelivery.cancer.gov/pcc/monograph.html (accessed on 12 February 2018).

24. Marvel, M.K.; Epstein, R.M.; Flowers, K.; Beckman, H.B. Soliciting the patient's agenda: Have we improved? *JAMA* **1999**, *281*, 283–287. [CrossRef] [PubMed]

25. Beckman, H.B.; Frankel, R.M. The effect of physician behavior on the collection of data. *Ann. Intern. Med.* **1984**, *101*, 692–696. [CrossRef] [PubMed]

26. Nelson, A.M. *Improving Patient Satisfaction Now: How to Earn Patient and Payer Loyalty*; Jones & Bartlett Learning: Burlington, MA, USA, 1997.

27. IHI Open School. PFC101: Introduction to Patient Centered Care. Available online: http://app.ihi.org/lmsspa/#/6cb1c614-884b-43ef-9abd-d90849f183d4/8eb52137-21d7-4b30-afcd-fd781de6d6d5 (accessed on 31 December 2017).

28. Evidence-Based Practice and Information Mastery: POEMs and DOEs. Available online: https://wilkes.libguides.com/c.php?g=191942&p=1266516 (accessed on 31 December 2017).

29. Holzmueller, C.G.; Wu, A.W.; Pronovost, P.J. A Framework for encouraging patient engagement in medical decision making. *J. Patient Saf.* **2012**, *8*, 161–164. [CrossRef] [PubMed]

30. Price, A.I.; Djulbegovic, B.; Biswas, R.; Chattergee, P. Evidence-based medicine meets person-centered care: A collaborative perspective on the relationship. *J. Eval. Clin. Pract.* **2015**, *21*, 1047–1051. [CrossRef] [PubMed]

31. De Oliveira, D.R.; Shoemaker, S.J. Achieving patient centeredness in pharmacy practice: Openness and the pharmacist's natural attitude. *J. Am. Pharm. Assoc.* **2006**, *46*, 56–66. [CrossRef]

32. The Pharmacist Patient Care Process. Available online: https://jcpp.net/wp-content/uploads/2016/03/PatientCareProcess-with-supporting-organizations.pdf (accessed on 31 December 2017).
33. Accreditation Council for Pharmacy Education. Accreditation Standards and Guidelines for the Professional Program in Pharmacy Leading to the Doctor of Pharmacy Degree. Available online: http://ccapp-accredit.ca/wp-content/uploads/2016/01/CCAPP_accred_standards_degree_2014.pdf (accessed on 12 February 2018).
34. Kurtz, S.M.; Silverman, J.; Draper, J. *Teaching and Learning Communication Skills in Medicine*, 2nd ed.; Radcliffe Medical: Oxford, UK; San Francisco, CA, USA, 2005.
35. Silverman, J.; Kurtz, S.M.; Draper, J. *Skills for Communicating with Patients*, 2nd ed.; Radcliffe Medical: Oxford, UK; San Francisco, CA, USA, 2005.
36. Silverman, J. The Calgary-Cambridge guides: The 'teenage years'. *Clin. Teach.* **2007**, *4*, 87–93. [CrossRef]
37. Silverman, J.; Kurtz, S.; Draper, J. *Skills for Communicating with Patients*, 3rd ed.; CRC Press, Taylor & Francis: Boca Raton, Fl, USA, 2013.
38. Greenhill, N.; Anderson, C.; Avery, A.; Pilnick, A. Analysis of pharmacist-patient communication using the Calgary-Cambridge guide. *Patient Educ. Couns.* **2011**, *83*, 423–431. [CrossRef] [PubMed]
39. Stein, T.; Frankel, R.M.; Krupat, E. Enhancing clinician communication skills in a large health care organization: A longitudinal case study. *Patient Educ. Couns.* **2005**, *58*, 4–12. [CrossRef] [PubMed]
40. Krupat, E.; Frankel, R.M.; Stein, T.; Irish, J. The four habits coding scheme: Validation of an instrument to assess clinicians' communication behavior. *Patient Educ. Couns.* **2006**, *62*, 4–12. [CrossRef] [PubMed]
41. Frankel, R.M.; Stein, T.M. Getting the most out of the clinical encounter: The four habits model. *J. Med. Pract. Manag.* **2001**, *16*, 184–191. [CrossRef]
42. Grice, G.R.; Gattas, N.M.; Prosser, T.; Voorhees, M.; Kebodeaux, C.; Tiemeier, A.; Berry, T.M.; Wilson, A.G.; Mann, J.; Juang, P. Design and validation of patient-centered communication tools (PaCT) to measure students' communication skills. *AJPE* **2017**, *81*, 33–48. [CrossRef] [PubMed]
43. Traynor, A.P.; Sorensen, T.D.; Larson, T. The main street pharmacy: Becoming an endangered species. *Rural MN J.* **2007**, *2*, 83–100.
44. HRSA. Health Literacy. Available online: https://www.hrsa.gov/about/organization/bureaus/ohe/health-literacy/index.html (accessed on 31 December 2017).
45. King, A.; Hoppe, R.B. Best practice for patient-centered communication: A narrative review. *JGME* **2013**, *5*, 385–393. [CrossRef] [PubMed]

pharmacy

MDPI

Article

Patient Education on Oral Anticoagulation

Emily M Hawes [1,2]

[1]   University of North Carolina Eshelman School of Pharmacy, Chapel Hill, NC 27514, USA;
       emily_hawes@med.unc.edu
[2]   University of North Carolina School of Medicine, Chapel Hill, NC 27599, USA

Received: 29 March 2018; Accepted: 19 April 2018; Published: 20 April 2018

Abstract: Given the potential harm associated with anticoagulant use, patient education is often provided as a standard of care and emphasized across healthcare settings. Effective anticoagulation education involves face-to-face interaction with a trained professional who ensures that the patient understands the risks involved, the precautions that should be taken, and the need for regular monitoring. The teaching should be tailored to each patient, accompanied with written resources and utilize the teach-back method. It can be incorporated in a variety of pharmacy practice settings, including in ambulatory care clinics, hospitals, and community pharmacies.

Keywords: pharmacy; anticoagulation; patient education; counseling; communication

1. Introduction

Anticoagulants, which are considered "high alert medications," can often lead to adverse drug events in the inpatient and outpatient healthcare setting if not managed appropriately. High alert medications refer to drugs that have an increased risk of causing significant harm when used in error [1]. Many of anticoagulation-associated adverse effects result from medication errors, suggesting they are preventable [2]. Therefore, national patient safety goals for the Joint Commission emphasize decreasing the possibility of patient harm due to anticoagulants (including apixaban, dabigatran, edoxaban, rivaxoraban, and warfarin) and recommend accurate and accessible patient education [3].

2. Anticoagulation Management Services

The majority of both inpatient and outpatient anticoagulation management services (AMS) utilize providers with anticoagulation expertise and incorporate patient and outcome tracking, comprehensive patient education, and quality improvement (QI) activities [4]. Studies have consistently demonstrated improved clinical outcomes with AMS compared to usual care [5]. With disease-state and medication knowledge regarding anticoagulation, pharmacists are well-suited to manage AMS. Studies have reported that patients who receive pharmacist-led warfarin management services whether in the community, inpatient or outpatient setting achieve significantly better International Normalized Ratio (INR) control compared with those patients who receive usual care [6–14]. In addition to achieving therapeutic INR range, pharmacist-led anticoagulation management has also been found to reduce adverse events associated with anticoagulation, resulting in both decreased hospitalizations and decreased hospital length of stay [15]. Furthermore, these services have been shown to reduce the rates of anticoagulation-related emergency department (ED) visits and hospitalizations, with significant financial impact. In a 2010 study, pharmacist-managed services averted $141,277 in hospitalization costs and $10,183 in ED costs versus a nurse-managed service, and $95,579 in hospitalization costs and $5511 in ED costs compared with usual care [16].

Even less comprehensive methods, such as a single patient counseling session at discharge, have noted positive outcomes. Enhanced patient understanding of warfarin has resulted in better INR control and decreased hospital readmission rates [17–19]. In one study, patients who did not receive pharmacist education in the hospital prior to discharge required more interventions related to adherence concerns, incorrect administration, and continued use of interacting drugs versus those who did (36.4% vs. 12.9%, $p = 0.0005$). In the same population, patients who had not received pharmacist counseling had higher readmission rates and ED visits due to anticoagulation problems within 3 months of discharge (12.12% vs. 1.85%, $p = 0.0069$) [19]. In the inpatient setting, patient education resulted in significantly reduced interacting medications, extreme INRs, and adverse events during warfarin therapy [20]. Wang et al. highlighted patients' concerns and deficits in knowledge regarding warfarin treatment, and also demonstrated their association with warfarin adherence and INR control. Patients had inadequate understanding of warfarin-diet and warfarin-drug interactions. The most common concerns regarding taking warfarin were related to warfarin-drug interactions (36.1%), forgetting to take warfarin (26.2%) and concerns about adverse effects (25.7%) [21]. Pharmacist-managed warfarin services, which includes patient education, have shown positive outcomes with respect to safety, efficacy, and cost savings.

Thus, some institutions have implemented AMS for both patients receiving warfarin as well as the direct oral anticoagulants (DOAC). For DOAC management, it is not clearly defined when and how to best provide patient education, how often to evaluate for bleeding or thrombosis, or how often to screen for interacting medications and changes in organ function [22–26]. In patients on DOACs, it is recommended to regularly assess for changes in organ function and evaluate for clinically-relevant drug interactions [27–32]. A recent study found that older age and higher number of concomitant medications were associated with higher DOAC adherence. Predictors of lower adherence were higher number of comorbidities and being a naïve anticoagulant (AC) user (no prior AC use). Prior exposure and management in anticoagulation clinics increases patient understanding of anticoagulation and the potential consequences of noncompliance. Therefore, these factors may lead to increased patient motivation to adhere to DOAC therapy [22].

According to the Joint Commission, education should be provided regarding anticoagulant therapy to prescribers, staff, patients, and families. Effective anticoagulation patient education involves face-to-face interaction with a trained professional who ensures that the patient understands the risks involved, the precautions that should be taken, and the need for regular monitoring [5]. Anticoagulation education is often provided as a standard of care and emphasized across healthcare settings [5,30]. Although the majority of research is associated with counseling in the ambulatory care clinic or hospital setting, patient education can be implemented in any setting, including at the community pharmacy [13,14].

3. Patient Counseling

Effective medication counseling can empower patients to be active partners in their care and enhance treatment compliance. Studies demonstrate that patients who are engaged in their health have enhanced care experiences, better outcomes and reduced overall healthcare costs [33,34]. Establishing a therapeutic relationship built on trust can be critical to promoting understanding and empowering self-management. This mutually beneficial exchange in which the patient gives authority to the provider and the provider gives information and commitment to the patient is central to effective medication management [35–37]. Patients should be empowered as partners in their care, with appropriate teaching and resources. Education involves assessing the patient's understanding about his or her health problems and medications, the ability to use the prescribed medications correctly, and attitudes toward the health-related issues and associated pharmacotherapy [24,35,36].

Asking open-ended questions is a method that can be used to evaluate patient understanding, reinforce key concepts, and decide what information is needed for patients. For example, "what questions do you have for me?" versus "do you have any questions?" can invite richer conversation [36]. When initiating a new drug, an inquiry about each medication's indications, the patient's expectations and asking the patient to show self-administration can promote understanding. This methodology can be repeated during follow up visits, to identify medication-related problems or concerns that arise.

Visual aids and demonstration devices can promote patient understanding. Opening pill bottles, for instance, can emphasize the medication color, size, and shape to the patient. For injectable medications, this may comprise showing patients the exact marking on the measuring devices to ensure accurate dosing. Devices such as low-molecular weight heparin syringes may necessitate a demo of the assembly and correct administration. The direct observation of drug-use can also reveal accurate usage and strengthen teaching of important points. Patient-friendly written resources as an adjunct to verbal communication can also help improve patient awareness [35,36]. In fact, multiple modalities of education, such as verbal, written and video should be used to emphasize important points. The combination of education methods improves patient and/or caregiver knowledge and satisfaction, but this is not always done [38]. According to an ISMP survey, 25% of nurses note that they do not provide written materials to accompany verbal education to patients about their medications [39]. Unfortunately, drug information sources are often inconsistent, complex, incomplete, unavailable, and written at a college reading level or not available in the patient's language [35,39]. Creation of a medication list, using graphics or simple phrases to show the medicine, its indication, how much to take, and when to take it can be useful resource [40,41].

Understanding patients' cultural background, especially health and illness beliefs, attitudes, and practices can help tailor educational strategies. Health care professionals should adjust their content and style to patients' communication skills, often with the use of teaching aids, interpreters, or cultural guides. Assessing a patient's cognitive abilities, health literacy, learning style, and physical status can also help individualize the educational method to meet the patient's needs. Some patients may learn best by listening to information, by seeing a picture or model, and/or by touching the pills and devices [36,40].

Some patients may lack the visual ability to correctly read prescription labels on bottles, find syringe markings, or follow written instructions. An impaired ability to read information on medication bottles or package inserts increases the likelihood for self-management errors. These patients may benefit from services such as blister packaging by community pharmacies. In addition, they may rely on family members or caregivers to read instructions, memorize how the pill feels in their hand, or use enhanced lighting devices and magnifiers. Other patients may use technology (such as talking pill bottles or home INR devices) or computer software that converts printed information to Braille. Promoting the use of a weekly pill box and encouraging patients to bring it to clinic appointments can help improve adherence and can assist the provider in confirming that the patient is organizing medications as prescribed [35,36].

Functional limitations can reduce patient dexterity or strength which makes it challenging to open child-resistant containers, and may require special lids for bottles. Patients may also have hearing difficulties which reduces understanding of oral education and forces reliance on a written instructions. Challenges in verbal communication between providers and patients can also lead to mistakes in the execution of the prescribed regimen. Although approaches for meeting the medication needs of patients with hearing or visual impairment are challenging, efforts should be made to tailor self-management to each patient's limitations [34].

Medication self-management requires physical and cognitive skills, including higher-level cortical processing and integration. With cognitive impairment, parts of the brain responsible for thinking and executive functions (such as memory, reasoning, learning) can be diminished and may interfere with self-management of medications. Even memory changes associated with normal aging can impair effective drug use. Behavior modification, caregiver education and support, and utilizing adherence tools such as weekly pill boxes, can assist in improved management of medications in patients with cognitive impairment [35,40]. The education level and patients' knowledge can impact the global management of the anticoagulation [42]. Thus, every effort should be made to clearly educate and evaluate understanding. When interacting with patients, health care providers should explain concepts clearly without using medical jargon. Terms such as use vs. utilize, side effect vs. adverse reaction, when you need it vs. PRN, and by mouth vs. oral are often easier to understand for patients [40]. Standardized terminology about dosing schedules (e.g., morning, noon, night, and bedtime) improves understanding and reduces administration errors. Imprecise information about dosing frequency (e.g., every 4 to 6 h) should be avoided for those patients with low health literacy. A prescription label that has explicit instructions such as "Take one tablet in the morning and one at 5 PM" instead of "Take one tablet twice daily" decreases the possibility of improper dosing frequency and administration. For a patient taking rivaroxaban for atrial fibrillation, including instructions to "Take rivaroxaban once a day with your evening meal" is more specific than "Take rivaroxaban once a day with food" [40,41]. Providers should be mindful of the pace and content and volume of speech, especially when communicating to patients with limited health literacy. Key information should be repeated with succinct explanations [40,41].

A "teach back" technique is an effective way to evaluate patient understanding, clarify key points, and remove any communication gaps between the patient and health educator. In this approach, patients are asked to repeat instructions in their own words to confirm understanding. A health care professional, for example, may say something as follows: "I want to make sure that I have explained everything clearly. If you were trying to explain to your partner how to take this medication, what would you say [24,40]? If a patient cannot accurately repeat what was presented, the information is clarified, and the patient is invited to teach back again. This process continues until the patient can accurately describe the directions [36,40]. The teach back may be an effective strategy to identify errors in drug administration, since studies have found a gap between a patient's ability to verbalize instructions correctly, and his or her ability to accurately show the correct number of pills to be taken daily [40,41].

4. Anticoagulation Information

The medication counseling session should ideally include the information listed below, and can be modified based on each patient's anticoagulant and monitoring plan and the educator's clinical judgement [23,24,36,37,43].

- The drug's brand and generic name and, when needed, its therapeutic class
- The drug's purpose and how it pertains to thrombus formation
- The drug's anticipated onset and what to do if the expected result does not occur
- The drug's route, dosage form, dose, frequency, and duration of treatment
- Directions for preparing and using the drug (such as low-molecular weight heparin)
- Missed-dose management
- Precautions to be aware of when using the drug and the potential measures to decrease bleeding risk and trauma
- Common side effects that may occur (including signs and symptoms of bleeding) and steps to follow if they occur, actions to prevent or reduce their occurrence, and what to do if they occur, including when to notify a healthcare professional
- Strategies for self-monitoring and the importance of regular monitoring to reduce bleeding and thrombosis
- Potential drug–drug (including OTC), drug–food, and drug–disease interactions or contraindications
- Need to inform provider if you are pregnant or plan to become pregnant
- Need to inform provider before a procedure or hospitalization
- Need to notify all health care providers of use
- Need to wear medical identification
- Importance of not stopping without consulting health care provider
- Need to consult health care provider before starting any new drug
- Inform provider of all medication changes, including over-the-counter and herbals

- Importance of taking exactly as prescribed and use of an adherence aid if needed
- Prescription refills authorized and the process for obtaining refills
- Proper drug storage and disposal
- Other helpful information unique to the specific patient or therapy

According the Joint Commission, anticoagulation education should include the necessity of follow-up monitoring, adherence, drug-food interactions, and the potential for side effects and drug interactions [5]. Effort should be made to integrate patient-centered educational methods to promote understanding of how to handle high-risk situations that may compromise safety related to anticoagulation [43]. There are some similarities in counseling a patient on DOAC and warfarin, but some important differences need to be noted.

5. Specific Drug Considerations

Anticoagulant counseling should be tailored to each patient, medication specific, and at an appropriate literacy level. Table 1 includes practical considerations for each of the oral anticoagulants. As the number of indications and data supporting DOAC use expands, educational tools need to be relied on and updated frequently. An important patient education point is that DOACs should not be discontinued unless specifically directed by a healthcare professional because of the rapid decline of protective anticoagulation that can occur (within 12–24 h after the last dose). The necessity for strict adherence should be implicitly explained to patients on DOACs. DOACs have a very predictable anticoagulant effect and monitoring of coagulation assays is not routinely required to guide therapy. This could wrongly lead some patients to determine that no follow up is needed. Patients should be educated regarding the need for ongoing monitoring of organ function, drug interactions, adherence, and bleeding/thrombosis [23,24,27–30]. The European Heart Rhythm Association guidelines recommend assessment of hemoglobin, liver function, and renal function at least annually for all patients. For patients with CrCl of 30 to 60 mL/min, those patients > 75 years, or fragile, they recommend more frequent evaluation of renal function every 6 months. For patients with CrCl of 15 to 30 mL/min, evaluation of renal function every 3 months should be considered [23]. Although there is no clear consensus regarding how and when to follow up, patients should be informed of a prespecified follow-up schedule.

Table 1. Practical Considerations of Oral Anticoagulants [27–30].

Drug	Warfarin	Dabigatran	Rivaroxaban	Apixaban	Edoxaban
Dosing Frequency (For venousthromboembolism treatment or atrial fibrillation thromboprophylaxis)	Daily, adjusted based on INR	Twice daily	Daily or twice daily depending on indication	Twice daily	Daily
Missed Dose	Take if before midnight on the same day	Take as soon as possible (asap) on same day but at least 6 h before next scheduled dose	If missed a 15 mg tablet, take asap but can take two 15 mg tablets together. Patients on once daily regimen should take asap on same day.	Take asap on same day	Take asap on same day
Administration	With or without food	With a full glass of water; with or without food	With food	With or without food	With or without food
Weekly pill box	Can aid adherence	MUST store in original container and keep sealed.	Can aid adherence	Can aid adherence	Can aid adherence
Drug-Drug Interactions	Numerous; primarily via CYP2C9; minor pathways include CYP2C8, 2C18, 2C19, 1A2, and 3A4	Important drug:drug interactions: P-gp inducers and inhibitors (especially if renal function compromised)	Avoid dual P-gp and strong CYP 3A4 inducers or inhibitors	Avoid dual P-gp and strong CYP 3A4 inducers or inhibitors	Important drug:drug interactions: P-gp inducers and inhibitors
Can you crush?	Yes	No; Swallow whole; do not cut, open, or crush	Yes	Yes	Yes

6. Conclusions

Education for warfarin, a narrow therapeutic index medication, is routinely incorporated in the outpatient and inpatient setting. The need for INR monitoring often allows for greater access to health care providers and subsequently more education. The below list includes additional counseling points for patients on warfarin [43–45]:

- Regular INR tests are needed to ensure warfarin is working properly
- The goal INR range is often between 2 and 3; risk for clotting is greater when INRs are less than 2, risk for bleeding is higher when INRs are greater than 3; doses of warfarin are modified based on INR test results
- Each strength of warfarin has a unique color; with each refill make sure the tablets are the same color
- Foods with a lot of vitamin K like kale, collard greens, and spinach may interfere with warfarin; you do not need to avoid foods with vitamin K, but need to try to maintain consistent dietary habits on a weekly basis
- Alcohol increases the risk for bleeding and interferes with warfarin therapy; no more than 1–2 drinks per day, and avoid binge drinking

Given the need to make adjustments to the dosing, it is recommended to provide written instructions for the patient, as shown in Figure 1 [43]. A wealth of evidence-based resources are available in assisting practitioners on how to effectively educate patients on warfarin [43,45].

Date: _____INR: ____INR Goal: _____Tablet (dose/strength/color): _____

	Sunday	Monday	Tuesday	Wednesday	Thursday	Friday	Saturday
Dose							
Tablet							

Call the Anticoagulation Clinic with any questions regarding your medications at 123-456-789.

Next appointment: _____Other instructions._____

Figure 1. Sample Warfarin Dose Instruction Card.

Given the potential harm associated with anticoagulant use, patient education should be incorporated in a variety of pharmacy practice settings, including in ambulatory care clinics, hospital settings, and community pharmacies. The verbal face-to-face teaching sessions should be tailored to each patient, be accompanied with written resources and use the teach-back method.

Conflicts of Interest: The authors declare no conflict of interest.

References

1. *How-to Guide: Prevent Harm from High-Alert Medications*; Institute for Healthcare Improvement: Cambridge, MA, USA, 2012. Available online: http://www.ismp.org/Tools/highalertmedications.pdf (accessed on 29 March 2018).
2. Piazza, G.; Nguyen, T.N.; Cios, D.; Labreche, M.; Hohlfelder, B.; Fanikos, J.; Fiumara, K.; Goldhaber, S.Z. Anticoagulation-associated adverse drug events. *Am. J. Med.* **2011**, *124*, 1136–1142. [CrossRef] [PubMed]
3. The Joint Commission. National Patient Safety Goals 2018. Available online: https://www.jointcommission.org/assets/1/6/NPSG_Chapter_HAP_Jan2018.pdf (accessed on 19 April 2018).
4. Garcia, D.A.; Witt, D.M.; Hylek, E.; Wittkowsky, A.K.; Nutescu, E.A.; Jacobson, A.; Moll, S.; Merli, G.J.; Crowther, M.; Earl, L.; et al. Delivery of optimized anticoagulant therapy: Consensus statement from the Anticoagulation Forum. *Ann. Pharmacother.* **2008**, *42*, 979–988. [CrossRef] [PubMed]

5. Saokaew, S.; Permsuwan, U.; Chaiyakunapruk, N.; Nathisuwan, S.; Sukonthasarn, A. Effectiveness of pharmacist-participated warfarin therapy management: A systematic review and metaanalysis. *J. Thromb. Haemost.* **2010**, *8*, 2418–2427. [CrossRef] [PubMed]

6. Bishop, M.A.; Streiff, M.B.; Ensor, C.R.; Tedford, R.J.; Russell, S.D.; Ross, P.A. Pharmacist-managed international normalized ratio patient self-testing is associated with increased time in therapeutic range in patients with left ventricular assist devices at an academic medical center. *ASAIO J.* **2014**, *60*, 193–198. [CrossRef] [PubMed]

7. Bungard, T.J.; Gardner, L.; Archer, S.L.; Hamilton, P.; Ritchie, B.; Tymchak, W.; Tsuyuki, R.T. Evaluation of a pharmacist-managed anticoagulation clinic: Improving patient care. *Open Med.* **2009**, *3*, e16–e21. [PubMed]

8. Challen, L.; Agbahiwe, S.; Cantieri, T.; Olivetti, J.G.; Mbah, T.; Mendoza-Becerra, Y.; Munoz, C.; Nguyen, M.; Partee, K.; Lal, L.; et al. Impact of Point-of-Care Implementation in Pharmacist-Run Anticoagulation Clinics within a Community-Owned Health System: A Two-Year Retrospective Analysis. *Hosp. Pharm.* **2015**, *50*, 783–788. [CrossRef] [PubMed]

9. Chilipko, A.A.; Norwood, D.K. Evaluating warfarin management by pharmacists in a community teaching hospital. *Consult. Pharm.* **2014**, *29*, 95–103. [CrossRef] [PubMed]

10. Garton, L.; Crosby, J.F. A retrospective assessment comparing pharmacist-managed anticoagulation clinic with physician management using international normalized ratio stability. *J. Thromb. Thrombolysis* **2011**, *32*, 426–430. [CrossRef] [PubMed]

11. Holden, J.; Holden, K. Comparative effectiveness of general practitioner versus pharmacist dosing of patients requiring anticoagulation in the community. *J. Clin. Pharm. Ther.* **2000**, *25*, 49–54. [CrossRef] [PubMed]

12. Young, S.; Bishop, L.; Twells, L.; Dillon, C.; Hawboldt, J.; O'Shea, P. Comparison of pharmacist managed anticoagulation with usual medical care in a family medicine clinic. *BMC Fam. Pract.* **2011**, *12*, 88. [CrossRef] [PubMed]

13. Ingram, S.J.; Kirkdale, C.L.; Williams, S.; Hartley, E.; Wintle, S.; Sefton, V.; Thornley, T. Moving anticoagulation initiation and monitoring services into the community: Evaluation of the Brighton and hove community pharmacy service. *BMC Health Serv. Res.* **2018**, *18*, 91. [CrossRef] [PubMed]

14. Harrison, J.; Shaw, J.P.; Harrison, J.E. Anticoagulation management by community pharmacists in New Zealand: An evaluation of a collaborative model in primary care. *Int. J. Pharm. Pract.* **2015**, *23*, 173–181. [CrossRef] [PubMed]

15. Locke, C.; Ravnan, S.L.; Patel, R.; Uchizono, J.A. Reduction in warfarin adverse events requiring patient hospitalization after implementation of a pharmacist-managed anticoagulation service. *Pharmacotherapy* **2005**, *25*, 685–689. [CrossRef] [PubMed]

16. Rudd, K.M.; Dier, J.G. Comparison of two different models of anticoagulation management services with usual medical care. *Pharmacotherapy* **2010**, *30*, 330–338. [CrossRef] [PubMed]

17. Holbrook, A.; Schulman, S.; Witt, D.M.; Vandvik, P.O.; Fish, J.; Kovacs, M.J.; Svensson, P.J.; Veenstra, D.L.; Crowther, M.; Guyatt, G.H. Evidence-based management of anticoagulant therapy: Antithrombotic therapy and prevention of thrombosis, 9th ed: American College of Chest Physicians evidence-based clinical practice guidelines. *Chest* **2012**, *141* (Suppl. 2), e152S–e184S. [CrossRef] [PubMed]

18. Wittkowsky, A.K. Impact of target-specific oral anticoagulants on transitions of care and outpatient care models. *J. Thromb. Thrombolysis* **2013**, *35*, 304–311. [CrossRef] [PubMed]

19. Zdyb, E.G.; Courtney, D.M.; Malik, S.; Schmidt, M.J.; Lyden, A.E. Impact of Discharge Anticoagulation Education by Emergency Department Pharmacists at a Tertiary Academic Medical Center. *J. Emerg. Med.* **2017**, *53*, 896–903. [CrossRef] [PubMed]

20. Dharmarajan, T.S.; Gupta, A.; Baig, M.A.; Norkus, E.P. Warfarin: Implementing its safe use in hospitalized patients from nursing homes and community through a performance improvement initiative. *J. Am. Med. Dir. Assoc.* **2011**, *12*, 518–523. [CrossRef] [PubMed]

21. Wang, Y.; Kong, M.C.; Lee, L.H.; Ng, H.J.; Ko, Y. Knowledge, satisfaction, and concerns regarding warfarin therapy and their association with warfarin adherence and anticoagulation control. *Thromb. Res.* **2014**, *133*, 550–554. [CrossRef] [PubMed]

22. Manzoor, B.S.; Lee, T.A.; Sharp, L.K.; Walton, S.M.; Galanter, W.L.; Nutescu, E.A. Real-World Adherence and Persistence with Direct Oral Anticoagulants in Adults with Atrial Fibrillation. *Pharmacotherapy* **2017**, *37*, 1221–1230. [CrossRef] [PubMed]

23. Heidbuchel, H.; Verhamme, P.; Alings, M.; Antz, M.; Hacke, W.; Oldgren, J.; Sinnaeve, P.; Camm, A.J.; Kirchhof, P. European Heart Rhythm Association. European Heart Rhythm Association practical guide on the use of new oral anticoagulants in patients with non-valvular atrial fibrillation. *Europace* **2013**, *15*, 625–651. [CrossRef] [PubMed]

24. Burnett, A.E.; Mahan, C.E.; Vazquez, S.R.; Oertel, L.B.; Garcia, D.A.; Ansell, J. Guidance for the practical management of the direct oral anticoagulants (DOACs) in VTEtreatment. *J. Thromb. Thrombolysis* **2016**, *41*, 206–232. [CrossRef] [PubMed]

25. Simon, J.; Hawes, E.; Deyo, Z.; Bryant Shilliday, B. Evaluation of prescribing and patient use of target-specific oral anticoagulants in the outpatient setting. *J. Clin. Pharm. Ther.* **2015**. [CrossRef] [PubMed]

26. Howard, M.; Lipshutz, A.; Roess, B.; Hawes, E.; Deyo, Z.; Burkhart, J.; Moll, S.; Shilliday, B. Identification of Risk Factors for Inappropriate and Suboptimal Initiation of Direct Oral Anticoagulants. *J. Thromb. Thrombolysis* **2017**, *43*, 149–156. [CrossRef] [PubMed]

27. *Eliquis* [package insert]; Bristol-Myers Squibb Company: Princeton, NJ, USA, 2012.

28. *Pradaxa* [package insert]; Boehringer Ingelheim Pharmaceuticals Inc.: Ridgefield, CT, USA, 2010.

29. *Xarelto* [package insert]; Janssen Pharmaceuticals, Inc.: Titusville, NJ, USA, 2011.

30. *Savaysa* [package insert]; Daiichi Sankyo, Inc.: Basking Ridge, NJ, USA, 2017.

31. Chan, L.L.; Crumpler, W.L.; Jacobson, A.K. Implementation of pharmacist-managed anticoagulation in patients receiving newer anticoagulants. *Am. J. Health Syst. Pharm.* **2013**, *70*, 1285–1286, 1288. [CrossRef] [PubMed]

32. Lane, D.A.; Aguinaga, L.; Blomström-Lundqvist, C.; Boriani, G.; Dan, G.A.; Hills, M.T.; Hylek, E.M.; LaHaye, S.A.; Lip, G.Y.; Lobban, T.; et al. Cardiac tachyarrhythmias and patient values and preferences for their management: The European Heart Rhythm Association (EHRA) consensus document endorsed by the Heart Rhythm Society (HRS), Asia Pacific Heart Rhythm Society (APHRS), and Sociedad Latinoamericana de Estimulación Cardíaca y Electrofisiología (SOLEACE). *Europace* **2015**, *17*, 1747–1769. [CrossRef] [PubMed]

33. James, J. Patient engagement. Health Affairs 2013. Available online: http://www.healthaffairs.org/healthpolicybriefs/brief.php?brief_id=86 (accessed on 28 January 2018).

34. Hibbard, J.H.; Greene, J.; Overton, V. Patients with lower activation associated with higher costs; delivery systems should know their patients' "Scores". *Health Aff.* **2013**, *32*, 216–222. [CrossRef] [PubMed]

35. Institute of Medicine. *Committee on Identifying and Preventing Medication Errors. Preventing Medication Errors*; The National Academies Press: Washington, DC, USA, 2006.

36. American Society of Health-System Pharmacy. ASHP Guidelines on Pharmacist-Conducted Patient Education and Counseling. Available online: https://www.ashp.org/DocLibrary/BestPractices/OrgGdlPtEduc.aspx (accessed on 29 March 2018).

37. American Society of Hospital Pharmacists. ASHP statement on pharmaceutical care. *Am. J. Hosp. Pharm.* **1993**, *50*, 1720–1723. Available online: http://www.ashp.org/doclibrary/bestpractices/orgstpharmcare.aspx (accessed on 29 March 2018).

38. Johnson, A.; Sandford, J.; Tyndall, J. Written and verbal information versus verbal information only for patients being discharged from acute hospital settings to home. *Cochrane Database Syst. Rev.* **2003**. [CrossRef] [PubMed]

39. Institute for Safe Medication Practices (ISMP). 2003. Available online: https://www.ismp.org/Survey/surveyresults/NursingSurvey.asp (accessed on 28 January 2018).

40. *Health Literacy in Pharmacy*; Agency for Healthcare Research and Quality: Rockville, MD, USA. Available online: http://www.ahrq.gov/professionals/education/curriculum-tools/pharmlitqi/ppt-slides.html (accessed on 29 March 2018).

41. Davis, T.C.; Wolf, M.S.; Bass, P.F., III; Thompson, J.A.; Tilson, H.H.; Neuberger, M.; Parker, R.M. Literacy and misunderstanding prescription drug labels. *Ann. Intern. Med.* **2006**, *145*, 887–894. [CrossRef] [PubMed]

42. Hernández Madrid, A.; Potpara, T.S.; Dagres, N.; Chen, J.; Larsen, T.B.; Estner, H.; Todd, D.; Bongiorni, M.G.; Sciaraffiam, E.; Proclemerm, A.; et al. Differences in attitude, education, and knowledge about oral anticoagulation therapy among patients with atrial fibrillation in Europe: Result of a self-assessment patient survey conducted by the European Heart Rhythm Association. *Europace* **2016**, *18*, 463–467. [CrossRef] [PubMed]

43. Anticoagulation Toolkit: Reducing Adverse Drug Events & Potential Adverse Drug Events with Unfractionated Heparin, Low Molecular Weight Heparins and Warfarin. Available online: http://excellence.acforum.org/sites/default/files/Purdue%20Univ%20Anticoag%20Toolkit.pdf (accessed on 17 January 2018).

44. Moreland, C.J.; Kravitz, R.L.; Paterniti, D.A.; Li, C.S.; Lin, T.C.; White, R.H. Anticoagulation education: Do patients understand potential medication-related emergencies? *Jt. Comm. J. Qual. Patient Saf.* **2013**, *39*, 22–31. [CrossRef]

45. Witt, D.M.; Clark, N.P.; Kaatz, S.; Schnurr, T.; Ansell, J.E. Guidance for the practical management of warfarin therapy in the treatment of venous thromboembolism. *J. Thromb. Thrombolysis* **2016**, *41*, 187–205. [CrossRef] [PubMed]

pharmacy

Article

"Being in Control of My Asthma Myself" Patient Experience of Asthma Management: A Qualitative Interpretive Description

Damilola T. Olufemi-Yusuf [1], Sophie Beaudoin Gabriel [1], Tatiana Makhinova [1,2] and Lisa M. Guirguis [1,2,*]

[1]   Faculty of Pharmacy and Pharmaceutical Sciences, University of Alberta, Edmonton, AB T6G 1C9, Canada; damiade@ualberta.ca (D.T.O.-Y.); sophie.beaudoin@gmail.com (S.B.G.); tatiana.makhinova@ualberta.ca (T.M.)
[2]   Asthma Working Group of the Respiratory Health Strategic Clinical Network, Alberta Health Services, Calgary, AB T2W 1S7, Canada
*   Correspondence: lisa.guirguis@ualberta.ca; Tel.: +1-780-492-9693

Received: 29 September 2018; Accepted: 12 November 2018; Published: 15 November 2018

Abstract: Asthma control can be achieved with effective and safe medication use; however, many patients are not controlled. Patients' perceptions of asthma, asthma treatment, and pharmacist roles can impact patient outcomes. The purpose of this study was to explore patients' experiences and patient–pharmacist relationships in asthma care. Qualitative Interpretive Description method guided the study. Semi-structured individual interviews were conducted with 11 patients recruited from personal contacts, pharmacies, and asthma clinics. Categories and themes were identified using inductive constant comparison. Themes indicated patients had a personalized common sense approach to asthma management, "go-to" health care provider, and prioritized patient–pharmacist relationships. Patients described their illness experiences and asthma control based on personal markers similar to the common sense model of self-regulation. Patients chose a family physician, asthma specialist, respiratory therapist, or pharmacist as an expert resource for asthma management. Patient perceived pharmacists' roles as information provider, adviser, or care provider. Pharmacists who develop a collaborative relationship with their asthma patients are better positioned to provide tailored education and self-management support. Inviting patients to share their perspective could increase patient engagement and uptake of personalised asthma action plans to achieve asthma control.

Keywords: asthma; patient experience; patient-centred care; communication; patient education; patient-pharmacist relationship; self-regulation; qualitative interpretive description

---

1. Introduction

Asthma is a significant public health problem all over the world and an everyday reality for the 2.4 million Canadians living with asthma [1]. Asthma control can be achieved with effective and safe medications and treatment guidelines [2]. However, level of asthma control has not improved over the last decade and currently 9 out of 10 Canadians with asthma are out of control [3]. Poor asthma control is burdensome to patients and increases emergency room visits, hospitalizations, and absence from work or school [4].

The reasons for poor asthma management are multifaceted including the disease itself, presence of comorbidities, patients' self-management, healthcare professionals' care, or the interaction among these factors [5,6]. Medication therapy is the primary intervention used in asthma highlighting asthma patients have needs that pharmacists can address [7,8]. Pharmacists frequently encounter asthma patients and are not only well placed to identify patients with poorly controlled asthma but also resolve medication problems, educate patients on inhaler technique, monitor therapy, and develop personalised asthma action plans [8–10].

Pharmacist-delivered interventions in asthma management have improved patient outcomes [11–15] but only few have explored the patient experience of pharmacist care as one of the factors contributing to positive outcomes [16–18]. Understanding the patient, their beliefs and experience about asthma and asthma treatment reduces barriers to effective asthma treatment [19,20]. Patients involved in their care are more likely to communicate their goals, preferences, and concerns, to seek support in adhering to their care plan, and to take more ownership of their treatment [20–22]. More so, effective communication between patients and pharmacists provides an enabling context for optimizing therapy and achieving asthma control for patients [17,23,24]. The patient's experience in managing asthma and how they are supported by pharmacists needs to be explored further.

With the shift toward patient-centred care in Canada and around the world, pharmacists have taken on an expanded role in providing patient care services to those living with chronic conditions including asthma [25]. In the province of Alberta, where the scope of pharmacy practice is the widest (pharmacists can prescribe for minor ailments, renew, adjust, initiate or substitute prescriptions, administer vaccinations, order and interpret laboratory tests, conduct medication reviews, and develop care plans), the experiences of those living with asthma are important in order to enhance care [26]. Given that the patient's perspective has not been examined in this patient-focused practice model, we sought to understand how asthma patients have experienced pharmacists' care. Our findings could have potential application in the design of patient-centred interventions in pharmacy care and improve care for asthma patients. Our study objectives were:

1. To identify how patients manage their asthma
2. To describe what resources patients need to access for asthma management
3. To understand how patients view and experience pharmacists' roles in ongoing management of asthma.

2. Methods

2.1. Research Team and Reflexivity

The research team consisted of three researchers, one patient with asthma (i.e., only research team member with asthma), and one pharmacy student, who were all invested in improving the quality of care for people with asthma. All three researchers were pharmacists; however, none was practicing. The pharmacy student conducted the interviews and was trained and supervised by one of the authors (L.G.). The patient was identified as a patient adviser with the Alberta Health Services Respiratory Health Strategic Clinical Network (RSCN) where two researchers were active members. The patient participated in one interview and reviewed a subset of interviews to provide insights on patient perspectives.

2.2. Study Design

Interpretive Description was the qualitative methodology used to frame the study [27,28]. Its constructivist paradigm formed the basis of our theoretical approach to knowing how patients perceived and interpreted meaning created through their asthma experiences [27,28]. The constructivist position recognizes that multiple perspectives exist and fit with our study objective of understanding the different perspectives of asthma patients' self-management in community pharmacy practice. As an applied qualitative approach, interpretive description focuses on thoughtful consideration of factors that could influence practice such as practice models, professional mandates, and biases of individuals and disciplines [29,30]. The orientation toward practice settings ensures that the creation of knowledge that is relevant to real-world clinical practice as well as theory development or expansion.

We used an inductive approach without the influence of a priori theories though we were open to theory to inform the analysis and discussion. We favoured the use of theory as an analytical tool rather than as a theoretical framework made explicit from the beginning to allow for the generation and interpretation of new themes that fit into broader contexts [31,32]. This study was driven by the need to better understand the experiences and perspectives of patients on managing their asthma and the role of community pharmacists in order to generate knowledge that could improve care practices for asthma patients. Ethics approval for the study was granted by the University of Alberta Health Research Ethics Board (study ID Pro00065978) prior to recruitment.

2.3. Recruitment and Sample

Adults between 18 and 70 years old were eligible if they or their children had asthma, took at least one asthma medication, spoke English, and were able to consent. Patients were ineligible if they had limited capacity to communicate. Purposive and convenience sampling were used to recruit 11 patient participants from three settings. The first five patients (i.e., Patients 1–5) were recruited from personal networks of members of the RHSCN. It was noted that these patients had positive experiences with pharmacists and thus we purposively sample two patients (Patients 6 and 7) from a community pharmacy with a known high level of care. Finally, four patients were purposively recruited from an asthma clinic to capture the voices of patients who may have more complex or severe asthma (Patients 8–11) than those in primary health care sites.

2.4. Data Collection

Data collection consisted of semi-structured individual interviews conducted by the trained pharmacy student who did not know the participants. Interviews occurred face to face and interviews occurred by telephone as participants lived out of Edmonton or they preferred to do so for scheduling or personal reasons. Seven interviews were conducted between July and August 2016. Additional four patients were recruited and interviewed in June 2017. Interviews were guided by a semi-structured interview guide lasted between 16 and 38 min. The questions in the interview guide were developed based on literature and knowledge of asthma care and community pharmacy practice (Appendix A). We explored the patient's experience of asthma, management strategies, and interactions with community pharmacists. As data collection and analysis occurred concurrently, areas of emerging interest were noted and included as probes in the next interview. Thus, the interview guide was modified as the interviews progressed to reflect additional questions.

During and after each interview, handwritten field notes were taken to record important observations made at the interview such as non-verbal behaviour, interpersonal disposition, and the researcher's impressions of the participant within the context of the interview. All interviews were audio recorded and transcribed verbatim.

2.5. Data Analysis

Interpretive description methods and thematic analysis shaped the data analysis [27,28,33,34]. First, researchers wrote a summary of each patient interview, included information about each patient and potential themes. Each transcript was open coded to identify main ideas and develop a taxonomy of related codes. Similar codes were sorted and collapsed together to create categories. Categories were then compared and contrasted across transcripts to generate themes that ran through the data. Constant comparison was used to compare between patients, provider preferences, type of pharmacist relationships to refine themes. Themes moved beyond clustering similar categories to develop a conceptual understanding of the patients' experiences with asthma [33,34]. We also used theory to create themes which contributed to making sense of the data and contextualizing study findings within the body of knowledge. Without the use of theory and thematic analysis, the results of the research will have little meaning and application in real world practice [31,35,36]. We involved one patient participant in the data analysis to draw on her patient experiences in the interpretation of a subset of interview transcripts. This helped improve the study's transparency and trustworthiness.

2.6. Rigour

Rigour was ensured throughout the study. First, the study was designed to achieve congruence between the research question and the theoretical position. Recruitment was adapted to capture patients with varying levels of asthma control and types of pharmacist relationships. Data collection and analysis were conducted concurrently to ensure our ongoing interview explored both new and evolving ideas introduced by participants. Analysis involved interview summaries including field notes, four coders, and iterative coding process. The recognition of three types of patient–pharmacist relationships allowed for multi-faceted comparisons between patients. A patient who was interviewed also participated in the data analysis to bring her experiences and improve the study's transparency and trustworthiness.

3. Results

The sample was predominantly female (n = 8, 73%) with a mean age of 42 years (range = 24 to 56 years). Patients recruited by the members of the RHSCN formed the largest group followed by the asthma clinics and then the community pharmacy. Within two groups sampled from the RSCN and asthma clinics, we observed variation in patients' experiences of interacting with pharmacists. Four patients visited family physician clinics, another four saw an asthma specialist, and one patient used a respiratory therapist for routine asthma care. One patient used both a respiratory a family physician and pharmacist and another an asthma specialist and pharmacist. The characteristics of patients are shown in Table 1.

Table 1. Patients' demographics and provider relationships associated with asthma care.

Patient Identifier	Age	Gender	Recruitment Strategy	"Go-To" Healthcare Provider	Type of Pharmacist Relationship
Patient 1	24	F	RSCN	Family physician	Valuable
Patient 2	43	M	RSCN	Family physician	Information
Patient 3	41	M	RSCN	Family physician	Information
Patient 4	51	M	RSCN	Asthma specialist	Information
Patient 5 [a]	45, 18, 14	F, M, M	RSCN	Respiratory therapist	Valuable
Patient 6 [b]	54	F	Community Pharmacy	Pharmacist and Family physician	Collaboration
Patient 7 [b]	56	F	Community Pharmacy	Pharmacist and Asthma specialist	Collaboration
Patient 8	30	F	Asthma Clinic	Family physician	Valuable
Patient 9	56	F	Asthma Clinic	Asthma specialist	Information
Patient 10	30	F	Asthma Clinic	Asthma specialist	Information
Patient 11	36	F	Asthma Clinic	Asthma specialist	Information

[a] Patient has two teenage sons who have asthma; [b] Patients have the same pharmacist who is a Certified Asthma Educator.

3.1. Theme 1: Personalized Common Sense Approach to Asthma Management

The patients described their illness experiences in a personal way. Similar to Leventhal's Common sense model of self-regulation [37], their perceptions of asthma symptoms, level of control and emotions were modifiable based on their knowledge and feelings of what they experienced over time. Patients discussed how they made sense of asthma symptoms, came up with their own individual non-medical strategies for coping and monitoring improvements or worsening of symptoms. What was most striking is that the patients constructed representations of their asthma from their everyday experiences but these narratives were not always discussed in medical visits. Patient ideas were considered non-medical and diverged from biomedical conversations that predominantly occur in medical settings.

3.1.1. Sub-Theme 1: Personalized Markers for Self-Monitoring

Patients determined if their asthma was under control based on personal markers of control and severity. Patients regularly made connections between symptoms and severity of their condition, relying on these subjective experiences as an early warning of an impending attack. Here are three individual examples of patient symptoms:

> As soon as I start coughing, I know this is going to be a three-month adventure, trying to figure out why. (Patient 1)
> So as soon as I start to get a tickle in my throat, and kind of that feeling that there's feathers in there ... then I make sure that I take my Advair® at night time as well, (Patient 6)
> I know if I can't make it up the stairs without wheezing, or a problem with my breath, that's when I go to my primary care doc. (Patient 3)

After recognizing the seriousness of the condition, patients knew what steps to take to address symptoms. Patients' self-management practices combined both medical (e.g., mainly medications) and non-medical lifestyle strategies to control current symptoms and prevent future problems.

3.1.2. Sub-Theme 2: Personalized Non-Medical Measures

Mostly, non-medication related strategies were seen to be as beneficial as medications for day to day management. One patient took preventative measures.

> So probably lifestyle wise is my biggest thing—like, you know, I try and exercise, get my cardiovascular as much as I can, make sure that my core is strong and strengthen everything around there. (Patient 4)

Other patients had non-medication strategies for asthma attacks

> What I used to do was just to try to lay [sic] down, relax my muscles—there are a lot of times when you have an asthma attack, your core muscles are kind of working overtime to force air in and out of your lungs. Um, so, just the more relaxed I can make myself, the better. (Patient 2)

3.1.3. Sub-Theme 3: Personalized Access to Medication

Patients figured ways to obtain cheaper medications and avoid the hikes in travel health insurance premiums that result from asthma attacks and their association use of oral emergency medications. With insights into the ease of getting medications in less regulated markets outside of Canada (e.g., Mexico), Patient 3 and 9 were sensible to proactively stock up on asthma medications to ensure they always had sufficient supply to meet asthma needs. It was clear that these patients knew what they needed and actively pursued practical solutions.

> Now, the fun part about prednisone is, for some insurance companies, it's an indicator of disease severity—especially if you've taken it in the last six months and all that, and they won't insure you for travel. So, like I said, I handle my asthma, and I know when I need to hit it hard and hit it quick. And, so, what you end up doing too is you have some patients—such as maybe myself—going down to Mexico, getting prednisone. Because they know that, number one, it's an insurance flag if you take it. (Patient 3)

3.2. Theme 2: Patients Identify Their "Go-To" Health Care Provider

Although patients apply a common sense view to manage and monitor asthma symptoms, the chronic nature of asthma implies frequent contact with the health care system. In our study, all patients used their common sense approach to choose one or more healthcare providers for routine asthma care. This "go-to" person was a family doctor, asthma specialist, respiratory therapist or pharmacist whom they recognized as an expert resource for asthma management. The patients described benefits of the encounter such as prescribing new medication or refills, a demonstration of proper inhaler technique, monitoring asthma medications.

Would I have booked an appointment to come in, and sit down, and do this [asthma action plan] with them? Probably not. I think that's probably—you know, that's something again that I would reserve for my family doctor, but, (I) would appreciate that. (Patient 2)

When I go to [name of Asthma specialist] for the respiratory end of things, she'll ask if I need any prescriptions. (Patient 9)

The choice of provider was informed by their perceived needs and expertise of the healthcare provider. Four patients saw their family physician (Patients 1, 2, 3, and 8) as the go-to-healthcare provider. Patients 4, 9, 10, and 11 that did not trust their family physician to provide expert advice on asthma preferred to seek help from an asthma specialist who focuses on asthma patients. Another patient (Patient 5) saw a respiratory therapist. Patients 6 and 7 had positive relationships with their pharmacist thus listed the pharmacists and either their family physician or asthma specialist respectively. The preferred provider(s) for each patient is outlined in Table 1.

3.3. Theme 3: Patient–Pharmacist Relationship Comes First

Patient and pharmacist relationships ranged from non-existent to an ideal situation where the pharmacist partnered with the patient. These relationships influenced care and how their asthma needs were met (Figure 1). For instance, Patients 6 and 7 had the only collaborative relationship with their pharmacist and correspondingly were the sole patients to consider their pharmacist a "go-to" provider. Patient 4 aptly described how relationships are important to patient care.

I think it takes some time to build trust, that sometimes is built in that patient-physician, that's important … But if you're comfortable, I think a pharmacist is well within their scope of practice to help create an action plan, for sure. (Patient 4)

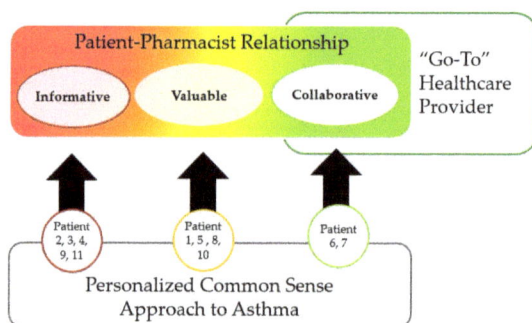

Figure 1. Relation of Spectrum of Patient–Pharmacist Relationships to Study Themes. Pharmacists were only considered the go-to healthcare providers when there was a collaborative relationship.

3.3.1. Sub-Theme 1: Information-Focused Relationship

Majority of the patient–pharmacist relationships clustered toward the bottom end of the spectrum where there is little existing positive relationship or a negative relationship. A group of patients described pharmacist interactions as "impersonal" and transactional. In such cases, they felt the relationship with the pharmacist was limited to dispensing without actively engaging the person behind the prescription.

It's [the interaction] very brief. It's just because I've had it for so long, that they know that I know what I'm doing with it. Um, but yeah, there's no real discussion regarding the medication. (Patient 2)

Generally, patients seemed to have low expectations of the pharmacist because they were satisfied with brief straightforward conversations and minimal interaction with the pharmacist.

The challenge is, it's [role of pharmacist] only appropriate in what's asked, right—I mean, nobody really wants anything forced on them, so, um . . . I imagine a pharmacist who is a certified respiratory educator would be a great thing, and [inaudible] lean on that background and work with them . . . But essentially in the end, I just want to know about the drug, interactions, possible side effects, and how to do it properly. (Patient 4)

Similar experiences evoked different reactions in patients. One patient explained that being disappointed by their pharmacist's inability to renew prescriptions for asthma medications in an emergency caused expectations to drop very low.

Didn't engage me on, yeah, "How well is he controlled? What is he doing about it? Does he know what he's doing?" Right? I rarely get that question. But once again, I think that's because in the last few years, I just . . . I just see that pharmacy as a dispensing outlet. (Patient 3)

The type of patient–pharmacist relationship can be also understood from the perspective of trust. People may have an inherent distrust in the involvement of pharmacists in the health care system. Those who hold this view believe that any advice beyond filling a prescription and drug interaction information is unsolicited and out of professional boundaries. Our study revealed one patient with such view. The patient opposed pharmacists monitoring asthma drug therapy, developing an asthma action plan and preferred to stick to her asthma specialist who has the specialised knowledge and expertise to assess and manage asthma.

"Well it's a nightmare to be honest with you. I find that whenever I've gone to a pharmacy in [city name] I have either had a pharmacist try to tell me what my asthma medication should be or they try to ask you tons of questions because you have asthma, but they don't know the whole picture. They only see the prescription that you're bringing in, they don't have your medical file, they don't know how many doctors you've been to or what steps you've taken so far. They just assume that because you have asthma, it's not under control and they can provide additional advice that is actually unsolicited. It's really irritating to be honest with you". (Patient 11)

3.3.2. Sub-Theme 2: Valuable Relationship

The middle group of patients had a relationship with their pharmacists where the pharmacist knew them by name and supported technical skills by demonstrating inhaler technique. These patients attested to the value of pharmacist-provided patient education since many patients have poor inhaler technique. For example, one patient alluded to the fact that using the Aerosol holding chamber recommended by a pharmacist eased taking her rescue medication and improved its effectiveness.

I do [use the AeroChamber®] yeah. Yeah I don't even see that as a concern because I've always used it. It was actually a pharmacist who told me about that, not my family doctor. Which is part of why I wanted to participate in this because they play such an important role and that's made such a difference for me. (Patient 8)

Patients in this category demonstrated curiosity and desired additional care that might improve their asthma condition beyond filling prescriptions. They wanted to ask questions on medication effectiveness, user-friendly devices, and latest advancements in asthma therapy. Patients hoped to involve the pharmacist in their care to a greater extent but felt the pharmacists was responsible for initiating conversations and creating more awareness of patient care services. Though the patients have not experienced pharmacist prescribing or care plans, they indicated these would be helpful if done in collaboration with their family physician who has more knowledge of the patient's medical history.

Or maybe even like when I get to a pharmacist, having an appointment with them when I go to pick it up, to go over things and maybe decide if this even going to help me, instead of spending three months trying to figure it out with my doctor, who maybe not as knowledgeable on that kind of stuff. So yeah, it'd be nice—I mean, I know they offer that kind of stuff, so maybe making it more known (Patient 1)

Reflecting on previous challenges in obtaining medications, some patients gave suggestions on ways to enhance access to pharmacy services. For example, relocating the pharmacy to the front of the building would facilitate access for urgent medication pickups. Additionally, pharmacists should have the mandate to refill medications for patients with controlled asthma in order to free up time for doctors to attend to sicker patients with greater medical needs.

> *I understand that there might be insurance stuff involved in that but I do believe that I should not have to make an appointment with my doctor just to get medication refills. I think that is ridiculous and it's a waste [of time]. There is legitimate sick people out there that really need to see the doctor and all that does is put stress on an already stressful system. So I really think the doctor should just be able to push a button to refill the prescriptions at the pharmacist or something. The pharmacy should be able to refill your medication without your doctor. (Patient 10)*

3.3.3. Sub-Theme 3: Collaborative Relationship

Two Patients (6 and 7) credited their ability to take control of their asthma to the written asthma action plan co-created with their pharmacist. They visited the same pharmacist who is a Certified Asthma Educator (CAE) and spoke very highly of the pharmacist's commitment and advocacy in helping them become empowered in managing their asthma and monitoring the effectiveness of medications.

> *Her [the CAE pharmacist's] role is to advocate for being in control of my asthma myself, and making sure that the things she or my doctor are prescribing are actually benefitting me in the way they're supposed to, because I have the right knowledge to use them properly". (Patient 6)*

These two patients valued the one-to-one consultation that could have with the pharmacist saying that these were helpful in reviewing and reinforcing the patients' knowledge of asthma and monitoring asthma goals. One patient specifically said that her pharmacist keeps encouraging her to be symptom-free and that goal motivates her to know all aspects of her condition and maintain control of symptoms.

> *You know, she's really, really educated me on all aspects of asthma—it's been a real eye opener. Because I've had it for so long, and for probably at least the first fifteen years or so, I was just . . . Kind of on my own. You know, I'd go to the doctor. "Oh hi, how you doing?" "Um yeah, kind of coughing." You know, he was pretty good, but he didn't help me understand why I was coughing, and why I was having these symptoms. Whereas she sits me down and says, "Okay, look. This is why you're doing this, this, and this. And this is what you need to do. And you should not cough, period." [laugh]. (Patient 7)*

Apart from providing a better understanding of the illness and medications, the patients acknowledged their relationship with the pharmacist was immensely supportive. One patient in particular worried and felt she had to tough it out on her own before having an action plan. Now she felt supported to change her medication-taking behaviour and successfully monitor symptoms. Being able to know when control is worsening and what specific actions to take to tackle asthma exacerbations were important benefits of the asthma action plan for these patients.

> *And I've always wanted one. I would ask the doctor, and . . . They either didn't know about it or didn't have time. But she [the pharmacist] will sit down with me every month or two and go through it and do any changes . . . . So the action plan gives me specific things to do when my chest gets tight, when I get short of breath—then I can be flexible with the Symbicort. And I don't have to be afraid to take more Ventolin, or take even less than, like, one an hour. If it gets bad, I can do more. (Patient 7)*

The pharmacist was described as being non-judgmental, caring, personable, attentive, and listening deeply to understand the patient's situation and encourage them toward their asthma goals. The two patients who had a positive and trusting relationship with their pharmacist have experienced comprehensive asthma care.

> *[Speaking about pharmacist] "and be very caring and personable during the process" (Patient 6)*

> *And [the pharmacist] is so good that way, she's always encouraging me to, you know—by the time the next action plan comes up, 'Oh yeah, I was supposed to do that, okay'. So she doesn't judge, she doesn't criticize, she just (says), 'Okay, well let's work on that'. (Patient 7)*

4. Discussion

This study extends the knowledge in pharmacy literature by exploring patients' experiences of asthma within the movement toward patient-centred care in pharmacy practice. Previous studies that examined pharmacists' contribution to asthma care found that pharmacists possess the skills and competencies required to support patients with self-management education, demonstrating inhaler technique, and monitoring asthma therapy and could do more for patients in therapy monitoring and follow-up [7,8,38]. Findings from prior studies highlight the need for community pharmacists to work together with patients to attain control of their asthma. This study adds to earlier work by privileging the patient's perspectives on how they experienced the community pharmacist's delivery of asthma care. We found three themes namely: patients had a personalized common sense approach to asthma management, had a "go-to" health care provider to address asthma needs, and considered patient–pharmacist relationships important in asthma care (Figure 1).

Patients mostly evaluate their level of asthma control based on personally defined parameters and represent and manage asthma in a way that is consistent with the common sense model of self-regulation [37]. This model describes how patients rely on a mentally constructed approach to assign meaning to their illness symptoms (or lack thereof) and how this affects care seeking and self-management behaviours. Previous studies have demonstrated the relationships between asthma patients' representation of illness and medication adherence [21,39]. Our study adds to prior knowledge that caring for asthma patients goes beyond understanding the disease, clinical presentation, or providing medications to understanding the patient. The study points to the need to develop a shared understanding with the person living with asthma including their perceptions of asthma and asthma treatment as well as shared goals of asthma control [19,40]. Knowing that many patients' representations are dynamic and based on experiences, pharmacists, and other healthcare professionals could employ patient-centred communication [41,42]. Patient-centred communication involves inviting the patient to share their perspective, addressing concerns about treatment, regularly monitoring asthma medications and level of control in individual patients [20,43,44]. Patients knowledge and experiences should be recognized as valid during routine encounters to make interactions more meaningful and patient-focused [45].

In addition to adopting personal definitions of asthma, patients with asthma drew on a variety of resources within the healthcare system to manage their condition [46]. This was also reflected in the range of preferred healthcare providers for patients in our study. This "go-to" person included a family physician, asthma specialist, respiratory therapist, or pharmacist, or at least two of these providers, who they recognized as an expert resource for asthma information, advice and support. The nature and development of relationships with the health care provider is influenced by the perceived asthma needs and perceived role of the health care provider as being able to provide good asthma care, level of trust, convenience, and ease of access [19]. It may be that patients who had at least two "go-to" health care providers may have had complex needs or reasoned that they need more than one healthcare professional to address their needs. While it is desirable for asthma specialists to care for people with complex asthma, they are neither sufficient in number nor accessible to patients when needed. More so, patients with chronic obstructive pulmonary disease receiving both care specialist and primary care were not shown to have better outcomes than those receiving primary care only, though the case for asthma may be different [47]. Patients mentioned the benefits of having a regular health care provider was to prescribe new medication or refills, check and demonstrate proper inhaler technique, monitor asthma medications. Patient can access these services in a community pharmacy in Alberta where a government funded model supports all pharmacists to extend prescriptions and provide care plans as well as approved pharmacists to initiate new medications [48]. The reliance of patients on different healthcare providers would be an important factor to consider if a shift to multidisciplinary team care delivery were to occur. Another factor would be if patients' choice of healthcare provider changes with time though our study did not examine this possibility.

Patients' expectations of pharmacist roles and the type of patient-pharmacist relationship influences perceptions on the quality of care and this was supported by our findings [49,50]. Majority of the patient-pharmacist relationships clustered toward the bottom end of the spectrum where there is little positive relationship or even a negative relationship. On the other end, two patients had positive relationships with their pharmacists that impacted their asthma care. Our study conceptualises patient–pharmacist relationship (Figure 1) as a continuum of information-focused, valuable, and collaborative relationships similar to patient's perceptions of pharmacist roles as retailers, medication experts, and care providers [49–57]. While policy changes to enhance care for people with chronic conditions has been a significant driver of pharmacists expanded role, every patient encounter is an opportunity to build the relationship and support the uptake of patient care services [58]. The use of patient-centred communication strategies are linked to higher therapy monitoring and the use of asthma action plans, an important self-management tool [23]. Compared with patients with a low engagement with pharmacists, those who had valuable and collaborative relationships reported they not only had better understanding of asthma and asthma treatment but also more confidence and skill in managing their asthma.

The themes in our study reflect that asthma patients value patient-centred communication in their encounter with pharmacists which has the potential to increase patient acceptance of professional roles [59,60]. This implies pharmacists could invite patients to share their perspective asthma and common sense approaches to achieving control. This could increase patient engagement and tailoring of asthma education focused on patient needs. The practice of pharmacy has expanded beyond traditional dispensing roles to a more collaborative relationship and pharmacists should become competent in incorporating specific markers of asthma control into personalized asthma action plans. What matters to patients in their asthma management is just as important as telling patients what to monitor.

Limitations

Our study focused on patients' perspectives only which are different from providers' perspectives [19]. Future work could compare the experiences of patients and pharmacists to provide a complete understanding on the dynamics of the patient–pharmacist interaction and how it influences the quality of asthma care. Another limitation was that all the patients were experienced, had an asthma diagnosis for a long period of time and mostly likely learned how to navigate the health system and adequately manage their asthma. Since their views may be different from newly diagnosed patients where pharmacists have been known to spend more time with patients, more research is needed to explore the initial interactions between new asthma patients and pharmacist in the era of higher public and patient interest in pharmacist roles. Although the patient and pharmacist relationships have been the focus in the patient-centred care, a broader range of "system" factors may affect the patient experience care but our study did not investigate how structural and political factors influence patient attitudes and experience of asthma care [61]. Further research is necessary to evaluate strategies at the organization and policy level that could foster the patient-centredness of care within pharmacy practice.

5. Conclusions

Patients had a personalized common sense approach to asthma management, a "go-to" health care provider to address asthma needs and considered patient-pharmacist relationships important in asthma care. Our study indicated that asthma patients viewed pharmacists as retailers, medication experts, or care providers and their perceptions were shaped by their beliefs and experience of the pharmacist role. Pharmacists routinely encounter asthma patients and would be better positioned to provide tailored education and self-management support if they developed a collaborative relationship with patients and invited patients to share their common sense approaches to asthma. This starting point could increase patient engagement and uptake of personalised asthma action plans to achieve asthma control.

Author Contributions: L.G. conceived the study; S.B.G. performed the data collection; S.B.G., L.G., D.A. and T.M. analysed the data; D.A. wrote the initial draft. All authors reviewed and approved the final draft of the paper.

Funding: This research received no external funding.

Acknowledgments: We thank the participating patients, pharmacists, asthma specialists, physicians and the Asthma Working Group of the Alberta Health Services (AHS) Respiratory Health Strategic Clinical Network. We appreciate the contribution of Mindy Tindall who participated in data analysis and interpretation.

Conflicts of Interest: The authors declare no conflict of interest

Appendix Patient Interview Guide

Demographic information

1. How old are you? _____
2. Gender: __Male __Female
3. How long have you had asthma?
4. What medications do you use for your asthma?

Part 1: Asthma

1. Tell me about how you manage asthma. Who helps you with that?
2. Tell me about your asthma medications
3. Tell me about how you manage your asthma when you have a flare up/out of control?
4. When thinking about your asthma and your life, what matters to you?
5. Do you use an asthma action plan? (Show a copy). If so, please tell me how it was created?
6. Who helps you manage your asthma?

    a. Family Physician, Asthma Clinic, Asthma Specialist, Nurse, Pharmacist?

Part 2: Pharmacist Care

1. Tell me about a typical interaction with your pharmacist about your asthma medications.
2. What is the pharmacist role in the interaction that occurs between pharmacists and patients?

    a. Has a pharmacist prescribed an inhaler for you? How did that happen?
    b. Have you had a med review or care plan session with your pharmacist? Has a pharmacist had a longer talk with you that concluded with signing a piece of paper? Please tell me about it.

3. What is your role in the interaction that occurs between pharmacists and patients?
4. Imagine that your pharmacist wants to do more for you. What could your pharmacist do to help with your asthma?
5. Tell me about any negative experiences you have in the pharmacy.
6. What would you think of creating an Asthma Action Plan with your pharmacist?

References

1. Statistics Canada. Asthma, by Age Group. Available online: https://www150.statcan.gc.ca/t1/tbl1/en/tv. action?pid=1310009608 (accessed on 24 August 2018).
2. Papaioannou, A.I.; Kostikas, K.; Zervas, E.; Kolilekas, L.; Papiris, S.; Gaga, M. Control of asthma in real life: Still a valuable goal? *Eur. Respir. Rev.* **2015**, *24*, 361–369. [CrossRef] [PubMed]
3. The Canadian Lung Association. Asthma Control in Canada Survey 2016. Available online: https://www.lung. ca/news/latest-news/survey-asthma-not-well-controlled-most-canadians (accessed on 24 August 2018).
4. Sawicki, G.S.; Vilk, Y.; Schatz, M.; Kleinman, K.; Abrams, A.; Madden, J. Uncontrolled asthma in a commercially insured population from 2002 to 2007: Trends, predictors, and costs. *J. Asthma* **2010**, *47*, 574–580. [CrossRef] [PubMed]
5. Braido, F. Failure in asthma control: Reasons and consequences. *Scientifica* **2013**, *2013*, 1–15. [CrossRef] [PubMed]
6. Pinnock, H.; Parke, H.L.; Panagioti, M.; Daines, L.; Pearce, G.; Epiphaniou, E.; Bower, P.; Sheikh, A.; Griffiths, C.J.; Taylor, S.J.C.; et al. Systematic meta-review of supported self-management for asthma: A healthcare perspective. *BMC Med.* **2017**, *15*, 64. [CrossRef] [PubMed]
7. Saini, B.; Krass, I.; Smith, L.; Bosnic-Anticevich, S.; Armour, C. Role of community pharmacists in asthma —Australian research highlighting pathways for future primary care models. *Australas. Med. J.* **2011**, *4*, 190–200. [CrossRef] [PubMed]
8. Watkins, K.; Bourdin, A.; Trevenen, M.; Murray, K.; Kendall, P.A.; Schneider, C.R.; Clifford, R. Opportunities to develop the professional role of community pharmacists in the care of patients with asthma: A cross-sectional study. *NPJ Prim. Care Respir. Med.* **2016**, *26*, 1–10. [CrossRef] [PubMed]
9. Armour, C.L.; Lemay, K.; Saini, B.; Reddel, H.K.; Bosnic-Anticevich, S.Z.; Smith, L.D.; Burton, D.; Song, Y.J.; Alles, M.C.; Stewart, K.; et al. Using the community pharmacy to identify patients at risk of poor asthma control and factors which contribute to this poor control. *J. Asthma* **2011**, *48*, 914–922. [CrossRef] [PubMed]
10. Apikoglu-Rabus, S.; Yesilyaprak, G.; Izzettin, F.V. Drug-related problems and pharmacist interventions in a cohort of patients with asthma and chronic obstructive pulmonary disease. *Respir. Med.* **2016**, *120*, 109–115. [CrossRef] [PubMed]
11. Saini, B.; Krass, I.; Armour, C. Development, Implementation, and Evaluation of a Community Pharmacy–Based Asthma Care Model. *Ann. Pharmacother.* **2004**, *38*, 1954–1960. [CrossRef] [PubMed]
12. Manfrin, A.; Tinelli, M.; Thomas, T.; Krska, J. A cluster randomised control trial to evaluate the effectiveness and cost-effectiveness of the Italian medicines use review (I-MUR) for asthma patients. *BMC Health Serv. Res.* **2017**, *17*, 9. [CrossRef] [PubMed]
13. Anum, P.O.; Anto, B.P.; Forson, A.G. Structured pharmaceutical care improves the health-related quality of life of patients with asthma. *J. Pharm. Policy Pract.* **2017**, *10*, 8. [CrossRef] [PubMed]
14. Benavides, S.; Rodriguez, J.C.; Maniscalco-Feichtl, M. Pharmacist involvement in improving asthma outcomes in various healthcare settings: 1997 to present. *Ann. Pharmacother.* **2009**, *43*, 85–97. [CrossRef] [PubMed]
15. Armour, C.; Bosnic-Anticevich, S.; Brillant, M.; Burton, D.; Emmerton, L.; Krass, I.; Saini, B.; Smith, L.; Stewart, K. Pharmacy Asthma Care Program (PACP) improves outcomes for patients in the community. *Thorax* **2007**, *62*, 496. [CrossRef] [PubMed]
16. Naik Panvelkar, P.; Armour, C.; Saini, B. Community Pharmacy-Based Asthma Services—What Do Patients Prefer? *J. Asthma* **2010**, *47*, 1085–1093. [CrossRef] [PubMed]
17. Onda, M.; Sakurai, H.; Hayase, Y.; Sakamaki, H.; Arakawa, Y.; Yasukawa, F. Effects of patient-pharmacist communication in the treatment of asthma. *Yakugaku Zasshi* **2009**, *129*, 427–433. [CrossRef] [PubMed]
18. Street, R.L.; Mazor, K.M. Clinician–patient communication measures: Drilling down into assumptions, approaches, and analyses. *Patient Educ. Couns.* **2017**, *100*, 1612–1618. [CrossRef] [PubMed]
19. Sapir, T.; Moreo, K.F.; Greene, L.S.; Simone, L.C.; Carter, J.D.; Mateka, J.J.L.; Hanania, N.A. Assessing Patient and Provider Perceptions of Factors Associated with Patient Engagement in Asthma Care. *Ann. Am. Thorac. Soc.* **2017**, *14*, 659–666. [CrossRef] [PubMed]
20. Horne, R.; Price, D.; Cleland, J.; Costa, R.; Covey, D.; Gruffydd-Jones, K.; Haughney, J.; Henrichsen, S.H.; Kaplan, A.; Langhammer, A.; et al. Can asthma control be improved by understanding the patient's perspective? *BMC Pulm. Med.* **2007**, *7*, 8. [CrossRef] [PubMed]

21. Horne, R.; Weinman, J. Self-regulation and self-management in asthma: Exploring the role of illness perceptions and treatment beliefs in explaining non-adherence to preventer medication. *Psychol. Health* **2002**, *17*, 17–32. [CrossRef]

22. Driesenaar, J.A.; De Smet, P.A.; van Hulten, R.; Noordman, J.; van Dulmen, S. Cue-Responding Behaviors During Pharmacy Counseling Sessions With Patients With Asthma About Inhaled Corticosteroids: Potential Relations With Medication Beliefs and Self-Reported Adherence. *Health Commun.* **2016**, *31*, 1266–1275. [CrossRef] [PubMed]

23. Berry, T.M.; Prosser, T.R.; Wilson, K.; Castro, M. Asthma Friendly Pharmacies: A Model to Improve Communication and Collaboration among Pharmacists, Patients, and Healthcare Providers. *J. Urban Health* **2011**, *88*, 113–125. [CrossRef] [PubMed]

24. Cole, A.; Shaw, M.; Wright, H. How you can encourage medicines optimisation for patients with asthma. *Pharm. J.* **2014**, *292*, 125. [CrossRef]

25. Canadian Pharmacists Association. Pharmacists' Scope of Practice in Canada. Available online: https://www.pharmacists.ca/pharmacy-in-canada/scope-of-practice-canada (accessed on 20 September 2018).

26. Morrison, J. Expanded pharmacy practice: Where are we, and where do we need to go? *Can. Pharm. J.* **2013**, *146*, 365–367. [CrossRef] [PubMed]

27. Thorne, S. *Interpretive Description*; Routledge: New York, NY, USA, 2016.

28. Thorne, S.; Kirkham, S.R.; MacDonald-Emes, J. Interpretive description: A noncategorical qualitative alternative for developing nursing knowledge. *Res. Nurs. Health* **1997**, *20*, 169–177. [CrossRef]

29. Hunt, M.R. Strengths and Challenges in the Use of Interpretive Description: Reflections Arising from a Study of the Moral Experience of Health Professionals in Humanitarian Work. *Qual. Health Res.* **2009**, *19*, 1284–1292. [CrossRef] [PubMed]

30. Kahlke, R.M. Generic Qualitative Approaches: Pitfalls and Benefits of Methodological Mixology. *Int. J. Qual. Meth.* **2014**, *13*, 37–52. [CrossRef]

31. Lau, S.R.; Traulsen, J.M. Are we ready to accept the challenge? Addressing the shortcomings of contemporary qualitative health research. *Res. Soc. Adm. Pharm.* **2017**, *13*, 332–338. [CrossRef] [PubMed]

32. Collins, C.S.; Stockton, C.M. The Central Role of Theory in Qualitative Research. *Int. J. Qual. Meth.* **2018**, *17*. [CrossRef]

33. Braun, V.; Clarke, V. What can "thematic analysis" offer health and wellbeing researchers? *Int. J. Qual. Stud. Health* **2014**, *9*. [CrossRef] [PubMed]

34. Braun, V.; Clarke, V. Using thematic analysis in psychology. *Qual. Res. Psychol.* **2006**, *3*, 77–101. [CrossRef]

35. Green, J.; Karen, W.; Emma, H.; Small, R.; Welch, N.; Lisa, G.; Daly, J. Generating best evidence from qualitative research: The role of data analysis. *Aust. N. Z. J. Public Health* **2007**, *31*, 545–550. [CrossRef] [PubMed]

36. Morse, J.M. Confusing categories and themes. *Qual. Health Res.* **2008**, *18*, 727–728. [CrossRef] [PubMed]

37. Leventhal, H.; Phillips, L.A.; Burns, E. The Common—Sense Model of Self-Regulation (CSM): A dynamic framework for understanding illness self-management. *J. Behav. Med.* **2016**, *39*, 935–946. [CrossRef] [PubMed]

38. Guirguis, L.M. Assessing the knowledge to practice gap: The asthma practices of community pharmacists. *Can. Pharm. J.* **2018**, *151*, 62–70. [CrossRef] [PubMed]

39. McAndrew, L.M.; Musumeci-Szabo, T.J.; Mora, P.A.; Vileikyte, L.; Burns, E.; Halm, E.A.; Leventhal, E.A.; Leventhal, H. Using the common sense model to design interventions for the prevention and management of chronic illness threats: From description to process. *Br. J. Health Psychol.* **2008**, *13*, 195–204. [CrossRef] [PubMed]

40. Bodenheimer, T.; Lorig, K.; Holman, H.; Grumbach, K. Patient self-management of chronic disease in primary care. *JAMA* **2002**, *288*, 2469–2475. [CrossRef] [PubMed]

41. Naughton, A.C. Patient-Centered Communication. *Pharmacy* **2018**, *6*, 1–8. [CrossRef] [PubMed]

42. King, A.; Hoppe, R.B. "Best practice" for patient-centered communication: A narrative review. *J. Grad. Med. Educ.* **2013**, *5*, 385–393. [CrossRef] [PubMed]

43. Phillips, L.A.; Leventhal, H.; Leventhal, E.A. Physicians' communication of the common-sense self-regulation model results in greater reported adherence than physicians' use of interpersonal skills. *Br. J. Health Psychol.* **2012**, *17*, 244–257. [CrossRef] [PubMed]

44. de Oliveira, D.R.; Shoemaker, S.J. Achieving Patient Centeredness in Pharmacy Practice: Openness and the Pharmacist's Natural Attitude. *J. Am. Pharm. Assoc.* **2006**, *46*, 56–66. [CrossRef]

45. Houben-Wilke, S.; Augustin, I.M.L.; Wouters, B.B.; Stevens, R.A.H.; Janssen, D.J.A.; Spruit, M.A.; Vanfleteren, L.E.G.W.; Franssen, F.M.E.; Wouters, E.F.M. The patient with a complex chronic respiratory disease: A specialist of his own life? *Expert Rev. Respir. Med.* **2017**, *11*, 919–924. [CrossRef] [PubMed]

46. Cheong, L.H.; Armour, C.L.; Bosnic-Antcevich, S.Z. Patient asthma networks: Understanding who is important and why. *Health Expect.* **2015**, *18*, 2595–2605. [CrossRef] [PubMed]

47. Gershon, A.S.; Macdonald, E.M.; Luo, J.; Austin, P.C.; Gupta, S.; Sivjee, K.; Upshur, R.; Aaron, S.D. Concomitant pulmonologist and primary care for chronic obstructive pulmonary disease: A population study. *Fam. Pract.* **2017**, *34*, 708–716. [CrossRef] [PubMed]

48. Alberta Health. Pharmacy Services and Prescription Drugs. Available online: http://www.health.alberta.ca/services/pharmacy-services.html (accessed on 28 September 2018).

49. Assa-Eley, M.; Kimberlin, C.L. Using interpersonal perception to characterize pharmacists' and patients' perceptions of the benefits of pharmaceutical care. *Health Commun.* **2005**, *17*, 41–56. [CrossRef] [PubMed]

50. Tarn, D.M.; Paterniti, D.A.; Wenger, N.S.; Williams, B.R.; Chewning, B.A. Older patient, physician and pharmacist perspectives about community pharmacists' roles. *Int. J. Pharm. Pract.* **2012**, *20*, 285–293. [CrossRef] [PubMed]

51. Guirguis, L.M.; Chewning, B.A. Role theory: Literature review and implications for patient-pharmacist interactions. *Res. Soc. Adm. Pharm.* **2005**, *1*, 483–507. [CrossRef] [PubMed]

52. Shah, B.; Chewning, B. Conceptualizing and measuring pharmacist-patient communication: A review of published studies. *Res. Soc. Adm. Pharm.* **2006**, *2*, 153–185. [CrossRef] [PubMed]

53. Worley, M.M.; Schommer, J.C.; Brown, L.M.; Hadsall, R.S.; Ranelli, P.L.; Stratton, T.P.; Uden, D.L. Pharmacists' and patients' roles in the pharmacist-patient relationship: Are pharmacists and patients reading from the same relationship script? *Res. Soc. Adm. Pharm.* **2007**, *3*, 47–69. [CrossRef] [PubMed]

54. Antunes, L.P.; Gomes, J.J.; Cavaco, A.M. How pharmacist–patient communication determines pharmacy loyalty? Modeling relevant factors. *Res. Soc. Adm. Pharm.* **2015**, *11*, 560–570. [CrossRef] [PubMed]

55. Mossialos, E.; Courtin, E.; Naci, H.; Benrimoj, S.; Bouvy, M.; Farris, K.; Noyce, P.; Sketris, I. From "retailers" to health care providers: Transforming the role of community pharmacists in chronic disease management. *Health Policy* **2015**, *119*, 628–639. [CrossRef] [PubMed]

56. McCullough, M.B.; Petrakis, B.A.; Gillespie, C.; Solomon, J.L.; Park, A.M.; Ourth, H.; Morreale, A.; Rose, A.J. Knowing the patient: A qualitative study on care-taking and the clinical pharmacist-patient relationship. *Res. Soc. Adm. Pharm.* **2016**, *12*, 78–90. [CrossRef] [PubMed]

57. Schindel, T.J.; Yuksel, N.; Breault, R.; Daniels, J.; Varnhagen, S.; Hughes, C.A. Perceptions of pharmacists' roles in the era of expanding scopes of practice. *Res. Soc. Adm. Pharm.* **2017**, *13*, 148–161. [CrossRef] [PubMed]

58. Kelly, D.V.; Young, S.; Phillips, L.; Clark, D. Patient attitudes regarding the role of the pharmacist and interest in expanded pharmacist services. *Can. Pharm. J.* **2014**, *147*, 239–247. [CrossRef] [PubMed]

59. Mead, N.; Bower, P. Patient-centredness: A conceptual framework and review of the empirical literature. *Soc. Sci. Med.* **2000**, *51*, 1087–1110. [CrossRef]

60. Tinelli, M.; Bond, C.; Blenkinsopp, A.; Jaffray, M.; Watson, M.; Hannaford, P. Patient Evaluation of a Community Pharmacy Medications Management Service. *Ann. Pharmacother.* **2007**, *41*, 1962–1970. [CrossRef] [PubMed]

61. Greene, S.M.; Tuzzio, L.; Cherkin, D. A Framework for Making Patient-Centered Care Front and Center. *Perm. J.* **2012**, *16*, 49–53. [CrossRef] [PubMed]

pharmacy

MDPI

Article

Barriers and Facilitators for Information Exchange during Over-The-Counter Consultations in Community Pharmacy: A Focus Group Study

Liza J Seubert [1,*], Kerry Whitelaw [1], Fabienne Boeni [2], Laetitia Hattingh [3], Margaret C Watson [4] and Rhonda M Clifford [1]

1   Division of Pharmacy, The University of Western Australia, M315, 35 Stirling Hwy, Crawley,
    WA 6009, Australia; kerry.whitelaw@uwa.edu.au (K.W.); rhonda.clifford@uwa.edu.au (R.M.C.)
2   Department of Pharmaceutical Sciences, Pharmaceutical Care Research Group, University of Basel,
    Klingelbergstrasse 50, CH-4056 Basel, Switzerland; fabienne.boeni@unibas.ch
3   School of Pharmacy and Pharmacology, Griffith University, Gold Coast Campus, Southport, QLD 4222,
    Australia; L.Hattingh@curtin.edu.au
4   Department of Pharmacy and Pharmacology, University of Bath, 5W 3.33, Claverton Down,
    Bath BA2 7AY, UK; m.c.watson@bath.ac.uk
*   Correspondence: liza.seubert@uwa.edu.au; Tel.: +61-8-6488-7500

Received: 27 October 2017; Accepted: 1 December 2017; Published: 6 December 2017

Abstract: Consumers are confident managing minor ailments through self-care, often self-medicating from a range of over-the-counter (OTC) medicines available from community pharmacies. To minimise risks, pharmacy personnel endeavour to engage in a consultation when consumers present with OTC enquiries however they find consumers resistant. The aim was to determine stakeholder perspectives regarding barriers and facilitators for information exchange during OTC consultations in community pharmacies and to understand the elicited themes in behavioural terms. Focus groups were undertaken with community pharmacist, pharmacy assistant and consumer participants. Independent duplicate analysis of transcription data was conducted using inductive and framework methods. Eight focus groups involving 60 participants were conducted. Themes that emerged indicated consumers did not understand pharmacists' professional role, they were less likely to exchange information if asking for a specific product than if asking about symptom treatment, and they wanted privacy. Consumers were confident to self-diagnose and did not understand OTC medicine risks. Pharmacy personnel felt a duty of care to ensure consumer safety, and that with experience communication skills developed to better engage consumers in consultations. They also identified the need for privacy. Consumers need education about community pharmacists' role and responsibilities to motivate them to engage in OTC consultations. They also require privacy when doing so.

Keywords: communication; nonprescription drugs; over-the-counter drugs; pharmacists; pharmacy; focus group

1. Introduction

Many consumers are confident in the management of their minor ailments through self-care and self-medication [1,2]. This is facilitated by an interest in personal health, accessible health information through the internet and access to a variety of over-the-counter (OTC) medicines available without prescription [3]. Self-care and self-medication of minor ailments have benefits such as consumer empowerment, convenience and reducing healthcare costs associated with clinic or general practice visits [2,4]. Possible risks must also be considered such as the potential for incorrect self-diagnosis and subsequent delay in accessing appropriate treatment, interactions with concomitant medicines, and inappropriate use of medicines [2,4].

Pharmacists and other pharmacy personnel are readily accessible in community pharmacies and as such ideally placed to support consumers with self-care. The World Health Organisation describes several functions of pharmacists involved with self-care requests [5], the primary function being a 'communicator'. The pharmacist engages with a consumer to obtain information relevant to the enquiry and provides information to assist the consumer to select appropriate medication or refer the consumer to another health professional when necessary. Similarly, professional organisations, recognise the pharmacist's role in the provision of OTC medicines and the supervision of pharmacy personnel in the supply of these products [6].

Globally, countries are increasing access to medicines which were previously only available as prescription medicines to enable self-care and reduce national drug budgets [7–9]. The range of OTC medicines is available to consumers with varying levels of pharmacist involvement required prior to supply, depending on the classification and country [10–13].

Pharmacists are entrusted with considerable responsibility to facilitate the appropriate use of OTC medicines as well as providing many other professional services such as dispensing of prescription medicines, medication reviews, screening and risk assessment, and compounding [6]. As pharmacists adopt more extended roles, they rely on other pharmacy personnel, such as pharmacy assistants, to provide certain services.

OTC requests can be complex and interventions to improve OTC consultations and support consumers to engage in self-care have been implemented in the community pharmacy setting with variable success [14–18]. Pharmacists and pharmacy personnel report difficulties in engaging consumers in dialogue, particularly when consultation involves a request for a medicine by name (hereafter referred to as a product based request) [14,19,20].The reasons for this lack of engagement require exploration and it is reasonable to suggest that there is not one simple reason, but rather a range of factors that interact.

Models and theories can provide greater understanding of the determinants of different behaviours such as consumer engagement in OTC consultations. The development of the Theoretical Domains Framework (TDF) identified the main factors that influence behaviours of healthcare professionals (Supplementary file 1) [21,22]. The Behaviour Change Wheel [23] is a synthesis of a number of behaviour change frameworks with the COM-B model of behaviour at its centre (Supplementary file 2). The COM-B model (Figure 1) recognises that behaviour is a result of the interacting components of capability, opportunity and motivation (COM), and that behaviour (B) in turn may also influence capability, opportunity and motivation [23,24]. Cane et al. mapped the COM-B system to the TDF domains when validating the TDF [22]. Mapping the TDF to COM-B can assist researchers to identify the target for interventions that aim to change behaviour. While it is recognised that the use of behavioural theory may assist to understand behaviours, few community pharmacy-specific interventions utilise behavioural theory to develop or report interventions [25].

The aim of this study was to determine stakeholder perspectives regarding barriers and facilitators for information exchange during OTC consultations in community pharmacies. A secondary aim was to understand the elicited barriers and facilitators in behavioural terms.

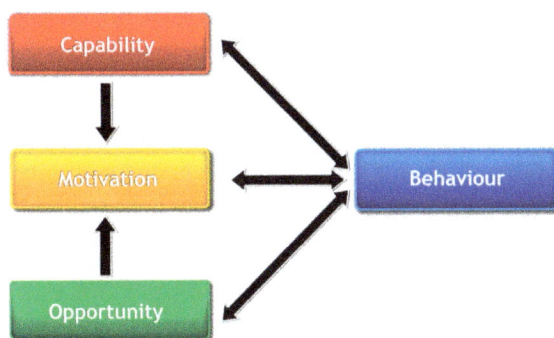

Figure 1. The COM-B system—a framework for understanding behaviour [24].

2. Materials and Methods

The data collected from this research will be used to inform the development of an intervention to enhance OTC consultations between pharmacy personnel and consumers in community pharmacies.

2.1. Study Design

A series of focus group discussions were undertaken to elicit a broad range of perspectives from key stakeholders to enable a deeper understanding of the topic. The main focus of these discussions was to explore the barriers and facilitators to the exchange of information between consumers and pharmacy personnel when consumers present in a community pharmacy with a request for a specific product (product based request) or assistance with a symptom (symptom based request)—hereafter referred to as an OTC consultation.

Approval for the conduct of this study was obtained from the Human Research Ethics Office at the University of Western Australia (RA/4/1/5298).

2.2. Participants

The key stakeholders of OTC consultations are consumers, pharmacists and pharmacy assistants. As such, these were the participants recruited to this study using purposive sampling to recruit 4–12 participants for each focus group. Participants were recruited from Perth, Western Australia. Pharmacist participants were recruited by email invitation from a member of The University of Western Australia (UWA) pharmacy practice teaching team to her contacts. This included more than 40 community pharmacists with whom Master of Pharmacy students were placed for practicums and pharmacists who taught into the course. Pharmacy assistant participants were recruited by pharmacist participants and the UWA pharmacy practice teaching team. Inclusion criteria for pharmacy personnel were that they had previous or current experience working in community pharmacy. Consumers were recruited via poster advertisements at UWA and within one Perth metropolitan community pharmacy with a UWA association during April and May of 2012 and again in April and May of 2013. Consumer participants were provided a $20 voucher for participation.

2.3. Focus Group Design

Focus group discussions were conducted by focus group moderators (LS, LG, HA). LS, an experienced focus group moderator, conducted training for LG and HA, Master of Pharmacy student researchers. The training was in the format of the provision of information about focus group facilitation, an observation of LS conducting a focus group, a pilot focus group consisting of Master of Pharmacy students as participants for practise (results not included in presented data), and feedback on technique. Each focus group commenced by discussing the focus group rules with a general outline of the project, including specific aims. During this time, participants were provided with participant information sheets and a demographic form. Consent forms were subsequently completed for both participation in and audio-recording of the focus group discussion. Consent forms were identical for all participant groups. Participant Information Sheets also had the same content, substituting lay person language for a few words in the consumer document. The focus group moderators followed a thematic interview guide which was adapted for the different participant groups (Table 1). The interview guide was developed by members of the research team (LS, RC, KW) with extensive community pharmacy experience and informed by a search of the literature for factors that influence OTC consultations [14,15,18,20,26–35]. The focus group discussions were conducted systematically beginning with a general discussion of participants' perceptions of asking/answering health-related questions during OTC consultations, followed by a more specific discussion of barriers and facilitators of the information exchange process.

Table 1. Thematic interview guide.

Participant Group	Main Themes	Support Questions
Pharmacist and pharmacy assistant	1. How do you feel about asking patients questions about their health?	- Do you think it is necessary? Why?
	2. What hinders patient assessment for over the counter enquiries?	- How does time affect asking questions? - Do you feel privacy is a factor? Why?
	3. What helps patient assessment for over the counter enquiries?	- How do you feel about taking a written patient history for primary care scenarios?
Consumers	1. How do you feel about being asked questions about your health by the pharmacist/pharmacy staff?	- Do you think it is necessary? Why?
	2. What closes the conversation about your health with the pharmacist/pharmacy staff?	- How does time affect asking questions? - Do you feel privacy is a factor? Why?
	3. What helps a conversation about your health with the pharmacist/pharmacy staff?	- How would you feel if the pharmacist took a written history from you for an over the counter enquiry?

2.4. Data Collection and Analysis

During the focus group discussions, a second researcher took notes on the participant responses. The discussions were also audio-recorded and then transcribed *verbatim*. A general inductive approach [36] was used for the analysis of the transcripts and was conducted independently by two researchers (LS, DA—a researcher with focus group expertise). Categories of key themes from the content of the discussions emerged into which the data was coded. Coding disagreements were discussed until consensus was reached.

The framework method of analysis [37] was also applied independently by two researchers (LS, KW) who coded data to the COM-B model and Theoretical Domains Framework (TDF) [22,23]. Coding disagreements were discussed until consensus was reached.

3. Results

Eight focus groups were held during 2012 and 2013 in Western Australia (Table 2). A total of 60 people participated in the focus group discussions (33 pharmacy personnel, 27 consumers). Statistics from the Pharmacy Board of Australia reports that in June 2013, 61% of Western Australian registered pharmacists were female [38]. Each focus group was approximately one hour in duration.

Table 2. Focus group participant demographics.

Stakeholder Group	Pharmacists	Pharmacy Assistant	Consumer
Number of focus groups conducted	4	1	3
Participant numbers	28	5	27
Female %	71	80	85
Mean age, years (range)	35 (21–62)	33 (20–57)	35 (17–82)
Median years since registration (IQR)	6 (25)	8 [#] (11)	NA
Currently working:			
• Full time	16	1	3
• Part time	11	4	14
• Not working	1 [*]	0	10

[*] on maternity leave, [#] mean years working in pharmacy.

Figure 2 illustrates the overlapping themes that emerged from the focus group discussions when participants were asked about barriers and facilitators for asking/answering health related questions during OTC consultations.

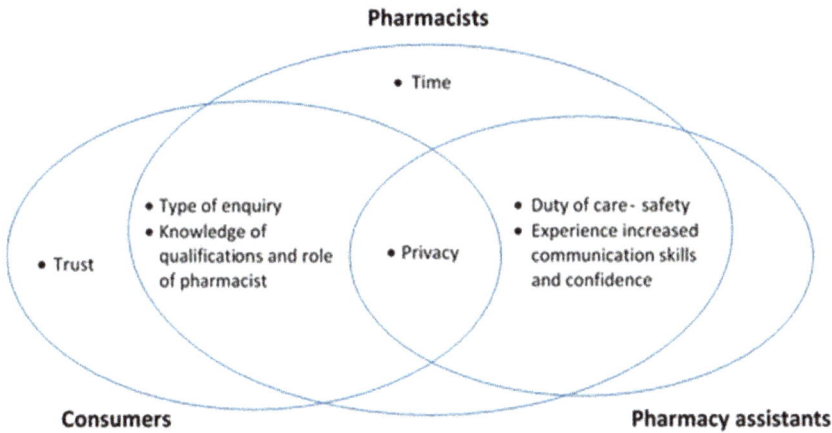

Figure 2. Thematic map of focus group themes and overlap.

The results of the TDF/COM-B analysis are summarised in Table 3 [23]. There was greater coding density for the Capability COM-B component from pharmacist participants than consumer participants which related to pharmacists' perception that consumer's lacked knowledge about the role of the pharmacist and also lacked knowledge about the potential risks with OTC medicines. Pharmacists also recognised the development of interpersonal (consultation) skills with experience. Environmental context and resources coding occurred frequently from the Opportunity domain and from the Motivation domain social/professional role and identity, belief about capabilities, and belief about consequences occurred frequently. Quotes are provided to illustrate the themes from both coding analyses.

Table 3. COM-B and Theoretical Domains Framework (TDF) coding from focus group transcripts.

COM-B	TDF		Participants (n)		
			Pharmacist (28)	Pharmacy assistant (5)	Consumer (27)
CAPABILITY	Physical	Physical skills	-	-	-
	Psychological	Knowledge	✓✓✓	-	✓
		Cognitive & interpersonal skills	✓✓✓	✓	-
		Memory, attention & decision processes	✓✓	✓	✓
		Behavioural regulation	✓	✓	✓
OPPORTUNITY	Social	Social influences	✓	-	✓
	Physical	Environmental context & resources	✓✓✓✓	✓	✓✓✓
MOTIVATION	Reflective	Social & professional role & identity	✓✓✓	✓	✓✓✓
		Belief about capabilities	✓✓	✓	✓✓
		Optimism	✓	-	-
		Belief about consequences	✓✓✓	✓	✓✓
		Intentions	✓	✓	✓
		Goals	✓	-	-
	Automatic	Reinforcement	✓	-	-
		Emotion	✓	✓	✓

COM-B: Capability. TDF: Cognitive and interpersonal skills

In the opening discussion of the focus group, pharmacy personnel reflected that as their communication skills developed with experience so too did their confidence and ability to develop a rapport with consumers and this facilitated asking consumers questions.

"I think to build a rapport with customers is important. The first contact [with the consumer] is quite important. If you can make a little difference on the first contact they will probably come back again and want to spend more time in the pharmacy. And that's the professionally rewarding bit." **Pharmacists' focus group 2, Participant 3 (hereafter quotes are labelled in the format Pharmacist 2, Participant 3)**

"I guess that's where the skill comes in . . . using a different approach with different people." **Pharmacist 3, Participant 8**

"It's [communication] a skill set that does take years of experience to develop." **Pharmacist 3, Participant 2**

"I think after working in pharmacy for five years . . . you get used to it. Initially it was difficult to develop that relationship to ask personal questions . . . but with time you become a bit more comfortable." **Pharmacist 4, Participant 4**

"[it helps to read] the body language of customers when you ask them the first question." **Pharmacy Assistant 1, Participant 1**

COM-B: Capability. TDF: Knowledge

Pharmacist participants expressed that they felt consumers' lack of knowledge about the qualifications, obligations and role of the pharmacist made consumers resistant to their questions.

"I think people probably underestimate the knowledge that pharmacists have." **Pharmacists 2, Participant 2**

" . . . people just don't know what we do. They don't know what our skill base is and how we can help them." **Pharmacists 2, Participant 1**

" . . . it really does depend on how they approach you and what they think you can offer. . . . most of the time people are very happy to offer some information but, you know, sometimes people are like: what right do you have to be asking me questions?" **Pharmacists 3, Participant 3**

To overcome this barrier pharmacists suggested publicising the role of the pharmacist.

"I think we need a massive PR [Public Relations] exercise on what pharmacists actually do, because people don't know what we do . . . they don't know what our skill base is and how we can help them" **Pharmacists 2, Participant 1**

" . . . *a massive public [relations exercise] on what the schedules are and what the role of the pharmacist is and that it isn't a retail transaction.*" **Pharmacists 3, Participant 6**

This was echoed by participants from consumer focus groups who indicated that they lacked an understanding of the role of the pharmacist in OTC symptom or product enquiries.

"*I'm not often sure what I can ask the pharmacist.*" **Consumer 2, Participant 4**

"*I wouldn't expect them to just hand it [OTC product] over . . . there would be a couple of corporate [standard] questions I would expect. Are you allergic, for instance. Those questions would be adequate, not about the actual problem. Not about the headache etc.*" **Consumer 1, Participant 2**

"*They don't have to ask for everyday things like Panadol® [paracetamol] and Nurofen® [ibuprofen] . . . because it's an everyday drug for a reason. Because it's OK for most people to take.*" **Consumer 2, Participant 3**

COM-B: Motivation. TDF: Social and professional role and identity. TDF: Beliefs about consequences

However, some consumer participants stated they thought that pharmacists had a duty of care to ensure the safety of the consumer.

"*I think pharmacists have a responsibility to ask questions because they can provide professional advice for certain diseases you may have. I think it's necessary.*" **Consumer 1, Participant 4**

"*The most important question with medications is [about] interactions. There are just so many of them*" **Consumer 3, Participant 2** "*and not everything is compatible and you're not aware that it would be really wrong to take them with something else that you're taking.*" added **Consumer 3, Participant 7**

Pharmacy assistant and pharmacist participants expressed an obligation to ensure the safety of the consumer.

"*It's a duty to ask them [health questions] to make sure we know what's going on with their life instead of giving them something that could kill them.*" **Pharmacy Assistant 1, Participant 1**

"*If somebody says 'I've had this before. Why are you asking me these questions?' If I say to them 'Well, because if this happens . . . you can end up in this scenario and that's why I'm asking. Just to keep you safe.'*" **Pharmacist 3, Participant 7**

COM-B: Motivation. TDF: Social and professional role and identity. TDF: Beliefs about capabilities

Pharmacy assistants expressed confidence in asking the pharmacist for assistance with OTC enquiries and that consumers may provide different information to the pharmacist.

"*I think it's important to make that decision to involve the pharmacist. People actually like that. They like to speak to the pharmacist . . . they really appreciate it when you involve the pharmacist.*" **Pharmacy Assistant 1, Participant 4**

"*It's amazing how their information changes from talking to us and talking to the pharmacist. It's like 'you never said that! I asked you that question and you said no, and now you're telling the pharmacist something different!'*" **Pharmacy Assistant 1, Participant 2**

A consumer participant stated willingness to provide health information to the pharmacist but not the pharmacy assistant. Other consumers noted that they could not identify who was a pharmacist and who was a pharmacy assistant (coded to COM-B: Opportunity. TDF: Environmental context and resources)

"*I guess it depends on who I am talking to. I'd be comfortable talking to the pharmacist . . . but if I'm talking to just an assistant . . . I wouldn't be as comfortable disclosing that information.*" **Consumer 1, Participant 9**

"You don't know if the person you're speaking to is the actual pharmacist or a staff person and you don't know how much they've studied." **Consumer 2, Participant 12**

" ... you can't tell the difference between pharmacist and assistants–there is an issue there I think." **Pharmacist 1, Participant 4**

COM-B: Motivation. TDF: Beliefs about capabilities. TDF: Beliefs about consequences

Pharmacist and consumer participants noted more willingness to exchange information with symptom based requests as opposed to product based requests. Pharmacist and consumer participants noted that the perceived risk, nature, or sensitivity of the problem also impacted the willingness of consumers to provide information. If a consumer asked for a product by name they were confident with their ability to manage the issue. However, if the request was for treatment of a symptom they were less confident.

In this context the need for privacy was universally raised.   (Privacy is coded to COM-B: Opportunity. TDF: Environmental context and resources)

"For cold and flu I'm perfectly happy to give over that information. But if it was something I deemed to be more personal . . . . I would be very resistant [to providing information] because I guess there is no privacy." **Consumer 1, Participant 2**

"For things like a cold and everyday things I really don't mind what questions they ask. But if it was a more personal thing it might be really specific and I'd be more reserved." **Consumer 2, Participant 8**

"I find it more [challenging asking questions] if they are asking for a particular product, then they aren't after the questions . . . . But if they come in with a problem then they want your help ... then they are up for the questioning." **Pharmacist 4, Participant 7**

"The other issue is privacy. I mean you ask these questions standing at a counter with other people around and it's not necessarily appropriate [consumers] giving [their] medical history." **Pharmacist 1, Participant 4**

"I think there's a good chunk of consumers who consider pharmacy as a transactional source of goods that they may not even view as a medicine. In their eyes 'I don't need a script [prescription] for it so just give it to me.'" **Pharmacist 3, Participant 7**

COM-B: Opportunity. TDF: Environmental context and resources

Pharmacists expressed concern with the limited time they had available to interact with consumers.

"Time is definitely a barrier because of the nature of our business. People rush in and you've got to serve everybody." **Pharmacist 1, Participant 1**

"There is a lot of pressure with people coming in and wanting to get their scripts in a timely manner [preventing time spent with OTC consumers]." **Pharmacist 4, Participant 5**

4. Discussion

This qualitative study on OTC consultation behaviour in community pharmacies explored barriers and facilitators to engaging in information exchange. A wide range of views from different perspectives were elicited during the discussions with convergent opinions between pharmacy personnel and consumers. The findings highlight consumer expectation of minimal interaction with OTC enquiries primarily due to a lack of knowledge about the professional role and obligations of pharmacists and other pharmacy personnel.

Pharmacy personnel are charged with supporting consumers in the management of their OTC enquiries through minimising the risks that consumers may not associate with self-care and self-medication. Pharmacy personnel and consumers expressed the view that pharmacists have a duty of care to ensure the safety of consumers with OTC enquiries. However, consumers seemed to relate this duty to only ensuring the consumer was not allergic to a medicine supplied or that it did not interact with their other medicines. While consumers were more willing to exchange health information if their request was for a symptom than for a specific product/medicine, it was evident that many consumers had a poor knowledge of the professional role of the pharmacist in diagnosis and whole of patient care.

Consumers' comments indicated an underestimation of the risks associated with taking OTC medicines and some were of the view that as these medicines were available without a prescription they had a right to obtain them without the need to engage in a discussion with the pharmacist. In behavioural terms, consumers are motivated to purchase an OTC medicine without consultation because they believe they have the capability to determine which medicine they require. This rise in health consumerism has been investigated by Hibbert et al. who found that many consumers were very confident in their ability for self-diagnosis and self-care of some conditions with purchased medicines [1]. Others have reported similar dis-interest of consumers to engage in a conversation about medicines [39], particularly when a specific product is requested as opposed to a request for treatment of a symptom [20,27,29].

A reluctance to engage in a discussion with OTC enquiries might also be related to the observation by all participant groups that consumers did not understand the role and responsibilities of pharmacists and other pharmacy personnel. The services offered by pharmacists have evolved from medicine supply to holistic patient care. It is broadly reported that consumers do not understand what services pharmacists are capable of providing [39,40]. To address this deficit in the knowledge TDF domain, campaigns have been implemented in many countries to improve the public knowledge of the pharmacist's role. For example, there is a Pharmacy Awareness Month in Canada [41], Australia has an 'Ask your Pharmacist' campaign [42] promoting pharmacists as a trusted source of health services and advice, and a similar campaign is run in the UK—'Dispensing Health' [43].

Pharmacist and pharmacy assistant participants recognised the need to develop a rapport with consumers when they present with an OTC enquiry. To develop this capability they said they needed to have well developed communication skills and that the more experience they had the better they reported having the required skill. This perception has been investigated by Nguyen who studied the development of pharmacist-patient consultation interactions in novice pharmacists (pharmacists in their first year of practice) and how they become 'expert' [44]. She found that the development of competence over their first year of practice occurred through repeated participation in interactions with patients. Novice pharmacists developed the skills of a two-way interaction involving the dynamics of turn taking, topic management, action sequencing, linguistic forms and participation frameworks. Novice pharmacists used their experiences to adjust future interactions resulting in a gradual change towards 'expertness' [44].

Privacy is a factor that affects the behaviour of consumers during OTC consultations. In Western Australia, where the study was conducted, pharmacies are required by law to have an area where consultations cannot reasonably be expected to be overheard [45]. While the legislation falls short of requiring a consultation room, in the time since the focus groups were conducted, immunisation by pharmacists has been implemented in Australia and requires community pharmacies where immunisation is provided to have a private consultation area [46]. Although this may provide a private area for some services it is likely that the majority of OTC consultations will continue to occur at the counter. When designing pharmacy layouts planning needs to provide easily accessible areas for private consultations to occur out of the hearing of the general public to provide consumers with the opportunity to engage in a consultation [47].

A strength of this study was the input from key participants involved in OTC consultations. The external validity of the analyses is strengthened by the use of theoretical frameworks. A limitation is that similar numbers from each participant group were not achieved resulting in a greater number of consumer and pharmacist participants than pharmacy assistants which may not fully represent the views of pharmacy assistants. Other limitations common to focus group methodology include the inability to generalise the qualitative data, and that the data could have been misinterpreted. This limitation was addressed by duplicate independent coding of the data.

5. Conclusions

In this study, many issues relating to information exchange during OTC enquiries in community pharmacy were identified. There was considerable overlap with the barriers and facilitators identified between participant groups. Much work has been conducted to improve the knowledge and skills (Capability) of pharmacists and pharmacy assistants when responding to OTC enquiries in community pharmacies with varying degrees of success [14,20,48–51]. There is, however, little research where the consumer is the target of the intervention. This study highlighted the consumer perspective as well as perspectives from pharmacy personnel. Educating (Capability) consumers about the role of the pharmacist and the potential risks associated with medicines (Motivation) whether they are available with or without a prescription is one type of intervention which might address these communication barriers.

Supplementary Materials: The following are available online at www.mdpi.com/2226-4787/5/4/65/s1. Supplementary file 1—Mapping of COM-B components to the Theoretical Domains Framework. Supplementary file 2—The COM-B system—a framework for understanding behaviour.

Acknowledgments: The authors would like to thank the participants of the focus group discussions for sharing their thoughts and experiences. The authors also thank Master of Pharmacy students at the University of Western Australia who assisted with data collection and transcription. No funding was received for this study. Author MW is funded by a Health Foundation Improvement Science Fellowship.

Author Contributions: Liza J Seubert conceived and designed the focus groups, analysed the results, and wrote the paper; Kerry Whitelaw performed duplicate analysis of data; Fabienne Boeni, Laetitia Hattingh, Margaret C Watson and Rhonda M Clifford contributed to analysis and write up of the paper.

Conflicts of Interest: The authors declare no conflict of interest. The authors confirm that all personal identifiers have been removed so that the persons described are not identifiable.

References

1. Hibbert, D.; Bissell, P.; Ward, P.R. Consumerism and professional work in the community pharmacy. *Soc. Health Illn.* **2002**, *24*, 46–65. [CrossRef]
2. Hughes, C.M.; McElnay, J.C.; Fleming, G.F. Benefits and Risks of Self Medication. *Drug Saf.* **2001**, *24*, 1027–1037. [CrossRef] [PubMed]
3. Therapeutic Goods Administration. Reasons for Scheduling Delegate's Final Decisions, June 2017. Available online: https://www.tga.gov.au/scheduling-decision-final/scheduling-delegates-final-decisions-june-2017 (accessed on 29 August 2017).
4. Bennadi, D. Self-medication: A current challenge. *J. Basic Clin. Pharm.* **2014**, *5*, 19–23. [CrossRef] [PubMed]
5. World Health Organisation. *The Role of the Pharmacist in Self-Care and Self-Medication*, 4th ed.; WHO Consultative Group on the Role fo the Pharmacist: The Hague, The Netherlands, 1998.
6. Pharmaceutical Society of Australia. *Professional Practice Standards—Version 4—June 2010*; Pharmaceutical Society of Australia: Deakin West, Australia, 2010.
7. Cohen, J.P.; Paquett, C.; Cairns, C.P. Switching prescription drugs to over the counter. *BMJ* **2005**, *330*, 39–41. [CrossRef] [PubMed]
8. Association of the European Self-Medication Industry. Available online: http://www.aesgp.eu/facts-figures/otc-ingredients/#undefined (accessed on 24 October 2017).
9. US Food and Drug Administration. OTC (Nonprescription) Drugs. Available online: https://www.fda.gov/Drugs/DevelopmentApprovalProcess/HowDrugsareDevelopedandApproved/ucm209647.htm (accessed on 23 October 2017).
10. Therapeutic Goods Administration. *Poisons Standard June 2017*; Australian Government Department of Health: Canberra, Australian, 2017.
11. US Food and Drug Administration. What Are over-the-Counter (OTC) Drugs and How Are They Approved? Available online: https://www.fda.gov/aboutfda/transparency/basics/ucm194951.htm (accessed on 23 October 2017).

12. U.K. Government. Medicines Act 1968. Available online: http://www.legislation.gov.uk/ukpga/1968/67/ introduction (accessed on 23 October 2017).

13. Pharmacy Board of Australia. *Guidelines on Practice Specific Issues*; Pharmacy Board of Australia: Melbourne, VIC, Australia, 2015.

14. Watson, M.C.; Cleland, J.A.; Bond, C.M. Simulated patient visits with immediate feedback to improve the supply of over-the-counter medicines: A feasibility study. *Fam. Pract.* **2009**, *26*, 532–542. [CrossRef] [PubMed]

15. Schneider, C.R.; Everett, A.W.; Geelhoed, E.; Padgett, C.; Ripley, S.; Murray, K.; Kendall, P.A.; Clifford, R.M. Intern pharmacists as change agents to improve the practice of nonprescription medication supply: Provision of salbutamol to patients with asthma. *Ann. Pharmacother.* **2010**, *44*, 1319–1326. [CrossRef] [PubMed]

16. Ratanajamit, C.; Chongsuvivatwong, V.; Geater, A.F. A randomized controlled educational intervention on emergency contraception among drugstore personnel in southern Thailand. *J. Am. Med. Womens Assoc. (1972)* **2002**, *57*, 196–199.

17. Westerlund, T.; Andersson, I.-L.; Marklund, B. The quality of self-care counselling by pharmacy practitioners, supported by IT-based clinical guidelines. *Pharm. World Sci.* **2007**, *29*, 67–72. [CrossRef] [PubMed]

18. Krishnan, H.S.; Schaefer, M. Evaluation of the impact of pharmacist's advice giving on the outcomes of self-medication in patients suffering from dyspepsia. *Pharm. World Sci.* **2000**, *22*, 102–108. [CrossRef] [PubMed]

19. Kaae, S.; Saleem, S.; Kristiansen, M. How do Danish community pharmacies vary in engaging customers in medicine dialogues at the counter—An observational study. *Pharm. Pract. (Granada)* **2014**, *12*, 422. [CrossRef] [PubMed]

20. Berger, K.; Eickhoff, C.; Schulz, M. Counselling quality in community pharmacies: Implementation of the pseudo customer methodology in Germany. *J. Clin. Pharm. Ther.* **2005**, *30*, 45–57. [CrossRef] [PubMed]

21. French, S.D.; Green, S.E.; O'Connor, D.A.; McKenzie, J.E.; Francis, J.J.; Michie, S.; Buchbinder, R.; Schattner, P.; Spike, N.; Grimshaw, J.M. Developing theory-informed behaviour change interventions to implement evidence into practice: A systematic approach using the Theoretical Domains Framework. *Implement. Sci.* **2012**, *7*, 38. [CrossRef] [PubMed]

22. Cane, J.; O'Connor, D.; Michie, S. Validation of the theoretical domains framework for use in behaviour change and implementation research. *Implement. Sci.* **2012**, *7*, 37. [CrossRef] [PubMed]

23. Michie, S.; Atkins, L.; West, R. *The Behaviour Change Wheel. A Guide to Designing Interventions*, 1st ed.; Silverback Publishing: Surrey, UK, 2014.

24. Michie, S.; van Stralen, M.M.; West, R. The behaviour change wheel: A new method for characterising and designing behaviour change interventions. *Implement. Sci.* **2011**, *6*, 42. [CrossRef] [PubMed]

25. Seubert, L.J.; Whitelaw, K.; Hattingh, L.; Watson, M.C.; Clifford, R.M. Interventions to enhance effective communication during over-the-counter consultations in the community pharmacy setting: A systematic review. *Res. Soc. Adm. Pharm.* **2017**, submitted.

26. Watson, M.C.; Johnston, M.; Entwistle, V.; Lee, A.J.; Bond, C.M.; Fielding, S. Using the theory of planned behaviour to develop targets for interventions to enhance patient communication during pharmacy consultations for non-prescription medicines. *Int. J. Pharm. Pract.* **2014**, *22*, 386–396. [CrossRef] [PubMed]

27. Watson, M.C.; Bond, C.M.; Grimshaw, J.; Johnston, M. Factors predicting the guideline compliant supply (or non-supply) of non-prescription medicines in the community pharmacy setting. *Qual. Saf. Health Care* **2006**, *15*, 53–57. [CrossRef] [PubMed]

28. Rutter, P.M.; Horsley, E.; Brown, D.T. Evaluation of community pharmacists' recommendations to standardized patient scenarios. *Ann. Pharmacother.* **2004**, *38*, 1080–1085. [CrossRef] [PubMed]

29. Watson, M.C.; Hart, J.; Johnston, M.; Bond, C.M. Exploring the supply of non-prescription medicines from community pharmacies in Scotland. *Pharm. World Sci.* **2008**, *30*, 526–535. [CrossRef] [PubMed]

30. Schneider, C.R.; Everett, A.W.; Geelhoed, E.; Kendall, P.A.; Murray, K.; Garnett, P.; Salama, M.; Clifford, R.M. Provision of primary care to patients with chronic cough in the community pharmacy setting. *Ann. Pharmacother.* **2011**, *45*, 402–408. [CrossRef] [PubMed]

31. Queddeng, K.; Chaar, B.; Williams, K. Emergency contraception in Australian community pharmacies: A simulated patient study. *Contraception* **2011**, *83*, 176–182. [CrossRef] [PubMed]

32. Kippist, C.; Wong, K.; Bartlett, D.; Bandana, S. How do pharmacists respond to complaints of acute insomnia? A simulated patient study. *Int. J. Clin. Pharm.* **2011**, *33*, 237–245. [CrossRef] [PubMed]

33. Kelly, F.S.; Williams, K.A.; Benrimoj, S.I. Does advice from pharmacy staff vary according to the nonprescription medicine requested? *Ann. Pharmacother.* **2009**, *43*, 1877–1886. [CrossRef] [PubMed]

34. Watson, M.C.; Bond, C.M.; Grimshaw, J.M.; Mollison, J.; Ludbrook, A.; Walker, A.E. Educational strategies to promote evidence-based community pharmacy practice: A cluster randomized controlled trial. *Fam. Pract.* **2002**, *19*, 529–536. [CrossRef] [PubMed]

35. Watson, M.C.; Bond, C.M. The evidence-based supply of non-prescription medicines: Barriers and beliefs. *Int. J. Pharm. Pract.* **2004**, *12*, 65–72. [CrossRef]

36. Thomas, D. A General Inductive Approach for Analyzing Qualitative Evaluation Data. *Am. J. Eval.* **2006**, *27*, 237–246. [CrossRef]

37. Gale, N.K.; Heath, G.; Cameron, E.; Rashid, S.; Redwood, S. Using the framework method for the analysis of qualitative data in multi-disciplinary health research. *BMC Med. Res. Methodol.* **2013**, *13*, 117. [CrossRef] [PubMed]

38. Pharmacy Board Of Australia. Pharmacy Registrant Data: June 2013. Available online: http://www.pharmacyboard.gov.au/About/Statistics.aspx (accessed on 6 November 2017).

39. Kaae, S.; Traulsen, J.M.; Nørgaard, L.S. Challenges to counseling customers at the pharmacy counter—Why do they exist? *Res. Soc. Adm. Pharm.* **2012**, *8*, 253. [CrossRef] [PubMed]

40. Assa-Eley, M.; Kimberlin, C.L. Using Interpersonal Perception to Characterize Pharmacists' and Patients' Perceptions of the Benefits of Pharmaceutical Care. *Health Commun.* **2005**, *17*, 41–56. [CrossRef] [PubMed]

41. Canadian Pharmacists Association. Pharmacist Awareness Month. Available online: https://www.pharmacists.ca/news-events/events/pharmacist-awareness-month-pam/ (accessed on 13 September 2017).

42. Pharmacy Guild of Australia. Ask Your Pharmacist. Available online: http://askyourpharmacist.com.au/ (accessed on 13 September 2017).

43. Pharmacy Health. Dispensing Health. Available online: http://www.dispensinghealth.org/ (accessed on 13 September 2017).

44. Nguyen, H.T. Constructing 'expertness': A novice pharmacist's development of interactional competence in patient consultations. *Commun. Med.* **2006**, *3*, 147–160. [CrossRef] [PubMed]

45. Government of Western Australia. *Pharmacy Regulations 2010*; State Law Publisher: Perth, Australia, 2010.

46. Pharmaceutical Society of Australia. Practice guidelines for the provision of immunisation services within pharmacy. In *Procedures and Requirements*; Pharmaceutical Society of Australia: Deakin West, ACT, Australia, 2014; p. 10.

47. Hattingh, H.L.; Emmerton, L.; Ng Cheong Tin, P.; Green, C. Utilization of community pharmacy space to enhance privacy: A qualitative study. *Health Expect.* **2016**, *19*, 1098–1110. [CrossRef] [PubMed]

48. Martin, B.A.; Chewning, B.A. Evaluating pharmacists' ability to counsel on tobacco cessation using two standardized patient scenarios. *Patient Educ. Couns.* **2011**, *83*, 319–324. [CrossRef] [PubMed]

49. Pham, D.M.; Byrkit, M.; Pham, H.V.; Pham, T.; Nguyen, C.T. Improving pharmacy staff knowledge and practice on childhood diarrhea management in Vietnam: Are educational interventions effective? *PLoS ONE* **2013**, *8*, e74882. [CrossRef] [PubMed]

50. Bertsche, T.; Nachbar, M.; Fiederling, J.; Schmitt, S.P.; Kaltschmidt, J.; Seidling, H.M.; Haefeli, W.E. Assessment of a computerised decision support system for allergic rhino-conjunctivitis counselling in German pharmacy. *Int. J. Clin. Pharm.* **2012**, *34*, 17–22. [CrossRef] [PubMed]

51. Watson, M.C.; Cleland, J.; Inch, J.; Bond, C.M.; Francis, J. Theory-based communication skills training for medicine counter assistants to improve consultations for non-prescription medicines. *Med. Educ.* **2007**, *41*, 450–459. [CrossRef] [PubMed]

pharmacy

MDPI

Article

Establishing a Pharmacy-Based Patient Registry System: A Pilot Study for Evaluating Pharmacist Intervention for Patients with Long-Term Medication Use

Manabu Akazawa [1,*], Akiko Mikami [1], Yuri Tamura [1], Natsuyo Yanagi [1,2], Shinichi Yamamura [3] and Hiroyasu Ogata [3]

[1] Meiji Pharmaceutical University, Noshio 2-522-1, Kiyose-city, Tokyo 204-8588, Japan;
    achito@nifty.com (A.M.); d176957@std.my-pharm.ac.jp (Y.T.); n-yanagi@chiba-u.jp (N.Y.)
[2] Graduate School of Medical and Pharmaceutical Sciences, Chiba University, Inohana 1-8-1,
    Chuo-ku, Chiba 260-8670, Japan
[3] Japanese Society for Applied Therapeutics, Hitotsubashi 1-1-1, Chiyoda-ku, Tokyo 100-0003, Japan;
    yamaroman@gmail.com (S.Y.); hi-ogata@wa2.so-net.ne.jp (H.O.)
*   Correspondence: makazawa@my-pharm.ac.jp

Received: 6 December 2017; Accepted: 24 January 2018; Published: 25 January 2018

Abstract: *Background:* In Japan, an increasing number of patients are prescribed a large amount of long-term medications by large hospitals that are then dispensed by a community pharmacy. This practice often leads to considerable wastage of medicine. As part of their professional role, community pharmacists are expected to contribute more to the appropriate use of medication by patients. Using a prospective cohort, we aimed to evaluate pharmacists' role in the community. *Methods:* We created a patient registry system for community pharmacies to monitor long-term medication use by patients with chronic conditions. Patient drug adherence and potential problems were monitored through regular home visits or telephone calls by the pharmacist at least once a month between patient hospital visits. Patient data were collected and stored in an internet-based system. *Results:* Over a one-year follow-up, 28 out of 37 registered patients from 14 community pharmacies were continuously monitored. In total, we extracted 19 problems relating to medication use, 17 to physical complaints, eight to patient concerns, and two others. *Conclusion:* The registry system was useful for identifying medication-related problems as well as patient concerns and changes in their condition. Pharmacists might play a key role in improving patient care in the community.

Keywords: community pharmacy; patient registry; pharmacist intervention; chronic condition; long-term medication

---

1. Introduction

The universal health insurance system is a unique feature of the Japanese healthcare system, and it allows patients to access any health services at a relatively low cost [1]. However, this system makes ineffective use of healthcare resources [2]. Many patients with minor disease conditions tend to seek health services at large-scale hospitals instead of local clinics. As a result, patients must wait hours to see doctors for only a minute; this situation is called 'three-hour wait, three-minute contact' [3]. In this healthcare environment, patients with chronic conditions often visit the hospital every two or three months and receive prescriptions to fulfil these periods. They then pick up a large amount of medications at a community pharmacy. However, Japan does not have a well-established primary care system that coordinates these patients in receiving long-term health services in the community [4]. Especially, even if a patient's condition becomes stable, referral from large hospitals to clinics does not function well. We do not have a system for family doctors and it is difficult to find an appropriate doctor in the community to care for one's condition. In addition, the introduction of a prescription refill system that allows patients to collect their medications repeatedly from a pharmacy without seeing their doctor is still under consideration [5].

Thus, patients with chronic conditions have primary responsibility for managing their medication use. Some patients do not use medications as instructed, while others stop taking them because of concerns about changes in their condition or treatment failures. This often leads to a large amount of wasted medicines, which are not used by patients [6–8]. According to a report from the Japan Pharmaceutical Association, the annual cost of the wasted medicines was estimated to be 47.5 billion yen in 2007 [9]. Community pharmacists must play a key role in adherence monitoring for patients requiring long-term medication because these patients cannot consult with doctors until their next appointment. Various studies have suggested that telephone counselling by pharmacists could improve patient adherence as well as their health and economic outcomes [10,11].

In April 2016, a new pharmacy system called 'Kakaritsuke-yakuzaishi' (family pharmacist) was introduced in Japan [12]. With this system, patients choose individual pharmacists (which requires an additional charge), who is then given the primary responsibility of managing patients' medications and health conditions. To be eligible to work as family pharmacists, pharmacists require the following: more than three years of work experience as a community pharmacist, a work time of more than 32 h per week, the requisite training, and involvement in community activities. All of this ensures high-quality services. However, the specific services that family pharmacists should provide to patients are not defined. According to Donabedian's framework, the quality of professional services can be evaluated in terms of structure, process, and outcome [13]. These requirements for family pharmacists merely ensure the structure of pharmacist services. To ensure high-quality pharmaceutical services, the process (i.e., the types of service/interventions that pharmacists should provide) and the outcomes (i.e., the benefits that patients can expect) should also be defined.

Therefore, to evaluate the pharmacist's role in community-based care, we established a patient registry system based in community pharmacies to monitor long-term medication use by patients with chronic conditions. This short report describes our experience of the first year of a pharmacist-led intervention using this registry as a pilot study.

2. Materials and Methods

We developed a patient registry system based in community pharmacies to evaluate the role of pharmacists in improving medication use among patients with chronic conditions [14]. A total of 14 pharmacists in 14 pharmacies, all of whom are members of the Japanese Society for Applied Therapeutics [15] or the Alliance of Pharmacy Executives [16], voluntarily participated in this pilot study. Patients who had been prescribed medications for 36 days or longer from large-scale hospitals and those who met the inclusion criteria of age 40 years or older, having chronic conditions, and having a potential problem with their medical treatment were selected by these community pharmacists. When patients were registered, information related to their medication adherence, including medication history, health condition, lifestyle, and potential problems/concerns, was obtained through a survey (as an initial assessment). Then, between patients' hospital visits, pharmacists contacted the patients by telephone calls or home visit at least once a month to check their medication use, as well as physical and mental problems (as follow-up assessments). As described in detail at Appendix A, all information taken from the patients was recorded and shared among the pharmacists via an internet-based system (DropBox^R). Pharmacists recorded patient information using Excel sheets at initial and follow-up assessments. Since information could be shared among pharmacists in different pharmacies, they could check each other's records to identify the best approach, to identify appropriate patients for registry, and to provide effective interventions. This study was approved by the Institutional Review Board at Meiji Pharmaceutical University (study number 2515), and written consent was obtained from all participants.

The data were collected by pharmacists from patient registration until the end of the monthly follow-up period—that is, about one year for each patient. Patient characteristics including medication adherence, health condition, and lifestyle were assessed via interviews and described. We counted the number of potential problems/concerns identified by the pharmacists and the number of cases improved by the pharmacists' interventions as a quantitative analysis. In addition, we described good examples of what kinds of interventions were provided and how they worked as a qualitative analysis. In the case that patients requested a withdrawal, the pharmacist recorded the reason for it in detail. When patients did not attend the next visits or did not answer the phone calls (dropouts), the pharmacists continued to try to contact them or other family members until they were found.

3. Results

During the four months between November 2013 and February 2014, 37 patients from 14 community pharmacies were registered (mean age = 72 years, 59% male). The mean number of different medications was 6.2 (maximum 14) and the mean duration of prescriptions was 67 days (with a maximum of 99 days). As for the background characteristics of patients, they had at least one chronic condition including hypertension (76%), hyperlipidaemia (51%), or diabetes (51%), as summarized in Figure 1. By the end of January 2015 (the one-year follow-up), 28 patients remained in the registry. The reasons for the nine dropouts were as follows: no patient follow-up data after registration (three cases), changes in hospital (two cases), and one case each of long-term hospitalization, house move, patient request for withdrawal, and the pharmacist moving to another pharmacy.

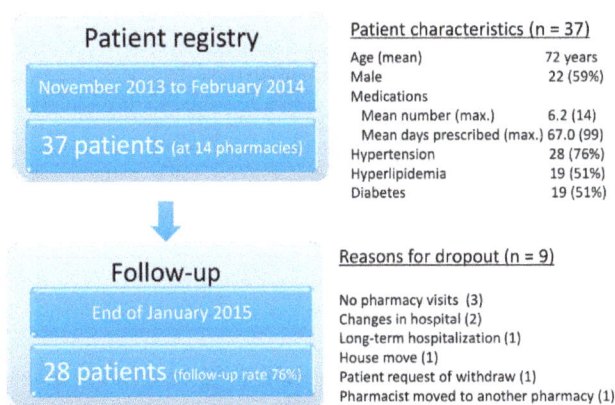

Figure 1. Patient characteristics and participation in the patient registry in the first-year pilot study.

At the initial assessment, pharmacists suspected problems related to medication uses, patient concerns (e.g., drug safety or effectiveness of medication), physical complaints (e.g., symptom improvement), or others (e.g., lifestyle). In addition, after registration, pharmacists could recognize these problems through close communication with patients during follow-up and provide suggestions or recommendations for improvement as described in Figure 2. In fact, 17 patients were registered due to suspected problems of medications use (non-adherence) and 20 patients were registered by their potential problems (patient concern, physical complaint, others). The potential problems identified by pharmacists during the follow-up period could be classified as medication use, patient concern (eight cases), physical complaints (17 cases), and others (two cases). There were 19 potential medication use problems among 16 patients; 12 cases of forgetfulness, six cases of self-adjustment/interruption, and one case of incorrect medication use. During follow-up, pharmacists discussed with patients as needed, identified why patients could not take medications as instructed, and worked together to look for methods of improvement. In fact, seven problems related to medication use were solved through this approach.

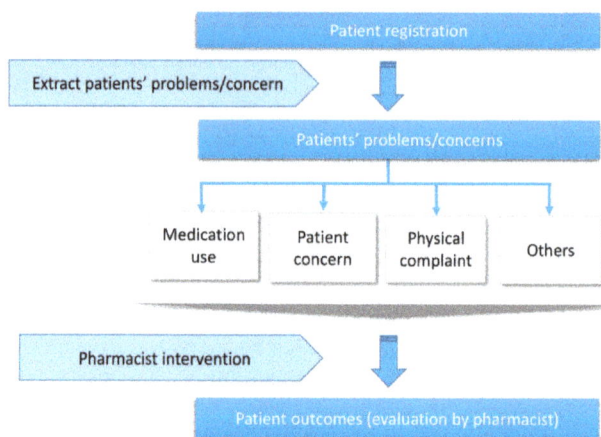

Figure 2. Flowchart of identifying problems and pharmacist interventions.

Specific cases are listed as examples of identifying problems, providing pharmacist interventions, and observing patient outcomes in Table 1. Note that we did not use any objective measures to evaluate patient adherence in this pilot study; this was based on the pharmacist's impression. In addition, lab results were obtained from patients if available. Some clinical results were based on the changes in lab data. However, most of the clinical findings were based on the pharmacists' judgments based on discussions with patients.

Table 1. Examples of potential problems, pharmacist interventions, and patient outcomes.

Category	Potential Problems	Pharmacist Intervention (Suggestion or Recommendation)	Patient Outcomes
1. Medication Use			
	Forget to take medicine when eating out	Keep some tablets in the bag constantly	Adherence was improved.
	Forget to take medicine when busy with work	Put the medicine in a conspicuous place Notice that the medicine could be taken also before eating	Adherence was improved.
2. Concerns			
	High blood sugar level despite efforts	Wait for the result of the next health check-up, and consider the possibility of hyperglycemia after a meal, as the current average blood sugar level is still better than before	The blood sugar level fell to the normal range on the next measurement.
	Blood pressure variation (low in the morning and high in the night)	Receive counseling from the family doctor	Concern disappeared after hearing that it was not necessary to mind this.
3. Physical Complaint			
	Chest ache after exercise	Get medical consultation for angina pectoris fear	The patient underwent detailed examination and was diagnosed and operated on for angina pectoris.
	Dizziness	Drink more water or tea because of possible side effect	Dizziness disappeared after several weeks.
4. Others			
	No interest in the results of the health check	Promote health education	The patient became interested in the value of health check-ups (e.g., purchased books); motivation to receive medical treatment increased.

The pharmacists involved in the pilot study were able to identify many potential problems among patients who received a large amount of medications, but could not consult with doctors and pharmacists for a long time. These problems are related to patient health conditions, medication use, and safety concerns. Some patient problems were identified during the follow-up telephone calls. When dispensing medications at the pharmacy, pharmacists did not have enough time to discuss these potential problems or ask about patients' concerns. However, when pharmacists were able to establish a good relationship with patients through frequent contact, patients gradually began to speak more about their daily life and medication-related problems. In some cases, pharmacists found many unused drugs at the patient's home, even though the patients had reported good adherence when asked at the pharmacy counter. Notably, in one case, a male patient reported an unusual condition after taking medication; based on his account, the pharmacist suspected that the patient had angina and reported it to his doctor, leading to early diagnosis and treatment.

4. Discussion

This pilot study was conducted to establish a pharmacy-based patient registry system, and then, this system was used to evaluate pharmacist interventions to improve potential problems related to long-term medication use. Therefore, we attempted to collect real-world evidence about potential problems of patients, pharmacist interventions, and patient outcomes. We determined what kinds of information should be collected and how often pharmacists should contact patients. In addition, we did not evaluate effectiveness of pharmacist interventions objectively and there were no comparison groups. Thus, it was difficult to determine whether observed outcomes were due to the intervention. However, from this pilot study, we could identify target patient populations and outcome measures that had been used for the new registration system.

One of the merits of this registry system is that pharmacists can learn from each other by sharing information. We asked pharmacists who participated in the pilot study what kinds of information should be collected at the initial and follow-up assessments. In this way, pharmacists could understand how to monitor patients. In addition, the pharmacists needed to collect information about medications prescribed outside of the pharmacies by asking patients or checking patients' medication notes. Therefore, they had a strong incentive to collect this information to identify patients' potential problems and monitor them through the registry system.

The patient registry system noted in this study is an effective approach for promoting active intervention by community pharmacists. When pharmacists identify patients who have potential problems and need special care, these patients should be registered and monitored. However, such patient selection and adherence monitoring would create an additional workload for pharmacists. A support system to help pharmacists is essential to continue this registry system. Only a limited number of patients could be recruited and followed-up in the pilot study, which impeded the generalization of the findings. Therefore, we completed the pilot study in March 2015 and developed a new online registry system for initial and follow-up data collection. This new registry system involves nearly 100 pharmacies, and was initiated in May 2015 with 300 registered patients. As of December 2017, the follow-up is still on going.

The goal of the new registry system is to provide a successful model for the family pharmacist from a perspective of quality of professional services, especially the process and the outcomes suggested by Donabedian. Therefore, to evaluate the pharmacists' roles in community-based care, cumulative evidence is needed showing how many patients have improved relationships with their pharmacists (quantitative data) and how they can establish such good relationships (qualitative data).

5. Conclusions

This is the first patient registry system to evaluate the pharmacist's role in community-based care in Japan. Medication wastage related to long-term prescriptions for chronic conditions is one of the target issues for Japanese healthcare reform, and we expect that family pharmacists might play a key role in promoting appropriate medication use and reducing costs related to wasted medication. Our findings could inform appropriate measures to evaluate health and cost benefits of pharmacist interventions with regard to patient care in the community.

Acknowledgments: We thank all of the pharmacists who participated in the pilot study at Minami Pharmacy, Olive Pharmacy, Primary Pharmacy, Tamura Pharmacy, and Nihon Chouzai Co., Ltd. We also would like to thank Editage (www.editage.jp) for English language editing. This work was supported by the Japan Society for the Promotion of Science (JSPS) KAKENHI grant number 26460236 (2014–2016).

Author Contributions: All the authors have approved the manuscript and agree with its submission.

Conflicts of Interest: There are no conflicts of interest to declare.

Disclosure: A part of this study was presented at the 30th International Conference on Pharmacoepidemiology and Therapeutic Risk Management in Taipei (Taiwan, 2014) and at the FIP Congress in Düsseldorf (Germany, 2015) as poster presentations.

Appendix A. Data Collection at the Initial and Follow-Up Assessments

At the initial assessment, pharmacists should collect and record the following data.

1. Patient's ID (automatically assigned at registration)
2. Age and sex
3. Clinical conditions for long-term medication use
4. Date of informed consent
5. Contact information if needed
6. List of all medications used by the patient (not only dispensed medication at the pharmacy, but also those dispensed at different pharmacies)
7. Treatment history
8. Other conditions not for long-term medication use
9. Lab results (blood pressure, lipid, HbA1c, etc.)
10. Treatment conditions (one-pack doses, number of clinics used, etc.)
11. Living environments related to treatment (living alone, job, home care, etc.)
12. Potential problems reported by patient
13. Potential concerns identified by pharmacist
14. Preferred methods for follow-up contacts
15. Others

At the follow-up assessments, pharmacists should monitor and record the following data.

1. Date of contacts
2. Method for monitoring (telephone or visit)
3. Changes in medications
4. Patient reported adherence or number of medications not used
5. Reason for not taking medications as instructed
6. Conditional changes (if any)
7. Lab results (reported by patients)
8. Pharmacist advice given to patients
9. Next appointment dates

When patients request a withdrawal, or have no further pharmacy visits, pharmacists should ask the reasons at the last visit or try to contact patients or family members as much as possible.

Pharmacy **2018**, *6*, 12

References

1. Abe, S. Japan's strategy for global health diplomacy: Why it matters. *Lancet* **2013**, *382*, 915–916. [CrossRef]
2. Organisation for Economic Co-operation and Development (OECD). *OECD Reviews of Health Care Quality: Japan–Assessment and Recommendations*; OECD: Paris, France, 2014.
3. Nomura, H.; Nakayama, T. The Japanese healthcare system: The issue is to solve the "tragedy of the commons" without making another. *BMJ* **2005**, *331*, 648–649. [CrossRef] [PubMed]
4. Cabinet Office, Government of Japan. General Overview and Examples of the Regulatory Reform Council's Second Report of Recommendations—Health and Medical Field. Available online: http://www8.cao.go.jp/kisei-kaikaku/english/index-en.html (accessed on 27 October 2017). (In Japanese)
5. Ministry of Health, Labour and Welfare. Unused Drugs and Split Dispensing (as a Document Used in Central Social Insurance Medical Council on 22 July 2015). Available online: http://www.mhlw.go.jp/stf/shingi2/0000092094.html (accessed on 27 October 2017). (In Japanese)
6. Koyanagi, K.; Kubot, T.; Kobayashi, D.; Kihara, T.; Yoshid, T.; Miisho, T.; Saito, Y.; Uchigoshi, H.; Takaki, J.; Seo, T.; et al. SETSUYAKU-BAG Campaign—Investigation of leftover drugs retained by outpatients and promotion of proper reuse leftover drugs to reduce medical expenses. *Yakugak. Zasshi* **2013**, *133*, 1215–1221. [CrossRef]
7. Nakamura, K.; Urano, K.; Tanaka, M.; Nishiguchi, K.; Sakai, Y.; Katano, T.; Nabekura, T.; Yamamura, K.; Kunimasa, J. The Reduction Impact in Medical Expenses of Pharmaceutical Inquiries on Leftover Medicines at a Community Pharmacy. *Jpn. J. Pharm. Health Care Sci.* **2014**, *40*, 522–529. [CrossRef]
8. Onda, M.; Imai, H.; Kasuga, M.; Yasuda, M.; Shimomura, M.; Okamoto, N.; Takada, Y.; Nanaumi, Y.; Tanaka, Y.; Arakawa, Y. Examining the effect of pharmacists' visits to housebound patients on the elimination of unused drugs. *Jpn. J. Drug. Inform.* **2015**, *17*, 21–33.
9. Japan Pharmaceutical Association. Study on the Effect of Pharmacist Drug Management for Elderly Patients at Home. Report March 2008. Available online: http://www.nichiyaku.or.jp/action/wp-content/uploads/2008/06/19kourei_hukuyaku1.pdf (accessed on 27 October 2017). (In Japanese)
10. Elliott, R.A.; Barber, N.; Clifford, S.; Horne, R.; Hartley, E. The cost effectiveness of a telephone-based pharmacy advisory service to improve adherence to newly prescribed medicines. *Pharm. World Sci.* **2008**, *30*, 17–23. [CrossRef] [PubMed]
11. Yamamoto, N.; Nitta, M.; Hara, K.; Watanabe, F.; Akagawa, K.; Kurata, N.; Kamei, M. Community pharmacists provided telephone treatment support for patients who received long-term prescribed medication. *Integr. Pharm. Res. Pract.* **2016**, *5*, 27–32. [PubMed]
12. Ministry of Health, Labour and Welfare 2015: Kanjanotameno Yakkyokubijon (as a Document, "a Vision of Community Pharmacy for Patients" on 23 October 2015). Available online: http://www.mhlw.go.jp/file/04-Houdouhappyou-11121000-Iyakushokuhinkyoku-Soumuka/vision_1.pdf (accessed on 27 October 2017). (In Japanese)
13. Donabedian, A. Evaluating the quality of medical care. *Milbank Mem. Fund Q.* **1966**, *44*, 166–206. [CrossRef]
14. Pharmacist Intermediate Intervention Study (PIIS). Available online: http://piis.skr.jp/public.health/home.html (accessed on 25 January 2018). (In Japanese)
15. Japanese Society for Applied Therapeutics. Available online: http://www.applied-therapeutics.org (accessed on 25 January 2018). (In Japanese)
16. Alliance of Pharmacy Executives. Available online: http://yakukeiren.com (accessed on 25 January 2018). (In Japanese)

pharmacy

MDPI

Article

A National Survey of Community Pharmacists on Smoking Cessation Services in Thailand [†]

Surarong Chinwong and Dujrudee Chinwong *

Department of Pharmaceutical Care, Faculty of Pharmacy, Chiang Mai University, Chiang Mai 50200, Thailand; surarong@gmail.com
* Correspondence: dujrudee.c@cmu.ac.th; Tel.: +66-53-944-342; Fax.: +66-53-944-390
† A part of this study was presented as a poster presentation at the 44th ESCP Symposium on Clinical Pharmacy, Lisbon, Portugal, 28–30 October 2015.

Received: 12 August 2018; Accepted: 13 September 2018; Published: 17 September 2018

Abstract: Providing smoking cessation services is one role of community pharmacists in Thailand. This cross-sectional study aimed to investigate activities and barriers related to smoking cessation services provided in community pharmacies in Thailand, as well as to compare these activities and barriers between those pharmacists providing and those not providing smoking cessation services. A postal questionnaire was conducted to collect information from community pharmacists across Thailand. In all, 413 valid responses were received from 5235 questionnaires, giving a 7.9% response rate. Of the 413 respondents, 152 (37%) pharmacists provided smoking cessation services in their pharmacy. The activities of smoking cessation services varied. Time for counseling each smoker varied, a mean of 15.1 ± 10.9 min (range 1–60) per person for the first time, and 8.9 ± 6.7 min (range 1–30) for each follow-up visit. Community pharmacists, providing smoking cessation services, were more likely to have pharmacist assistants, be a member of the Thai Pharmacy Network for Tobacco Control, and have more than 1 pharmacist on duty. The most dispensed pharmaceutical product for smoking cessation was nicotine gum. Their most perceived barriers were being unable to follow-up and inadequate staff. In conclusion, only a minority of community pharmacists in Thailand are engaged in smoking cessation activities, even though some perceived barriers existed.

Keywords: smoking cessation; community pharmacists; tobacco control

---

1. Introduction

Tobacco smoking is a preventable cause of death and causes more than six million deaths annually [1]. Smoking accounted for one in ten of all deaths in Thailand, and is related with increasing health expenditure [2]. Therefore, smoking cessation is one strategy to reduce the cause of preventable death from tobacco use. Offering help to quit tobacco use is one strategy for tobacco cessation, as recommended by the World Health Organization (WHO) [3]. Thailand has adopted the WHO policy for tobacco control, and has been recognized for its success in tobacco control for many years [4].

Community pharmacists play key roles in helping smokers to quit smoking [5,6]. Pharmacy professionals are in an optimal position to aid smoking cessation, due to their roles in providing counselling and smoking aid products to support cessation. It has been well established that interventions for smoking cessation by pharmacists are cost-effective [7]. As community pharmacists are in locations where patients could easily access, evidence in many countries has shown the success of smoking cessation services provided by community pharmacists [8,9]. Smoking cessation services were provided by health care workers, including pharmacists in many countries, such as in the UK, USA, Finland, as well as Thailand [5,6,8–17].

In Thailand, community pharmacies are in all provinces across the country and are primary places where people can go when they have a minor illness. Some community pharmacies provide smoking cessation services. Likewise, providing smoking cessation services in Thai community pharmacies is of interest to both professionals and patients. Community pharmacists can dispense nicotine replacement therapy (NRT) and non-nicotine products to strengthen their smoking cessation services, for those smokers needing pharmacotherapy to stop smoking. Research has confirmed that Thai community pharmacists engage in many smoking cessation services [8,10].

Smoking cessation services provided in community pharmacies in Thailand have been encouraged by the Thai Pharmacy Network for Tobacco Control (TPNTC) since 2004. Community pharmacists have been trained by the TPNTC using both lectures and practice. The first national survey in 2010 on community pharmacists' roles in providing smoking cessation services, showed that the community pharmacist at least engaged in helping patients to quit smoking by offering brief advice [8]. Thananithisak et al. [10] conducted a study among 42 community pharmacists in Bangkok, to learn about the experiences of community pharmacists. They focused on pharmacists' perceptions of their roles, barriers, and tobacco control activities. This study identified eight barriers in the provision of smoking cessation services, the most important three being: Lack of patient demand, lack of educational materials, and lack of smoking cessation products. This study did not cover community pharmacies across Thailand. Other studies in other countries, also identified barriers preventing community pharmacists from achieving the highest level of offering their practices of smoking cessation services. For example, these barriers included time constraints, no interest from smokers, lack of knowledge and skills needed to help smokers to quit, lack of confidence, inadequate staffing, and no reimbursement [8,10,18–21]. Since 2004, provision of smoking cessation by community pharmacists has increased encouraged by the TPNTC, and the pharmacy faculties at many universities have added smoking cessation content in their curriculum [22].

However, smoking cessation services are only available in some community pharmacies in Thailand. Thus, this study aimed to investigate activities and barriers related to smoking cessation services provided in community pharmacies in Thailand, as well as to compare these activities and barriers between those pharmacists providing and those not providing smoking cessation services. This will provide policy makers and organizations, such as the TPNTC and pharmacy faculties, with important information about increased roles of community pharmacists in promoting smoking cessation.

2. Materials and Methods

2.1. Participants and Procedures

A cross-sectional survey was conducted among community pharmacies in Thailand, between 2013 and 2014. This study aimed to explore roles of community pharmacists in tobacco control, especially in providing smoking cessation services. The participants included community pharmacists across Thailand. A list of all community pharmacies and their addresses were received from the Thai Food and Drug Administration (Thai FDA), Ministry of Public Health, Faculty of Pharmacy, Chiang Mai University, and the Office of Pharmacy Accreditation (Thailand). Therefore, the questionnaires were sent to all community pharmacies, according to the list compiled from these organizations.

2.2. Questionnaire Development and Data Collection

The questionnaire used to collect information from participants was designed to be self-administered, and all responses were voluntary. The questionnaire was developed by the research team based on the objectives of the study and literature reviews. The content validity of the questionnaire was also reviewed by the research team and experts in tobacco control. The questionnaire was then tested with ten pharmacists, for the use of appropriate language, before sending the questionnaire to participants. The aim of this process was to ensure that the pharmacists properly understood each item in the questionnaire.

The questionnaire included general information regarding pharmacists, and information on activities of community pharmacists providing smoking cessation services. The demographic information included sex, age, length of being a community pharmacist, having a pharmacist assistant, location of the pharmacy, number of pharmacists on duty, being a member of the TPNTC, and products for smoking cessation available in their community pharmacies. The information on activities related to smoking cessation services in their community pharmacies, for those providing smoking cessation services, included number of people asking for help with smoking cessation, time spent with the smoking cessation services and services to aid smoking cessation. In addition, an open-ended question was asked about motivation of pharmacists to help smokers to quit, for those pharmacists offering smoking cessation services in their drugstores. The last part focused on perceived barriers by community pharmacists in providing smoking cessation services; this part was for all pharmacists to answer. Eleven Likert scale items (4-points: strongly agree, agree, disagree, and strongly disagree) inquired about perceived barriers for smoking cessation services. In all, 38 questions included a mix of multiple choice, open-ended, and Likert scale items.

Pharmacists providing smoking cessation services were identified by the question "Do you provide a smoking cessation service in your pharmacy?", where a "Yes" response was classified as providing smoking cessation services; whilst a "No" was classified as not providing smoking cessation services.

Questionnaires with cover letters explaining the purpose of the study and confidentiality were sent by post to 5450 community pharmacies, according to their addresses on the list. To increase the response rate, pharmacists were later contacted by telephone and given reminders. Unfortunately, many telephone numbers of pharmacists were incorrect or missing.

2.3. Statistical Analysis

STATA Software, Version 12 (StataCorp LP, College Station, TX, USA) was used for statistical analyses. The significance level was set as two-tailed, and at *p*-value of <0.05. For descriptive statistics, means ± standard deviations for continuous variables, and frequencies with percentages for categorical variables were reported. The differences between the two groups (such as pharmacists providing services and those not), were compared using Fisher's exact test for categorical variables, or independent *t*-test for continuous variables. For the 4-point Likert scale, data were grouped in two groups only (agree vs. disagree).

2.4. Ethics

This study protocol was approved by the Ethics Review Committee, Faculty of Pharmacy, Chiang Mai University, Thailand, before commencing the study. All participants were informed about the study protocol through the subject information sheet, and that their completing the questionnaire was voluntary.

3. Results

3.1. Response Rate

From the initial questionnaires sent to 5450 pharmacists, failure delivery notifications were received for 215 (3.9%), giving a denominator of 5235 pharmacists. Of the 435 returned questionnaires, duplicate submission to the same community pharmacies (10) and incomplete questionnaires unsuitable for the analysis (10) were removed. Hence 413 questionnaires were included in the analysis, representing a 7.9% response rate (413/5235). Hence, percentages presented are based on numbers of respondents answering each question.

3.2. Characteristics of the Respondents

Of the 413 community pharmacists, who answered the questionnaire, 152 (37%) reported having smoking cessation services provided in their community pharmacies. More pharmacists were women than men (60% and 40%), and the average age was 40.9 ± 12.7 years, ranging from 22 to 82. Most had graduated as a pharmacist before 1994, that is, graduated more than 20 years previously. Almost one half served as community pharmacists for less than 10 years. Most pharmacists (97%) agreed that providing smoking cessation services was one role of community pharmacists. Community pharmacists providing smoking cessation services, were more likely to have pharmacist assistants, be a member of the TPNTC, and have more than 1 pharmacist on duty. Details are shown in Table 1.

Table 1. Participants' characteristics in providing smoking cessation services (*n* = 413).

Characteristic	Total (*n* = 413)	Pharmacists Providing Smoking Cessation Services (*n* = 152)	Pharmacists not Providing Smoking Cessation Services (*n* = 261)	*p*-Value
Sex				
Male	171 (41.4)	59 (38.8)	112 (42.9)	0.469
Female	242 (58.6)	93 (61.2)	149 (57.1)	
Age (years)				
<30	92 (22.4)	48 (31.8)	44 (17.0)	0.009
30–39	120 (29.3)	38 (25.2)	82 (31.7)	
40–49	95 (23.2)	31 (20.5)	64 (24.7)	
>49	103 (25.1)	34 (22.5)	69 (26.6)	
mean ± SD	40.9 ± 12.7	38.7 ± 12.0	42.2 ± 13.0	0.007
Being a pharmacist (years)				
<10	190 (46.6)	74 (49.0)	116 (45.1)	0.759
10–19	120 (29.4)	43 (28.5)	77 (30.0)	
>19	98 (24.0)	34 (22.5)	64 (24.9)	
Having pharmacist assistant				
No	144 (34.9)	37 (24.3)	107 (41.0)	0.001
Yes	269 (65.1)	115 (75.7)	154 (59.0)	
Number of pharmacists on duty				
1	284 (68.8)	76 (50.0)	208 (79.7)	<0.001
>1	129 (31.2)	76 (50.0)	53 (20.3)	
Location of pharmacy				
Bangkok	126 (30.7)	48 (31.6)	78 (30.1)	0.733
North	110 (26.8)	41 (27.0)	69 (26.6)	
Central	89 (21.6)	29 (19.1)	60 (23.2)	
Northeast	45 (10.9)	20 (13.2)	25 (9.6)	
South	41 (10.0)	14 (9.2)	27 (10.4)	
Location of pharmacy				
Shopping center	46 (12.1)	21 (15.6)	25 (10.2)	0.141
Community	333 (87.9)	114 (84.4)	219 (89.8)	
Membership in TPNTC				
Yes	115 (27.9)	93 (61.2)	22 (8.4)	<0.001
No	298 (72.1)	59 (38.8)	239 (91.6)	
Smoking cessation products available				
Yes	316 (76.5)	145 (95.4)	171 (65.5)	<0.001
No	97 (23.5)	7 (4.6)	90 (34.5)	
Providing smoking cessation is a role of community pharmacists				
Yes	400 (96.9)	152 (100.0)	248 (95.0)	0.003
No	13 (3.1)	0 (0.0)	13 (5.0)	

Note: TPNTC, Thai Pharmacy Network for Tobacco Control. Percentages presented are based on numbers of respondents answering each question.

Smoking cessation products were available in 316 pharmacies (77%), and these products included nicotine gum, nicotine patch, bupropion, nortriptyline, varenicline, and herbal mixture for smoking cessation. Nicotine gum (73%) was the most dispensed pharmaceutical product to aid smoking cessation (Table 2). The most frequent activities pharmacists reported having performed for smoking cessation in their community pharmacies were providing materials to aid smokers to quit, e.g., brochures, posters, and video (Table 3).

Table 2. Smoking cessation products provided at the community pharmacy.

Smoking Cessation Products	Total (*n* = 413)	Pharmacists Providing Smoking Cessation Services (*n* = 152)	Pharmacists not Providing Smoking Cessation Services (*n* = 261)	*p*-Value
Nicotine gu	300 (72.6)	140 (92.1)	160 (61.3)	<0.001
Bupropion	111 (26.9)	75 (49.3)	36 (13.8)	<0.001
Nicotine patch	81 (19.6)	54 (35.5)	27 (10.3)	<0.001
Herbal mixture for smoking cessation	72 (17.4)	43 (28.3)	29 (11.1)	<0.001
Nortriptyline	56 (13.6)	41 (26.9)	15 (5.7)	<0.001
Varenicline	10 (2.4)	8 (5.3)	2 (0.8)	0.006
Others	42 (10.2)	29 (19.1)	13 (5.0)	<0.001

Note: Percentages presented are based on numbers of respondents answering each question.

Table 3. Activities of smoking cessation services (*n* = 147).

Activities	*n* (%)
Providing materials for smoking cessation (*n* = 147)	110 (74.8)
Brochures (*n* = 110	87 (79.1)
Video (*n* = 110)	5 (4.6)
Poster (*n* = 110)	85 (77.3)
Showing symbols in front of pharmacy (*n* = 147)	105 (71.4)
A designated area for smoking cessation (*n* = 147)	53 (36.0)
Engaging with the community (*n* = 147)	50 (34.0)

For those 152 pharmacists who provided smoking cessation services, an average of 3.4 ± 4.6 smokers monthly, for each pharmacy, received smoking cessation services; an average of 6.4 ± 6.9 smokers/month could stop smoking; whilst an average of 9.0 ± 9.0 smokers/month could reduce their smoking. Time spent in each cessation service was about 15 min per person for the first time, and 9 min for each follow-up visit (Table 4).

The top two perceived barriers on providing smoking cessation services, were being unable to follow-up patients after providing the cessation services and inadequate staffing. These barriers did not significantly differ between those providing and those not providing cessation services. This study showed six significant different perceived barriers between the two groups, i.e., lack of time, lack of population demand, no smoking cessation products available in the drugstore, lack of knowledge and skills, lack of self-confidence, and lack of media/equipment. Interestingly, no payment for providing smoking cessation services was the lowest perceived barriers (23%), and did not significantly differ between the two groups. Details are shown in Table 5.

Table 4. Number of smokers receiving smoking cessation services and time spent on smoking cessation services (*n* = 152).

	n	Mean (±SD)	Median (Q1, Q3)	Min	Max
Number of smokers receiving smoking cessation services (person/month)					
Total number of smokers receiving smoking cessation service (person/month)	135	3.4 ± 4.6	2 (1, 3)	0	30
Smokers can quit smoking (person/pharmacy)	90	6.4 ± 6.9	4 (2, 10)	0	40
Smokers can decrease smoking (person/pharmacy)	76	9.0 ± 9.0	5 (3, 10)	0	40
Time for providing smoking cessation service (min/person)					
The first service	141	15.1 ± 10.9	10 (5, 20)	1	60
Each follow-up visit	129	8.9 ± 6.7	5 (5, 10)	1	30

Table 5. Perceived barriers on providing smoking cessation services (*n* = 413).

	Total (*n* = 413)	Pharmacists Providing Smoking Cessation Services (*n* = 152)	Pharmacists not Providing Smoking Cessation Services (*n* = 261)	*p*-Value
1. Unable to follow-up	346 (84.6)	122 (81.9)	224 (86.1)	0.258
2. Inadequate staffing	299 (73.5)	111 (74.5)	188 (72.9)	0.816
3. Lack of time	262 (64.1)	115 (76.2)	147 (57.0)	<0.001
4. Lack of population demand	286 (69.8)	87 (57.6)	199 (76.8)	<0.001
5. No smoking cessation products	126 (30.7)	26 (17.2)	100 (38.5)	<0.001
6. Lack of knowledge and skills	216 (52.9)	64 (43.0)	152 (58.7)	0.003
7. Lack of self-confidence	166 (40.7)	48 (32.0)	118 (45.7)	0.007
8. Lack of media/equipment	299 (73.3)	102 (67.5)	197 (76.6)	0.049
9. No appropriate place	199 (48.7)	68 (45.0)	131 (50.8)	0.305
10. No motivation	177 (43.7)	64 (43.0)	113 (44.1)	0.836
11. No payment	95 (23.4)	41 (27.5)	54 (21.0)	0.146

Note: Percentages presented are based on numbers of respondents answering each question.

4. Discussion

4.1. Smoking Cessation Services Provided by the Community Pharmacists

This national survey across Thailand showed that approximately 37% of respondents provided smoking cessation services in their community pharmacies. A related study [8], also set in Thailand, showed a level of only 15%. In Thailand, community pharmacists are in an optimal position to provide smoking cessation services to patients, as pharmacists can be easily reached and asked for advice. However, not every community pharmacist can provide smoking cessation services, as smoking cessation requires not only knowledge and skills, but also time spent in assisting smokers to quit. This study showed that community pharmacists from all parts of Thailand engaged in providing smoking cessation services, mostly in Bangkok and northern Thailand. Community pharmacists at least had activities related to tobacco control or smoking cessation services provided to the public. These activities comprised (1) providing materials to aid smokers in quitting smoking, e.g., pamphlets, brochures, posters; (2) showing symbols in front of their pharmacies on helping smokers to quit smoking; (3) providing a designated area for smoking cessation services; and (4) engaging in community activities related to tobacco control, e.g., organizing a camp for students to learn the dangers of tobacco and to avoid smoking, and participating in the nonsmoking week in late May, as 31 May is World No Tobacco Day. Some community pharmacists were encouraging community members to reduce or stop smoking through radio broadcasts or journals in the community. Pharmacists who were members of the TPNTC were more likely to performing all four of these activities than nonmembers. A study conducted in the UK by Dewsbury et al., revealed that smoking cessation supported by community pharmacists had been viewed as being most valued by clients [9]. The results of this study showed that almost all pharmacists (97%) agreed that smoking cessation is an important role of community pharmacists. This finding is consistent with a related Thai study [10], suggesting that community pharmacists perceived they had important roles in helping smokers to quit smoking.

Many smoking cessation aid products were available in community pharmacies: Nicotine gum, Nicotine patch, Bupropion, Nortriptyline, Varenicline, and Herbal formulas for smoking cessation. In Thailand, these products do not require a prescription, but need to be dispensed by a pharmacist. Nicotine gum was found to be incorrectly used by smokers as it is quite difficult to use, and a patient needs to know how to use it properly to get the most effectiveness from the product, to avoid adverse effects that may occur. This constitutes a very important role of pharmacist to help patients. A study by Kurko et al. in Finland found inappropriate use of NRT products for other purposes, and not for smoking cessation, such as products misused or used in harm reduction purposes [23]. Thus, pharmacists should communicate with clients or smokers concerning the proper use of NRT products for smoking cessation purposes.

For those 152 community pharmacists who provided smoking cessation services daily, the number of smokers who stopped smoking after receiving smoking cessation services ranged from 0 to 40 individuals, for each pharmacy. Six smokers, monthly, on average, could quit smoking, and 9 smokers, monthly, could reduce their smoking. It seemed that the number of smokers receiving smoking cessation services was quite low, and some pharmacists did not provide smoking cessation services at the time the study was conducted. This implied that pharmacists should encourage and motivate their customers to participate in smoking cessation services.

This study revealed that pharmacists not providing smoking cessation services were older, nonmembers of the TPNTC, did not have a pharmacist assistant, had only one pharmacist on duty, and did not stock smoking cessation products, compared to pharmacists providing smoking cessation services. In Thailand, levels of smoking cessation services provided by community pharmacists have been increasing in the past 10 to 15 years. "New generation" pharmacists have learned about smoking cessation services during their university study, and universities have only begun teaching this area recently [22]. TPNTC member pharmacists were trained by the TPNTC and were further interested in providing smoking cessation services. Therefore, the more recent pharmacy graduates or pharmacists who were TPNTC members were more likely to provide smoking cessation services, as compared with others.

4.2. Perceived Barriers of Smoking Cessation Services by Community Pharmacists

Community pharmacists perceived some barriers preventing them from providing smoking cessation services. First, being unable to follow-up after providing the service was the most common issue considered to be a barrier, and did not differ between those pharmacists providing services and those not. Arranging follow-up was one part of the 5 A's (Ask, Advise, Assess, Assist, and Arrange) that pharmacists should perform, and pharmacists may have thought that this entailed a difficult task due to reasons, such as no time or no interest from clients. The 5 A's comprised asking all patients of their smoking status; advising smokers to stop smoking; assessing the willingness to quit; assisting smokers to quit; and arranging follow-up [24]. Therefore, having professional communication with community pharmacists that involved follow-up was essential to help motivate smokers to stop smoking. This included training them to understand the purpose of follow-up and how to conduct it.

Second, inadequate staffing was another perceived barrier, and did not differ between the two groups. Community pharmacies providing smoking cessation services had more than one pharmacist on duty and pharmacist assistants. Smoking cessation services require time spent with smokers to counsel them, especially for the first time, about 15 min and about 9 min for each follow-up visit. Normally in Thailand, only one pharmacist is on duty; therefore, providing smoking cessation services without other personnel was quite difficult. This was similar to other studies that reported a lack of staff as a barrier [8,10,15,20,25].

This study identified five barriers more common among those pharmacists not providing smoking cessation services: Lack of demand, lack of knowledge and skills, lack of self-confidence, no smoking cessation products available in the drugstore, and lack of media/equipment or educational materials for providing smoking cessation services. This was consistent with findings of studies conducted in Australia, Qatar, and the USA, which also found that lack of patient demand was a barrier for providing public health services, i.e., smoking cessation [15,18,25]. As smoking is unacceptable in Thai society, especially female smoking, where the provision of smoking cessation services is a role of pharmacists, identifying smoking status should be an initial step in pharmacy practice. This could identify more smokers and those who could be assisted to quit. Communication with pharmacists involving asking clients' smoking status is essential and could help smokers to quit smoking. This would also enhance the roles of pharmacists, regarding tobacco control.

Two identified barriers in providing smoking cessation services, i.e., lack of knowledge/skills and lack of self-confidence, were also identified by other studies [10,26,27]. As these barriers may be overcome by training; the TPNTC and the pharmacy faculties of universities could usefully provide more relevant training to pharmacists and pharmacy students.

Another perceived barrier to providing smoking cessation services was not having relevant medications, which was also identified in related studies [10,26]. However, this study found that Thai pharmacists perceived lack of smoking cessation medications as a weaker barrier, as per the findings of a related Thai study conducted in 2008 [10]. This was because medications for smoking cessation were only available in hospitals, at the time that the study was conducted. However, nicotine replacement products became available in community pharmacies starting July 2005.

This study also identified the lack of materials for smoking services as a barrier to service provision, a result consistent with a related study conducted in Thailand by Thananithisak et al. [10], and other studies [26,28]. This is despite that materials to aid smoking cessation could be requested without any charge from the Action on Smoking and Health Foundation Thailand (ASH Thailand). In Thailand, pharmacists and health personnel or people could receive educational materials or equipment for smoking cessation, such as posters, stickers, and videos from ASH Thailand through its website, free of charge [29]. Given that community pharmacists may be unaware of this fact, promotion and communication to pharmacists on this website should be increased.

Consistent with several other studies [10,18,20,21,25–27], this study found that lack of time was perceived to be a significant barrier to providing smoking cessation services. Interestingly, lack of time was more likely to be perceived as a barrier among those community pharmacists providing smoking cessation than those that did not. Further investigation should examine the reasons for providing smoking cessation services among pharmacists, even when they perceived time constrain was a barrier.

Apart from perceived barriers reported by the pharmacists, motivation to provide smoking cessation services was investigated. This study found that the motivation of community pharmacists in providing smoking cessation services was mainly to enhance the pharmacy profession in helping patients, smokers, individuals, society, and the nation, to be free from the dangers of tobacco. It also expanded the roles of community pharmacies in tobacco control and smoking cessation. In addition, community pharmacists could create awareness of the dangers of smoking and be willing to communicate with patients and smokers to help them to quit smoking, and prevent diseases caused by smoking. This study showed that the motivation for providing public health services was related to the pharmacy profession and not a financial issue, particularly considering those working in independent pharmacies. Similar to one study conducted in the UK [9], professional responsibility was the motivation for providing smoking cessation services in the community pharmacy. Financial issues were not the reason, because these cessation services at the community pharmacy were provided free of charge, unless smokers needed to use pharmacotherapy to stop smoking.

In Thailand, the TPNTC plays a vital role in motivating and providing training to pharmacists to be readily equipped with knowledge and skills for smoking cessation services. This study also confirmed that being a member of the TPNTC encouraged pharmacists to serve greater roles in helping smokers to quit. However, there remains a need to further motivate and encourage community pharmacists to continue their smoking cessation roles, and to expand and communicate with other community pharmacists to initiate smoking cessation services in their community pharmacies, as well as to overcome perceived barriers preventing them from providing smoking cessation services.

4.3. Limitations and Strengths

Some limitations should be acknowledged. First, the presented data were not representative of all community pharmacists in Thailand due to the survey's very low response rate of 7.9% (selection bias, overestimation). Although the study received a low response rate from the respondents, the responses were received from all throughout Thailand: Bangkok, North, Central, Northeast, and the south. In addition, participants who returned the questionnaire showed their interest in promoting the pharmacy profession concerning tobacco control, suggesting their opinions and practices were crucial. Another reason for the low response rate could be that they did not perform smoking cessation services, so they were uninterested in sharing their opinions. In addition, most community pharmacists in Thailand did not have assistants; thus, they did not have time to complete the questionnaire. Follow-up telephone calls were made to increase the survey response rate. Unfortunately, some telephone numbers were wrong. However, this low response rate was similar to a study conducted with community pharmacists using an online-questionnaire in Australia, with a response rate of 6% [15]. Second, given that the survey collected self-reported data, some measurement errors are likely. For example, the Table 4 item, "Smokers can quit or decrease smoking" depends on self-reports of pharmacists. Therefore, pharmacists could overestimate their success of providing smoking cessation services.

However, this study collected information from community pharmacists across Thailand. It constitutes a countrywide survey regarding the roles of community pharmacists in Thailand, in providing smoking cessation services to the public. Although the low response rate implied caution in interpreting the findings and generalizing of the results, the findings are still legitimate in reflecting the situation of the roles of community pharmacists in tobacco control and smoking cessation, and highlighting pharmacy professionals' need to extend smoking cessation services.

5. Conclusions

In conclusion, only a minority of community pharmacists in Thailand are engaged in smoking cessation activities, even though some perceived barriers existed. Community pharmacists who provided smoking cessation services were more likely to have pharmacist assistants, be a member of the TPNTC, and have more than one pharmacist on duty. Being unable to follow-up and inadequate staffing were the top two perceived barriers. Those pharmacists not providing smoking cessation services perceived five barriers more than those providing the services, i.e., lack of demand, no smoking cessation products available, lack of knowledge and skills, lack of self-confidence, and lack of media/equipment for providing smoking cessation services.

Actions to improve smoking cessation services in community pharmacies in Thailand could be implemented through the TPNTC or pharmacy faculties of each concerned university. For example, the TPNTC or the universities could provide short course trainings on smoking cessation services to practicing pharmacists, especially those who did not receive relevant training at undergraduate or graduate levels. As the educational materials or media/equipment to aid smoking cessation services could be requested from the ASH Thailand for free, their availability should be communicated to pharmacists. At universities, pharmacy students should be encouraged to practice the delivery of smoking cessation services through their clerkships in year 6. Finally, a health promotion campaign targeting smokers could advertise the availability of community pharmacists' smoking cessation services.

Author Contributions: Study concept and design: D.C., S.C. Data curation: D.C. Statistical analysis and interpretation of data: D.C. and S.C. Drafting of the manuscript: D.C. Critical revision of the manuscript for important intellectual content: D.C. and S.C. Funding Acquisition: S.C.

Funding: This research was funded by the Thai Pharmacy Network for Tobacco Control (TPNTC) under the Thai Health Promotion Foundation.

Acknowledgments: The authors wish to acknowledge the financial support from the Thai Pharmacy Network for Tobacco Control. We are grateful to the community pharmacists who participated in this study for their time and participation. We are thankful to Katha Bunditanukul, the Chairman of the Thai Pharmacy Network for Tobacco Control, for his useful information and knowledge. We are grateful to the Thai Food and Drug Administration (Thai FDA), Ministry of Public Health, and Faculty of Pharmacy, Chiang Mai University, and the Office of Pharmacy Accreditation (Thailand), for the list and address of community pharmacies.

Conflicts of Interest: The authors declare no conflict of interest. The funder had no role in the design of the study; in the collection, analyses, or interpretation of data; in the writing of the manuscript; and in the decision to publish the results.

References

1. Lim, S.S.; Vos, T.; Flaxman, A.D.; Danaei, G.; Shibuya, K.; Adair-Rohani, H.; Amann, M.; Anderson, H.R.; Andrews, K.G.; Aryee, M.; et al. A comparative risk assessment of burden of disease and injury attributable to 67 risk factors and risk factor clusters in 21 regions, 1990–2010: A systematic analysis for the global burden of disease study 2010. *Lancet* **2012**, *380*, 2224–2260. [CrossRef]

2. Bundhamcharoen, K.; Aungkulanon, S.; Makka, N.; Shibuya, K. Economic burden from smoking-related diseases in Thailand. *Tob. Control* **2016**, *25*, 532–537. [CrossRef] [PubMed]

3. World Health Organization. Tobacco Free Initiative (TFI): MPOWER in Action. Available online: http://www.who.int/tobacco/mpower/publications/brochure_2013/en/ (accessed on 10 April 2018).

4. Vathesatogkit, P.; Charoenca, N. Tobacco control: Lessons learnt in Thailand. *Indian J. Public Health* **2011**, *55*, 228–233. [CrossRef] [PubMed]

5. Peletidi, A.; Nabhani-Gebara, S.; Kayyali, R. Smoking cessation support services at community pharmacies in the UK: A systematic review. *Hell. J. Cardiol. HJC* **2016**, *57*, 7–15. [CrossRef]

6. Eades, C.E.; Ferguson, J.S.; O'Carroll, R.E. Public health in community pharmacy: A systematic review of pharmacist and consumer views. *BMC Public Health* **2011**, *11*, 582. [CrossRef] [PubMed]

7. Thavorn, K.; Chaiyakunapruk, N. A cost-effectiveness analysis of a community pharmacist-based smoking cessation programme in Thailand. *Tob. Control* **2008**, *17*, 177–182. [CrossRef] [PubMed]

8. Nimpitakpong, P.; Chaiyakunapruk, N.; Dhippayom, T. A national survey of training and smoking cessation services provided in community pharmacies in Thailand. *J. Community Health* **2010**, *35*, 554–559. [CrossRef] [PubMed]

9. Dewsbury, C.; Rodgers, R.M.; Krska, J. Views of english pharmacists on providing public health services. *Pharmacy* **2015**, *3*, 154–168. [CrossRef] [PubMed]

10. Thananithisak, C.; Nimpitakpong, P.; Chaiyakunapruk, N. Activities and perceptions of pharmacists providing tobacco control services in community pharmacy in Thailand. *Nicot. Tob. Res. Off. J. Soc. Res. Nicot. Tob.* **2008**, *10*, 921–925. [CrossRef] [PubMed]

11. Kurko, T.; Linden, K.; Pietila, K.; Sandstrom, P.; Airaksinen, M. Community pharmacists' involvement in smoking cessation: Familiarity and implementation of the national smoking cessation guideline in Finland. *BMC Public Health* **2010**, *10*, 444. [CrossRef] [PubMed]

12. Aquilino, M.L.; Farris, K.B.; Zillich, A.J.; Lowe, J.B. Smoking-cessation services in Iowa community pharmacies. *Pharmacotherapy* **2003**, *23*, 666–673. [CrossRef] [PubMed]

13. Sinclair, H.K.; Bond, C.M.; Stead, L.F. Community pharmacy personnel interventions for smoking cessation. *Cochrane Database Syst. Rev.* **2004**, *1*, Cd003698.

14. Dobbie, F.; Hiscock, R.; Leonardi-Bee, J.; Murray, S.; Shahab, L.; Aveyard, P.; Coleman, T.; McEwen, A.; McRobbie, H.; Purves, R.; et al. Evaluating long-term outcomes of NHS stop smoking services (ELONS): A prospective cohort study. *Health Technol. Assess.* **2015**, *19*, 1–156. [CrossRef] [PubMed]

15. Mc Namara, K.P.; Peterson, G.M.; Hughes, J.; Krass, I.; Versace, V.; Clark, R.A.; Dunbar, J. Cardiovascular disease risk assessment in Australian community pharmacy. *Heart Lung Circ.* **2017**, *26*, 667–676. [CrossRef] [PubMed]

16. Omboni, S.; Caserini, M. Effectiveness of pharmacist's intervention in the management of cardiovascular diseases. *Open Heart* **2018**, *5*, e000687. [CrossRef] [PubMed]

17. Brown, T.J.; Todd, A.; O'Malley, C.; Moore, H.J.; Husband, A.K.; Bambra, C.; Kasim, A.; Sniehotta, F.F.; Steed, L.; Smith, S.; et al. Community pharmacy-delivered interventions for public health priorities: A systematic review of interventions for alcohol reduction, smoking cessation and weight management, including meta-analysis for smoking cessation. *BMJ Open* **2016**, *6*, e009828. [CrossRef] [PubMed]

18. El Hajj, M.S.; Al Nakeeb, R.R.; Al-Qudah, R.A. Smoking cessation counseling in Qatar: Community pharmacists' attitudes, role perceptions and practices. *Int. J. Clin. Pharm.* **2012**, *34*, 667–676. [CrossRef] [PubMed]

19. Edwards, D.; Freeman, T.; Gilbert, A. Pharmacists' role in smoking cessation: An examination of current practice and barriers to service provision. *Int. J. Pharm. Pract.* **2006**, *14*, 315–317. [CrossRef]

20. Wibowo, Y.; Berbatis, C.; Joyce, A.; Sunderland, V.B. Analysis of enhanced pharmacy services in rural community pharmacies in Western Australia. *Rural Remote Health* **2010**, *10*, 1400. [PubMed]

21. Dent, L.A.; Harris, K.J.; Noonan, C.W. Tobacco treatment practices of pharmacists in Montana. *J. Am. Pharm. Assoc. JAPhA* **2010**, *50*, 575–579. [CrossRef] [PubMed]

22. Nimpitakpong, P.; Chaiyakunapruk, N.; Dhippayom, T. Smoking cessation education in Thai schools of pharmacy. *Pharm. Educ.* **2011**, *11*, 8–11.

23. Kurko, T.; Linden, K.; Vasama, M.; Pietila, K.; Airaksinen, M. Nicotine replacement therapy practices in Finland one year after deregulation of the product sales—Has anything changed from the community pharmacy perspective? *Health Policy* **2009**, *91*, 277–285. [CrossRef] [PubMed]

24. Curry, S.J.; Keller, P.A.; Orleans, C.T.; Fiore, M.C. The role of health care systems in increased tobacco cessation. *Annu. Rev. Public Health* **2008**, *29*, 411–428. [CrossRef] [PubMed]

25. Hudmon, K.S.; Prokhorov, A.V.; Corelli, R.L. Tobacco cessation counseling: Pharmacists' opinions and practices. *Patient Educ. Couns.* **2006**, *61*, 152–160. [CrossRef] [PubMed]

26. Odukoya, O.; Poluyi, E.; Aina, B.; Ejekam, C.; Faseru, B. Pharmacist-Led Smoking Cessation: The Attitudes and Practices of Community Pharmacists in Sagos State, Nigeria: A Mixed Methods Survey. Available online: http://www.tobaccopreventioncessation.com/Pharmacist-led-smoking-cessation-The-attitudes-and-practices-of-community-pharmacists-in-Lagos-state-Nigeria-A-mixed-methods-survey-,61546,0,2.html (accessed on 16 September 2018).

27. Bouchet-Benezech, B.; Champanet, B.; Rouzaud, P. Smoking cessation at the pharmacy: Feasibility and benefits based on a french observational study with six-month follow-up. *Subst. Abuse Rehabil.* **2018**, *9*, 31–42. [CrossRef] [PubMed]

28. Taha, N.A.; Guat Tee, O. Tobacco cessation through community pharmacies: Knowledge, attitudes, practices and perceived barriers among pharmacists in Penang. *Health Educ. J.* **2014**, *74*, 681–690. [CrossRef]

29. Action on Smoking and Health Foundation Thailand. Available online: http://www.ashthailand.or.th/en/ (accessed on 5 January 2018).

pharmacy

MDPI

Article

Assessing the Understanding of Pharmaceutical Pictograms among Cultural Minorities: The Example of Hindu Individuals Communicating in European Portuguese

Lakhan Kanji, Sensen Xu and Afonso Cavaco *

Department of Social Pharmacy, Faculty of Pharmacy, University of Lisbon. Av. Prof. Gama Pinto,
1649-003 Lisboa, Portugal; lakhan@hotmail.com (L.K.); sensen.58@hotmail.com (S.X.)
* Correspondence: acavaco@ff.ulisboa.pt; Tel.: +351-217-946-456

Received: 9 January 2018; Accepted: 27 February 2018; Published: 5 March 2018

Abstract: One of the sources of poor health outcomes is the lack of compliance with the prescribed treatment plans, often due to communication barriers between healthcare professionals and patients. Pictograms are a form of communication that conveys meaning through its pictorial resemblance to a physical object or an action. Pharmaceutical pictograms are often associated with a better comprehension of treatment regimens, although their use is still subject to limitations. The main goal of this study was to examine the potential understanding of pharmaceutical pictograms by a cultural minority when providing patient information while comparing the effectiveness of two reference systems (United States Pharmacopeia USP and International Pharmacy Federation FIP) for this purpose. A self-administered questionnaire was developed comprising 30 pictograms, 15 selected from the United States Pharmacopeia Dispensing Information and the equivalent from the International Pharmaceutical Federation. The questionnaire comprised plain instructions, socio-demographic data, self-reported language fluency and pictogram labels in Portuguese presented to conveniently selected members of the Hindu community of Lisbon (Portugal) until reaching a quota of 50. Participants showed difficulties in understanding some pictograms, which was related to the self-reported reduced fluency in Portuguese. Overall, the interpretation of USP pictograms was better than FIP ones, as well as for pictograms composed of multiple images, presenting a negative reading, or when conveying information unrelated to medication instructions. Even using internationally validated pictograms, added care should be taken when community pharmacists use such communication resources with cultural minorities. It is important not to disregard other forms of patient communication and information, considering pictograms as a complement to other forms of patient counselling.

Keywords: pharmaceutical pictograms; written health communication; Hindu community; USP; FIP PictoRx; Portugal

1. Introduction

It is well accepted that it is the responsibility of community pharmacists to actively contribute to the safe and effective use of medications [1,2]. While their primary mission is to assure the quality of the products dispensed, the current focus on pharmaceutical care practice adds a professional responsibility towards patient medication outcomes [3]. Community pharmacists are actively contributing to improving medication usage, including medication compliance, treatment effectiveness and adverse events monitoring [1,3]. Medication compliance can be defined as the extent to which a patient acts in accordance with the prescribed dosing regimen [4]. Inadequate compliance has important negative patient outcomes [5,6] and usually emerges from therapy costs and complexity of the regimen, being communication barriers between health professionals and patients also known to contribute to non-compliance [6].

Communication barriers may arise from speech or hearing impairments but are commonly a consequence of language issues related to schooling or literacy limitations [7]. Lack of therapy compliance is frequent for the elderly and those who do not speak the same language as the healthcare providers [8–11]. Despite efforts to implement Esperanto or basic English, communication issues persist based on language differences between communities including alphabet, lexical, syntactic and semantic variations, even between bordering counties [12]. To overcome communication issues, information can be conveyed using pictures, symbols, audiotapes or interpreters [9]. One widely known resource, frequently considered a beneficial solution, is the use of pictograms.

1.1. What are Pictograms?

Pictograms are graphic representations of objects or actions conveying a meaning which should be independent of any particular culture or language [12]. They are frequently used to quickly transmit important information such as the male or female gender (e.g., toilets info), safety hazards (e.g., health precautions) or road information (e.g., prohibitions and warnings). Although each cultural environment may promote differences in signs relevance [12,13], a basis for the use of pictograms is their universal interpretation, i.e., they should offer the same meaning regardless of language, culture or education [9,14].

Pictograms have been used to give instructions or warnings regarding health products usage [10,14]. Characteristics such as visual intricacy, concreteness, simplicity, the shape and color of the illustrations can help clarify the information conveyed or, if not well designed, misguide its assimilation [15–17]. As familiarity also plays a role in understanding visual aids, pictogram testing is required to determine its appropriateness [16,18]. Given most pictograms have been designed within Western societies, caution is suggested when using them in cross-cultural contexts [9,19,20].

Pharmaceutical pictograms are useful tools to reinforce both comprehension and recall of medicines-related information, attract attention and reduce misunderstandings regarding a drug treatment [13,15]. Attributes such as the design of the frames, marks expressing negation (e.g., crosses or strikethroughs), specific human body parts, and marks for pain and movement can lead to a decline in comprehension [21]. Pharmaceutical pictograms have been developed and disseminated by a few different organizations such as the Risk-benefit Assessment of Drugs-Analysis and Response (RAD-AR) Council of Japan pictograms, the United States Pharmacopeia Dispensing Information pictograms (USP) and the International Pharmaceutical Federation (FIP) pictograms [22]. The USP pictograms have been widely used in Western societies, although published studies regarding their usability and legibility in different settings revealed potential limitations for culturally diverse populations (e.g., South African) [9–11,23,24]. The FIP pictograms developed in June 2009 were last updated 7 February 2017, according to the website (https://www.fip.org/pictograms, accessed November 2017). This update fixed issues with the language and added Turk and Malayan, which suggest a greater potential to suit multi-cultural societies.

In Portugal, the legibility of USP pictograms was studied by Soares (2012) [25] using the overall Lisbon population. Patients' ability to understand a set of 15 pictograms was measured according to the International Standards Organization (ISO) 3864, which considers as legible the icons presenting over 67% of correct results. Only 10 pictograms were able to achieve the legibility threshold, thus suggesting limitations in USP understanding by the Portuguese population. This was particularly relevant with low literacy and foreign communities, those justifying the development of pictograms [25]. Despite the economic recession, the influx of foreign populations has been constant in mainland Portugal. For instance, the Hindu community has been growing in Lisbon with 6160 emigrants who were born in India (before 2010), as well as from other countries such as Mozambique, Pakistan and Bangladesh [26]. Cultural minorities, who are not well versed in Portuguese, often face communication issues with treatment adherence. The use of pictograms by community pharmacy practitioners may contribute to improving adherence if the pictograms are comprehensible by all patients.

1.2. Study Objectives

The aim of this study was to investigate if pharmaceutical pictograms, specifically United States Pharmacopeia (USP) and the International Pharmaceutical Federation (FIP), were understandable by a Hindu-based population living abroad thus defining a feasible form of pharmaceutical communication with culturally diverse populations in Portugal. Besides the cultural sensitivity of both USP and FIP, pictograms design and other characteristics which may contribute to an enhanced meaning discernment were also investigated.

2. Materials and Methods

The present study followed a cross-sectional design, using a survey approach.

2.1. Study Participants

This study was conducted with a convenience sample of 50 Hindu individuals living in Lisbon and Tagus Valley regions of Portugal. These individuals were selected from two different Hindu temples, the Radha Krishna Temple and the Shiv Temple in Lisbon, between March and August 2017, by direct invitation from the field researcher. The inclusion criteria considered people aged over 18 years, from both genders, with different levels of education and income. Individuals who lived in India, Pakistan and/or Bangladesh (major Hindu nationalities living in Portugal) for less than five consecutive years, declaring to be unable to read Portuguese, or presenting any limitations that might prevent them from interpreting the pictograms, were excluded from the study. The selected participants responded to the questionnaire, after voluntarily signing the informed consent. From all approached and able to participate, a drop out of 18 participants was registered before achieving the 50 participants quota. The study followed all ethical research principles, particularly concerning participants' full anonymity and data confidentiality, having received ethical approval by the Faculty of Pharmacy Ethical Committee, as well as with respect for the principles stated in the current Portuguese law of personal data protection.

2.2. Questionnaire

The research questionnaire consisted of three sections. The first one comprised participants' socio-demographic data i.e., age, gender, place of birth and citizenship, level of schooling and its location, time living in Portugal, household income, employment status, and healthcare-related variables. While most of these variables were evaluated through closed multiple-choice questions, a Likert-scale was used for participants' self-assessment of their perceived Portuguese proficiency, running from 0 (null aptitude) to 10 (native speaker). This variable was dichotomized in poor and good self-perceived Portuguese fluency, respectively ≤5 and >5 points, defining subsample B and subsample A, respectively.

The next section comprised 30 pictograms, 15 selected from the USP set and 15 from the FIP offline non-USA MEPS set. Both sets were obtained from the official websites, accessed in January 2017 (respectively, https://www.usp.org/download-pictograms and https://www.fip.org/www/?page=meps_pict_download_eu). The 15 USP pictograms were those used in previously published papers [24,25,27], 7 reported to be difficult to interpret and 8 more often correctly interpreted. The 15 FIP pictograms were those that conveyed an equal or similar meaning to the selected USP ones. It was checked if the pictograms comprised the graphics features of more than one illustration, non-affirmative marks (e.g., prohibition), and information such as warnings and precautions, besides directions. The pictograms were randomly sequenced in the questionnaire.

Each pictogram was followed by 3 descriptions, one correct and two incorrect options, written in plain European Portuguese. The pictograms correct option was obtained from the direct translation of each USP pictogram label. To develop the two incorrect options, a pilot study was conducted interviewing face-to-face 5 individual members of the Hindu community who speak and write both Portuguese and Hindi fluently. Each pictogram was shown and their interpretations noted. If their interpretation matched the correct label, two other possible options were requested, making sure those were incorrect in wording and/or meaning. If not matching the original description only one alternative interpretation was requested. This procedure produced two incorrect, but credible options, within cultural sensitivity. An informal consensus on the most suitable wrong options to use in the study was reached by the research team, which included two members of cultural minorities living in Lisbon, one from the Hindu community. The pilot study also confirmed the ease of use and completeness of the questionnaire for the members of the community.

Participants filling-in the questionnaire were asked to mark the option they considered to be correctly describing each pictogram. Each correct answer was scored with 3 points, while an incorrect answer would 1 point. A standardized final score between 1 and 3 points was obtained for all questionnaires. In the last section participants were asked about previous experiences with pictograms and to give feedback on the pictograms relevance as a patient information tool. Although this was a self-administered questionnaire, a field researcher was always present during questionnaire completion to answer any participants' voluntary doubts.

2.3. Data Analysis

The analysis started by detailing pictograms classification according to the three previous graphical features, i.e., being composed of either single or multiple image, the presence or absence of any negation mark (e.g., cross or strike) and disclosing directions (e.g., how to take or apply the medication) or relaying other medication information (e.g., contraindications or side-effects). The analysis included the whole set of 30 pictograms of the USP and FIP subsets (15 + 15) i.e., no paired comparisons were intended, although equivalent pictograms from both sets were chosen.

Questionnaire data were analyzed using the IBM SPSS software, version 24. The statistics performed included descriptive results, Students' *t*-test, Persons' Chi-Square, non-parametric ANOVA tests and Pearson linear correlations. A confidence level equivalent to $p < 0.05$ was used in all tests.

3. Results

3.1. Socio-Demographic Data

The sample comprised mostly males (62%), with an age range between 23 and 63 years of age. Thirty-six of them declared having an Indian passport (72%), while the rest declared being citizens from Pakistan, Bangladesh or Mozambique, the last being included after confirming their main language and culture was Hindu and having lived for at least five consecutive years in that country. Overall, 44% of the respondents have lived in Portugal for up to five years, 26% between 5 and 20 years and 30% lived there for more than 20 years. Almost half (46%) of the participants had more than 12 years of education, with 66% completing their education in India, 12% studied in Portugal and the remainder studied in Pakistan, Bangladesh or Mozambique. Table 1 presents participants' education, self-perceived Portuguese (PT) proficiency and time spent in Portugal across gender and citizenship.

Twenty-two (44%) participants rated their Portuguese fluency as 5 or below, while 28 (56%) rated their fluency as 6 or above. Hence, participants were divided into two subsamples: A speakers ($n = 28$) and B speakers ($n = 22$). The amount of time the respondents have lived in Portugal and their education level were positively associated with their self-perceived Portuguese fluency (respectively, $Chi^2 = 6.445$, $p = 0.04$ and $Chi^2 = 5.547$, $p = 0.019$). There was no significant association with the location where the participants acquired their Portuguese language skills, nor associations with other background variables, such as the reported household income (68% under 1000€ per month), employment status (all declared to have a job), and the healthcare provider, e.g., choosing a community pharmacist when afflicted by a minor ailment (72%) and having access to a general practice (GP) physician (64%).

If presenting an ill-health condition, 52% of the participants said they would also seek traditional Hindu medical care. Only one participant admitted having a chronic condition and 39 (78%) reported taking medicines less than once a month.

Table 1. Participants' demographics (*n* = 50) including variables associated with Portuguese fluency.

		Education (Years)		Self-Perc. PT Proficiency		Time Living in PT (Years)		
		≤9	>9	≤5	>5	≤5	≤20	>20
Gender	Male	15	16	15	16	15	8	8
	Female	12	7	7	12	7	5	7
	Total	27	23	22	28	22	13	15
Nationality	Portuguese	11	11	6	16	2	5	15
	Hindu	11	10	11	10	14	7	0
	Pakistani	5	0	4	1	4	1	0
	Bangladesh	0	2	1	1	2	0	0
	Total	27	23	22	28	22	13	15

3.2. Pictograms Data

The percentage of correct answers obtained for each individual pictogram are displayed in Table 2. Participants' average score was 1.83 (σ = 0.34), ranging from 1.27 (the lowest score) to 2.67 (the highest). The most frequently correctly interpreted pictograms were #27, correctly interpreted by 70% of the participants, and #15 by 66% both from the UPS set. The worst interpreted pictograms were #9 (USP), with 45 (90%) participants missing the correct label and #18 (FIP) with 41 (82%) participants missing the correct label option.

Table 2. Pictograms used, meaning and number of correct answers per pictogram (*n* = 50).

Pictogram Id	Images	Pictogram Meaning	Correct Answers Counts (%)
#1 (FIP)		Take this medicine in the morning, afternoon and at night	19 (38%)
#2 (USP)		Do not take this medicine if pregnant	24 (48%)
#3 (FIP)		If this medicine makes you dizzy, do not drive	25 (50%)

Table 2. *Cont.*

Pictogram Id	Images	Pictogram Meaning	Correct Answers Counts (%)
#4 (FIP)		Take this medicine with an empty stomach	19 (38%)
#5 (USP)		Store this medicine in the fridge	24 (48%)
#6 (USP)		Keep this medicine out of the reach of children	32 (64%)
#7 (FIP)		Do not drink alcoholic beverages during treatment with this medicine	15 (30%)
#8 (USP)		Do not break the tablets nor open the capsules	20 (40%)
#9 (USP)		Take this medicine 3 times per day	5 (10%)
#10 (FIP)		Do not take this medicine if breastfeeding	17 (34%)
#11 (USP)		Take this medicine with meals	20 (40%)

Table 2. *Cont.*

Pictogram Id	Images	Pictogram Meaning	Correct Answers Counts (%)
#12 (FIP)		Insert the medicine in the vagina	23 (46%)
#13 (USP)		Do not take this medicine with meals	26 (52%)
#14 (FIP)		This medicine can cause sleepiness	18 (36%)
#15 (USP)		Do not take this medicine if breastfeeding	33 (66%)
#16 (USP)		Do not drink alcoholic beverages during treatment with this medicine	23 (46%)
#17 (USP)		Wash your hands before and after applying this medicine on the ear	24 (48%)
#18 (FIP)		Keep this medicine out of the reach of children	9 (18%)
#19 (FIP)		Store this medicine in the fridge	18 (36%)

Table 2. *Cont.*

Pictogram Id	Images	Pictogram Meaning	Correct Answers Counts (%)
#20 (FIP)		Shake this medicine before using	26 (52%)
#21 (FIP)		Do not break the tablets nor open the capsules	26 (52%)
#22 (FIP)		Do not take this medicine if pregnant	14 (28%)
#23 (FIP)		Take this medicine with meals	12 (24%)
#24 (USP)		Drink this medicine with an extra glass of water	12 (24%)
#25 (USP)		Shake this medicine before using	22 (44%)
#26 (FIP)		Apply one drop of this medicine on the left and on the right ears	18 (36%)

Table 2. *Cont.*

Pictogram Id	Images	Pictogram Meaning	Correct Answers Counts (%)
#27 (USP)		Wash your hands before and after applying this medicine on the vagina	35 (70%)
#28 (USP)		This medicine can cause sleepiness	26 (52%)
#29 (USP)		If this medicine makes you dizzy, do not drive	17 (34%)
#30 (FIP)		Take this medicine with water	17 (34%)

USP—United States Pharmacopeia; FIP—International Pharmacy Federation.

No significant linear correlation was found between participants' age and the total score. A significant negative correlation existed between the total score and the time spent outside Portugal ($r = -0.584$, $p < 0.001$) corroborated by the positive correlation for the total score and the time lived in Portugal ($r = 0.385$, $p = 0.006$). No significant differences were found between; male and female participants, the level or place of schooling, or income and employment status. A statistically significant difference was found between those having good Portuguese fluency (A participants) and poor fluency (B participants) ($t = -3.008$, $p = 0.004$). Only one participant acknowledged having had previous contact with pictograms. Thirty-eight (76%) participants considered them to be helpful for correctly understanding treatment plans.

The average USP and FIP pictograms scores were, respectively, 1.92 ($\sigma = 0.37$) and 1.74 ($\sigma = 0.37$). The USP set had a statistically significantly higher score ($t = -3.40$, $p = 0.001$) compared to the FIP. Testing the self-reported language ability (subsamples A and B) against the USP and FIP average scores confirmed differences within both pictorial sets (respectively, $t = -2.98$, $p = 0.004$ and $t = -2.53$, $p = 0.01$). The poorer Portuguese speaking participants (subsample B) showed average scores for USP of 1.75 ($\sigma = 0.36$) and for FIP of 1.59 ($\sigma = 0.33$), a difference that was significantly lower ($t = -2.27$, $p = 0.03$). Several other variables (e.g., pictograms relevance, household income, minor ailments behavior, and having a GP) were tested against participants' average scores within all sample and subsamples and no significant associations were found.

3.3. Pictogram Design Data

Mean scores and standard deviations were calculated according to pictograms dichotomous graphical classifications. These were compared using Students' *t*-test for the entire sample as well as subsamples A and B. The results are presented in Table 3.

Table 3. Means and standard deviation according to pictograms design.

		Entire Sample		Subsample A		Subsample B	
		Average	σ	Average	σ	Average	σ
Images	1	1.68	0.43	1.79	0.46	1.55	0.36
	>1	1.92	0.35	2.05	0.29	1.75	0.34
Negation marks	Present	1.87	0.45	2.06	0.39	1.62	0.39
	Absent	1.80	0.32	1.86	0.32	1.72	0.31
Text	Directions	1.80	0.34	1.88	0.35	1.71	0.31
	Other info	1.86	0.43	2.04	0.37	1.62	0.39

There were 12 (40%) pictograms consisting of a single image and 18 (60%) with multiple images, the latter achieving a significantly higher total score (All: $t = -3.91$, $p = 0.001$; A: $t = -3.09$, $p = 0.005$; B: $t = -2.62$, $p = 0.016$). Thirteen (43%) pictograms had negation marks, with only a significantly higher mean interpretation score found between A participants and the entire sample (A: $t = -3.35$, $p = 0.002$) for multiple images. Sixty percent of pictograms had medication directions, while 40% had other information. As with non-affirmative signs, only the subsample A had significantly better interpretation of other information (A: $t = -2.42$, $p = 0.022$).

4. Discussion

Pharmaceutical pictograms are widely accepted as an important resource that provide patients with information regarding their drug therapies and believed to meaningfully contribute to safer and more effective medication use. The present study addressed the comprehension of well-known pharmaceutical pictograms by a population that does not necessarily share the cultural and linguistic background of the native population, thus requiring additional resources for effective communication.

In the present study, participants' self-reported Portuguese fluency was found to be associated with their schooling, as well as with the time spent in Portugal, but not related to the country of formal education. On the other hand, their pictogram comprehension was significantly related to the time participants have lived in and out of Portugal. In this sense, participants' Portuguese literacy might have been developed from an informal daily usage of the language, which suggests potential language limitations regarding less frequent and more specific contexts, such as being ill and using medication. The present study population could be an adequate means to study the usefulness of pharmaceutical pictograms.

4.1. Pictograms Comprehension

This study found only one pictogram (#27) out of 30 that could be immediately used in pharmacy practice, according to the ISO-3864 legibility criteria, i.e., using the 67% correct interpretation cut-off. This was lower than expected, given previous results from participants living in Portugal [25]. One cause might be the interpretation issues with reading Portuguese when choosing from the pictogram 3 label options. In fact, there was a clear association between the self-reported Portuguese fluency and average scores: the poor language proficiency group always scored worse. This confirms the common belief that effective communication issues resulting from language barriers, which frequently emerge within culturally diverse populations, may not be overcome without the effort to explain pictograms. These signs on their own might not be enough to guarantee appropriate patient information and the expected medication usage. Practitioners should keep in mind that pictograms comprehension was also independent of variables such as the frequency of using community pharmacies (for solving minor health ailments) or being in contact with a GP. Having more or less interaction with healthcare providers does not guarantee better or worse understanding of pharmaceutical pictograms, assuming the absence of translators in community pharmacies. The Hindu cultural minority, as many other minorities living in Portugal, will not necessarily be better informed just by using pictograms and hoping they will do their job. Moreover, no associations were found between different comprehension scores and appreciation of pictograms relevance, which were considered helpful to understand medication regimens. Thus, pharmaceutical pictograms are an important tool in patient counselling, although their full success requires further attention regarding the actual level of comprehension achieved by a certain population.

4.2. SP and FIP Comparison

FIP MEPS pictograms are a set of illustrations issued in 2009, more than one decade after the USP set released in 1997. FIP, a world-wide organization, released a pictogram software update on 7 February 2017 that fixed some language issues and included Turkish and Malayan as languages. Even if developers warn of cultural sensitivity issues, it was expected the pictograms would relay information more precisely. However, this was not confirmed: the average total comprehension score obtained with USP pictograms was significantly higher than the correspondent FIP result. This is also true when the individuals rated their Portuguese fluency as poor. This indicates that USP pictograms could be better suited to the Hindu population living in Lisbon than the FIP set, knowing pharmacists can access both freely.

4.3. Pictograms Design

The present study findings were not always in line with previous studies, acknowledging different research settings. The use of single images did not seem to be preferable to multiple images [17,20]. One possible explanation may be the use of several sequential frames helping the participant to better infer the meaning of subsequent images. Negatively marked pictograms were more easily interpreted, which also differs from previously published literature [18,21]. However, interpreting negative marks well (as well as medication-related information content) was achieved by those who considered themselves fluent in Portuguese. This could be a cultural feature from this sample, where these pictograms may resemble other common signs of caution to which Hindus are more sensitive. Finally, pictograms illustrating medication directions may convey more information than pictograms with warnings or precautions thus increasing complexity leading to diminished understanding among the sampled population. All these results are in line with previous findings mentioning that culture-specific and education level-specific pictograms may be essential for the effective communication of health information [28].

4.4. Study Limitations

Some resistance to full participation was found during the fieldwork. Bulky questionnaires with a high number of pages because of the room need for the pictures seemed to discouraged participants from completing them. As mentioned earlier, 18 selected participants dropped out before achieving the 50 participants quota, even with support from the field researcher where requested. During the pre-test, participants took an average of 11 min to complete the questionnaire but during data gathering people often took longer, mainly due to poorer understanding of the questions or to external interferences (e.g., others waiting). This apparent reluctance in completing the survey may also result from the infrequent contact due to disbelief in pictograms by community pharmacies. Using an interview approach instead of a self-administered questionnaire may have improved participation, although impact on findings is not possible to assess.

More importantly, participants showed some difficulties in reading and understanding the written information, including the wording of the options for each pictogram. While assuring a more genuine background (i.e., Portuguese is the dominant language in healthcare provision), it was not possible to control for the effects of functional cognitive abilities and literacy. No structured and independent assessment of Portuguese speaking proficiency was conducted which possibly contributed to less accurate reading of the options per pictogram and answering. This was minimized by translating questions to Hindu only when necessary, avoiding introducing undue variation in survey administration and additional response bias.

Extending the present results to all Hindu communities in Lisbon or Portugal, or other culturally diverse sub-populations, should be done with care since no representativeness or external validation was achieved in this study, resulting from anticipated time constraints. Finally, no qualitative approach was taken to investigate the reasons underlying such diverse interpretation on paired pictograms (e.g., #1 and #9 or #7 and #16), which adds further caution if the present findings are to be directly used in practice, even within the Hindu community.

5. Conclusions

Pictograms are potentially a good way to pass on treatment directions and precautions, in particular to culturally challenging populations, such as the Hindu Community in Portugal. Nevertheless, this study indicated that pictograms may fail their mission. Thus, it is recommended that prior to generalized usage, pictograms are tested with local populations. If local refinements are not possible, usage warnings should be issued by the responsible health authorities, alerting professionals to use them with attention.

Further field studies with pharmaceutical pictograms in Portuguese community pharmacies are needed to improve the validation and usefulness of this tool. Pictograms do not replace pharmacist–patient communication, but they cannot be ignored as an information resource in Portuguese pharmacy practice.

Acknowledgments: No sources of funding were used.

Author Contributions: A.C. conceived and designed the survey; L.K. and S.X. performed the data collection; L.K., S.X. and A.C. analyzed the data; and L.K. and A.C. wrote the paper.

Conflicts of Interest: The authors declare no conflict of interest.

References

1. O'Loughlin, J.; Masson, P.; Déry, V.; Fagnan, D. The role of community pharmacists in health education and disease prevention: A survey of their interests and needs in relation to cardiovascular disease. *Prev. Med.* **1999**, *28*, 324–331. [CrossRef] [PubMed]

2. Van Grootheest, A.C.; de Jong-van den Berg, L.T. The role of hospital and community pharmacists in pharmacovigilance. *Res. Soc. Adm. Pharm.* **2005**, *1*, 126–133. [CrossRef] [PubMed]

3. Bryant, L.J.; Coster, G.; Gamble, G.D.; McCormick, R.N. General practitioners' and pharmacists' perceptions of the role of community pharmacists in delivering clinical services. *Res. Soc. Adm. Pharm.* **2009**, *5*, 347–362. [CrossRef] [PubMed]

4. Cramer, J.A.; Roy, A.; Burrell, A.; Fairchild, C.J.; Fuldeore, M.J.; Ollendorf, D.A.; Wong, P.K. Medication compliance and persistence: Terminology and definitions. *Value Health* **2008**, *11*, 44–47. [CrossRef] [PubMed]

5. Balkrishnan, R.; Rajagopalan, R.; Camacho, F.T.; Huston, S.A.; Murray, F.T.; Anderson, R.T. Predictors of medication adherence and associated health care costs in an older population with type 2 diabetes mellitus: A longitudinal cohort study. *Clin. Ther.* **2003**, *25*, 2958–2971. [CrossRef]

6. Ho, P.M.; Rumsfeld, J.S.; Masoudi, F.A.; McClure, D.L.; Plomondon, M.E.; Steiner, J.F.; Magid, D.J. Effect of medication nonadherence on hospitalization and mortality among patients with diabetes mellitus. *Arch. Intern. Med.* **2006**, *166*, 1836–1841. [CrossRef] [PubMed]

7. Barros, I.M.; Alcântara, T.S.; Mesquita, A.R.; Santos, A.C.; Paixão, F.P.; Lyra, D.P. The use of pictograms in the health care: A literature review. *Res. Soc. Adm. Pharm.* **2014**, *10*, 704–719. [CrossRef] [PubMed]

8. Ng, A.W.; Chan, A.H.; Ho, V.W. Comprehension by older people of medication information with or without supplementary pharmaceutical pictograms. *Appl. Ergon.* **2017**, *58*, 167–175. [CrossRef] [PubMed]

9. Kassam, R.; Vaillancourt, L.R.; Collins, J.B. Pictographic instructions for medications: Do different cultures interpret them accurately? *Int. J. Pharm. Pract.* **2004**, *12*, 199–209. [CrossRef]

10. Yasmin, R.; Shakeel, S.; Iffat, W.; Hasnat, S.; Quds, T. Comparative Analysis of Understanding of Pictograms in Pharmacy and non-Pharmacy Students. *Intl. J. Sci. Basic Appl. Res.* **2014**, *13*, 197–204.

11. Barros, I.M.; Alcântara, T.S.; Mesquita, A.R.; Bispo, M.L.; Rocha, C.E.; Moreira, V.P.; Junior, D.P.L. Understanding of pictograms from the United States Pharmacopeia Dispensing Information (USP-DI) among elderly Brazilians. *Patient Prefer Adher.* **2014**, *8*, 1493–1501.

12. Kolers, P. Some formal characteristics of pictograms. *Am. Sci.* **1969**, *57*, 348–363.

13. Dowse, R.; Ehlers, M. Medicine labels incorporating pictograms: Do they influence understanding and adherence? *Patient Educ. Couns.* **2005**, *58*, 63–70. [CrossRef] [PubMed]

14. Fonseca, R. Reading Pictograms and Signs—The Need for Visual Literacy. Master's Thesis, University of Stavanger, Stavanger, Norway, 2011. Available online: https://brage.bibsys.no/xmlui/handle/11250/185313 (accessed on 1 September 2017).

15. Davies, S.; Haines, H.; Norris, B.; Wilson, J.R. Safety pictograms: Are they getting the message across? *Appl. Ergon.* **1998**, *29*, 15–23. [CrossRef]

16. McDougall, S.J.; Curry, M.B.; de Bruijn, O. Measuring symbol and icon characteristics: Norms for concreteness, complexity, meaningfulness, familiarity, and semantic distance for 239 symbols. *Behav. Res. Methods Instrum. Comput.* **1999**, *31*, 487–519. [CrossRef] [PubMed]

17. Rogers, Y. Icon Design for the User Interface. In *International Reviews of Ergonomics*; Oborne, D.J., Ed.; Taylor & Francis: London, UK, 1989; pp. 129–155.

18. Wolf, J.S.; Wogalter, M.S. Test and development of pharmaceutical pictorials. *Proc. Interface* **1993**, *93*, 187–192.

19. Foster, J.J.; Afzalnia, M.R. International assessment of judged symbol comprehensibility. *Int. J. Psychol.* **2005**, *40*, 169–175. [CrossRef]

20. Lee, S.; Dazkir, S.S.; Paik, H.S.; Coskun, A. Comprehensibility of universal healthcare symbols for wayfinding in healthcare facilities. *Appl. Ergon.* **2014**, *45*, 878–885. [CrossRef] [PubMed]

21. Montagne, M. Pharmaceutical pictograms: A model for development and testing for comprehension and utility. *Res. Soc. Adm. Pharm.* **2013**, *9*, 609–620. [CrossRef] [PubMed]

22. Health Sciences Library. Health Literacy and Patient Education Guide: Pictograms. 2017. Available online: http://hslibraryguides.ucdenver.edu/c.php?g=259516&p=1732398 (accessed on 22 August 2017).

23. Dowse, R.; Ehlers, M.S. The evaluation of pharmaceutical pictograms in a low-literate South African population. *Patient Educ. Couns.* **2001**, *45*, 87–99. [CrossRef]

24. Dowse, R.; Ehlers, M. Pictograms for conveying medicine instructions: Comprehension in various South African language groups. *S. Afr. J. Sci.* **2004**, *100*, 678–693.

25. Soares, M.A. Legibility of USP pictograms by clients of community pharmacies in Portugal. *Int. J. Clin. Pharm.* **2013**, *35*, 22–29. [CrossRef] [PubMed]

26. Instituto Nacional de Estatística. Censos—Resultados Definitivos. Região Lisboa—2011. Available online: http://censos.ine.pt/xportal/xmain?xpid=CENSOS&xpgid=ine_censos_publicacao_det&contexto=pu&PUBLICACOESpub_boui=156651739&PUBLICACOESmodo=2&selTab=tab1&pcensos=61969554 (accessed on 17 December 2016).

27. Yu, B.; Willis, M.; Sun, P.; Wang, J. Crowdsourcing participatory evaluation of medical pictograms using Amazon Mechanical Turk. *J. Med. Internet Res.* **2013**, *15*, e108. [CrossRef] [PubMed]

28. Richler, M.; Vaillancourt, R.; Celetti, S.; Besançon, L.; Arun, K.; Sebastien, F. The use of pictograms to convey health information regarding side effects and/or indications of medications. *J. Commun. Healthc.* **2012**, *5*, 200–226. [CrossRef]

![pharmacy logo] *pharmacy*

MDPI

Article

Uncertainty and Motivation to Seek Information from Pharmacy Automated Communications

Michelle Bones [1] and Martin Nunlee [2,*]

[1] Department of Veterans Affairs, Voluntary Service, 1601 Kirkwood Highway, Wilmington, DE 19805 USA; mcnunlef@umich.edu

[2] Department of Business Administration, College of Business, Delaware State University, 1200 North Dupont Highway, Dover, DE 19901-2277, USA

* Correspondence: mnunlee@desu.edu; Tel.: +1-302-857-6974; Fax: +1-302-857-6927

Received: 12 April 2018; Accepted: 23 May 2018; Published: 28 May 2018

Abstract: Pharmacy personnel often answer telephones to respond to pharmacy customers (subjects) who received messages from automated systems. This research examines the communication process in terms of how users interact and engage with pharmacies after receiving automated messages. No study has directly addressed automated telephone calls and subjects' interactions. The purpose of this study is to test the interpersonal communication (IC) process of uncertainty in subjects in receipt of automated telephone calls ATCs from pharmacies. Subjects completed a survey of validated scales for Satisfaction (S); Relevance (R); Quality (Q); Need for Cognitive Closure (NFC). Relationships between S, R, Q, NFC, and subject preference to ATCs were analyzed to determine whether subjects contacting pharmacies display information seeking behavior. Results demonstrated that seeking information occurs if subjects: are dissatisfied with the content of the ATC; perceive that the Q of ATC is high and like receiving the ATC, or have a high NFC and do not like receiving ATCs. Other interactions presented complexities amongst uncertainty and tolerance of NFC within the IC process.

Keywords: pharmacy; patient communication; pharmacy communications; interpersonal communications; automated telemarketing telephone calls; telephone messages; automated messages; communication theory; customer relation management; CRM; pharmacy practice

---

1. Introduction

Automated messaging is a major form of patient communication for community pharmacies. Voicemails, text messages or emails serve to notify patients. These forms of communication are by their nature unidirectional, from the pharmacy to the patient. For there to be bidirectional communication, the patient must contact the pharmacy—usually this contact is by telephone. How many times have personnel in pharmacies had to respond to customers who have called concerning communications from automated systems? Automated messages—specifically automated telephone messages dates back to 1924 [1]. Accordingly, the sentiments of the intent of the sender's message, " ... was believed ... to save considerable expense to the companies where many "repeat" calls are necessary" [1]. The use of recorded messages blossomed in the late 20th century and exploded in the 21st century [2]. Often pharmacies send automated messages via telephone to patients, as a form of communication. The telephone, as a medium, is "cool" or one of low definition [3]. Automated telephone calls from pharmacies provide information requiring so much to be filled in by the pharmacy customer. When a pharmacy customer responds to the automated telephone call (ATC) from a pharmacy, the medium requires the individual to "actively analyze and interpret what is presented, to make sense of what they ... hear" [4]. After receiving a message from a cool medium such as an ATC, the pharmacy customer can choose to respond to the message, thereby engaging in the interpersonal communication process. An alternative option is not to respond.

Very few studies directly addressed the role communication plays in pharmacy patients' interactions; this is one of the few studies in the pharmacy discipline that seeks to dive in-depth into the communication and interpersonal communication concepts [5,6]. By definition communication is the process of imparting or interchanging thoughts, opinions or information. Fields of study as disperse as psychology, business and engineering rely upon the same basic model of communication. A diagram of the communications process is outlined in Figure 1.

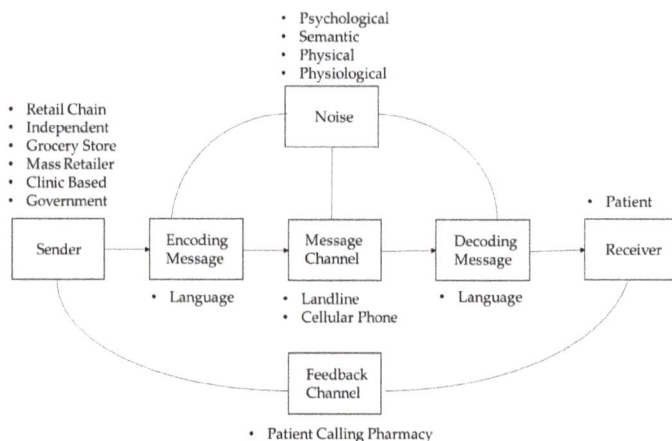

Figure 1. Diagram of communication process.

Figure 1 depicts the typical communication process. In this research we are concerned with how noise, specifically—psychological noise, influences patients' perceptions within the domain of ATCs. As indicated in the figure, noise can impact the encoding and decoding, and the message channel. Noise is anything that hinders the communication process. The four most common forms of noise are physical, physiological, semantic, and psychological. Physical noise is something that interferes with communication that is external to both the sender and receiver. Physiological noise is an internal condition of the receiver or sender that causes a distraction. Physiological noise could be caused by hunger, fatigue, malaise, medication or other factors that affect how people feel and think. In terms of oral exchanges these internal distraction, may cause senders to have problem in articulation, while receivers may have problem in hearing. Semantic noise is primarily cause by the sender. It occurs when senders encode messages in language in which the receiver is unfamiliar. Most of the work concerning the communication process in healthcare has focused on semantic noise—in the form of patient health literacy. In its most basic form, psychological noise consists of mental interference. The reader should understand that psychological noise could stem from wandering thoughts and preconceived ideas; as well as dislike of the sender, medium or receiver. To measure psychological noise, we use common constructs and in-turn scales from psychology and consumer behavior to assess patients' tendencies and attitudes and then gauge their response, by the number of feedback calls.

The motivation for why people would contact pharmacies varies. Is the ATC a channel for information seeking by pharmacy patients? Will pharmacy customers call the pharmacy seeking information pertaining to the ATC? According to Brasher et al. [6], within the health context framework, information is defined as stimuli from a person's environment that contribute to his or her knowledge or belief. Some customers will call to get clarification or confirmation, while other customers will call if they find the ATC from a pharmacy a bother or nuisance. What are the thoughts of the pharmacy patient following the receipt of an ATC from a pharmacy? If a pharmacy patient seeks information from the pharmacy, what are the contributions to the patient? Within the health context framework, "the information can be used to decrease uncertainty that is distressing, to increase certainty that allows for hope or optimism, and to invite reappraisal of uncertainty" [6]. Information seeking has been studied in the context of individuals' network of interpersonal relationships. Theories from the Social Science discipline of Interpersonal Communication will serve as the basis of analysis for the pharmacy-pharmacy patient interpersonal relationship. The selected perspective is represented by the arc of "noise" to "decoding message" outlined in Figure 1. The content of the message is not a specific focus. However, the medium of the message, via telephone, contributes to the knowledge or beliefs of the pharmacy patient. Before, discussing motivation there has to be a clear understanding of what is meant by communication.

What is communication? "A process as complex as communication is hard to summarize or define" [7]; from a business marketing perspective, "communication is the process by which we exchange or share meanings through a common set of symbols" [8]. The highest level of communication can be further delineated, from broadcasting one-way messages to interactive interpersonal communication. Focusing on interpersonal communication, it is direct, face-to-face communication between two or more people [8], and the participants receive maximum feedback [7]. A further delineation of interpersonal communication is the theory of uncertainty. Brashers [9] states that "uncertainty exist when details of situations are ambiguous, complex, unpredictable, or probabilistic; when information is unavailable or inconsistent; and when people feel insecure in their own state of knowledge or the state of knowledge in general". What factors, in an interpersonal communication relationship, can affect uncertainty? Need for Closure (NFC) is one factor. NFC is commonly defined "within the relationship exchange of information, [as] the desire for an answer on a given topic, any answer, as compared to confusion or ambiguity" [10].

Excluding pharmacy, "disciplines that have examined this depth of the uncertainty process in earnest include communications, psychology, sociology, family studies, library and information sciences, medicine, genetic counseling, business, economics and religious studies" [11]. Theories from the Social Science discipline of Interpersonal Communication serve as the basis of analysis for the pharmacy-pharmacy patient interpersonal relationship. To advance our understanding of the pharmacy-pharmacy patient communication process more empirical study is necessary. Further, socio-demographic characteristics should be examined within the framework of the information exchange process. This research focuses on the beliefs of the pharmacy patient and their motivation to contact pharmacies and directly addresses the role communication science plays in pharmacy patients' interactions in ATCs.

To examine communication processes, we will refer to pharmacy patients as "subjects". Kruglanski [10] states that subjects' desire for information or knowledge leads to NFC and is related to any particular belief properties. These properties may be content-related, structural, a novelty, desirable or formal features in given circumstances. Subjects generate theories that view their own attributes as more predictive of desirable outcomes, and they are reluctant to believe in theories relating their own attributes to undesirable events [12]. These desirable outcomes seem to be explained best by motivational ends according to Kunda [12], or otherwise stated the desire for information or knowledge is a driving motivation. The desire to seek information serves as an example of a motivational force. Motivational forces do not completely blind people to undesirable evidence or information; however, motivational forces could lead people to play down negative information. It should be noted, people's tendency to link their attributes to desirable outcomes was found only for people who cared about the outcomes. Furthermore, people threatened by undesirable evidence are reluctant to believe this evidence. The desire to seek information is tainted by self-protective motivational forces [12]. Otherwise stated, subjects are satisfied with their current state of knowledge, and do not seek information.

The framework of attribute satisfaction by consumers has been examined. Attribute satisfaction, then, is the consumer's subjective satisfaction judgment resulting from observations of attribute performance (role or event) and can be the fulfillment response consumers make when assessing performance [13]. In his research Oliver [13] looked at the role of events (e.g., attribute performance experiences) as causal agents for positive states. This analogy is extended to the summary attribute level, where the sum of positive product experiences (i.e., satisfactory attribute performances) should relate to positive affect, and negative experiences (i.e., dissatisfactory attribute performances) to negative affect [13]. If consumer's posses dissatisfactory attribute performances and negative outcomes, will they seek information to affect uncertainty?

Cosby and Stephens [14] examined stimulus influences on satisfaction decisions in a study model related to services by an entity. The communication stimuli enhanced satisfaction to services. Subjects given valid information about the services reduced search and evaluation of alternate services within the model. Henceforth in the interpersonal communication process this level of enhanced satisfaction lead to declining levels of uncertainty, with corresponding decreasing information seeking behavior [10].

In our examination, the content of the belief properties or attributes of the ATC are general satisfaction, and relevance of information. In this case, information seeking or desire for exchange of information means calling the pharmacy. Therefore, we hypothesize the following about the subjects' belief properties toward the ATC from pharmacies.

Hypothesis 1. *If subjects are dissatisfied with the content of the ATC received from a pharmacy, then they will seek information.*

Pyszczynski and Greenberg [15] conducted a study to determine causal perceptions of relevant information by subjects, including selection of information. Subjects observed an individual's behavior in a scenario. Then subjects read personality-related answers provided by the individual in the scenario. A few relevant items help explain the just-observed scenario, and the other items were irrelevant to the scenario. Next the subjects were asked something about the personality of the individual in the scenario. This study design measures the subject's motivation to voluntarily select information for use in analyzing and providing the answer to the question about the personality of the individual in the scenario. The findings revealed that when faced with disconfirming expectations subjects will seek attribution-relevant information [15]. This research demonstrated when people are confused they search for relevant information. Likewise, the relevance of the information is related to information seeking. This leads to the following hypothesis.

Hypothesis 2. *If subjects feel that the content of the ATC received from a pharmacy is relevant, then they will seek information.*

In addition, communication quality is another belief property associated with the ATC. Webster and Kruglanski [16] conducted an experiment comparing subjective certainty and susceptibility to persuasion in people with different levels of the need for closure. The experimental design was accomplished by introducing participants to differing amounts and quality of information about a situation. The investigators concluded that people with a high NFC are susceptible to the persuasion of differing quality of information, because each persuasive message gives them a chance to achieve closure [16]. This leads us to the third hypothesis, which is as follows.

Hypothesis 3a. *If a subject perceives that the quality of the ATC received from a pharmacy is high, the subject will seek information.*

Likewise, a pre-existing knowledge structure can serve as a motivating factor for search of information. If a subject has both a high affinity for receiving information, and high perception of quality, then we theorized the following:

Hypothesis 3b. *If a subject perceives that the quality of ATC received from a pharmacy is high, and like receiving the ATC, the subject will seek information.*

The extant literature on NFC, indicates the higher the need for closure, the greater the information seeking. Alternatively, a summarization of another finding by Kruglanski [8], states that if the subjects' confidence in belief properties rank high, along with a high NFC, the tendency to seek information is decreased. If the initial confidence in belief properties ranks low and NFC is high, subjects possess an increased tendency for information seeking. In examining the properties of ATC communication, we decided to test the basic premise of NFC, which leads to the following hypothesis.

Hypothesis 4a. *If subjects, NFC are high after receipt of the ATC from a pharmacy, the subjects will seek information.*

The interaction of variables surfaced from findings in an experiment [17] examining NFC effects and dependent variables to engage informational search by subjects, a multivariate analysis of variance (MANOVA) yielded a significant interaction among variables or belief properties. This unpublished study used a 2 × 2 factorial analysis with two independent and dependent variables to examine interactive effects of need-for-closure. The independent variables were need-for-closure and the subjects' confidence in the process. The two dependent variables were measures of the subjects' tendency to engage in information search. The analysis of data showed the two-way interactions were significant ($p < 0.01$) [17]. We chose to examine subjects' NFC based on preexisting conditions. In particular, the preexisting condition consists of whether patients receiving the ATC from pharmacies like or dislike of receiving the ATC from pharmacies. Besides generally testing NFC, we will test whether people who do not have an affinity for receiving the ATC and have a high NFC would call the pharmacy. These would most likely be the people that we mentioned earlier who call because they find ATCs a bother or nuisance. This leads us to the following sub-hypotheses.

Hypothesis 4b. *If a subject perceives that the quality of the ATC received from a pharmacy is low, and has a high NFC, the subject will seek information.*

Theses related aspects of attribute beliefs found in satisfaction, relevance, and quality along with the theory of need for closure within the theory of uncertainty as embodied in the concept of Interpersonal Communication were analyzed in a random population. We chose validated constructs scales of Satisfaction (Generalized), Information Relevance, Communication Quality and NFC to examine the pharmacy subjects' response to engaging in the interpersonal communication process. See Table 1 for a summary of the hypotheses.

Table 1. Summary of hypotheses for phenomena of behaviors of pharmacy patients in receipt of an automated telephone call (ATC).

Item	Hypothesis
1.	If subjects are dissatisfied with the content of the ATC received from a pharmacy, then they will seek information.
2.	If subjects feel that the content of the ATC received from a pharmacy is relevant, then they will seek information.
3a.	If a subject perceives that the quality of the ATC received from a pharmacy is high, the subject will seek information.
3b.	If a subject perceives that the quality of ATC received from a pharmacy is high, and like receiving the ATC, the subject will seek information.
4a.	If subjects, NFC are high after receipt of the ATC from a pharmacy, the subjects will seek information.
4b.	If a subject perceives that the quality of the ATC received from a pharmacy is low, and has a high NFC, the subject will seek information.

2. Materials and Methods

A 46-item questionnaire was compiled as a tool for the survey. Refer to Supplementary Materials for the complete survey. The questionnaire contains six validated construct scales. Validated scales have been tested with successful results many times. Validated construct scales are both reliable and reproducible. The psychometric qualities of each validated construct scales have been provided to verify the validity and reliability of each measure, giving rise to testable theories. This compilation method was utilized to collect data for analysis and inclusion in the 46-item questionnaire survey tool.

Google survey served as the platform for the survey design, and response collection. The survey was titled "Automated Telephone Calls from Pharmacies" for administration to subjects. The survey design consisted of three sections, Section 1—Pre-Interactions, Section 2—Post-interactions and Section 3—Demographics. Questions in Section 1 of the survey served to separate subjects. If subjects indicated that they have never received prescription medication or never received an ATC from a pharmacy, they were directed to Section 3 of the survey for collection of demographic data. Also, subjects were directed to Section 3 of the survey if they had never received ATCs from a pharmacy. Completion of Section 2 was limited to subjects meeting the criteria set forth in question 1 and/or 2 of Section 1. Only subjects who completed Section 2 responded to all 46-items of the survey. The completion of Section 3 of the survey was required for all subjects in fulfillment of survey completion. The estimated time for completion of the survey was 10-min. The survey was administered using Amazon Mechanical Turk (MTurk) for Social/Behavioral Research projects. MTurk is a web service that provides on-demand scalable human subjects to complete surveys. Keywords, a phrase and a short description were used to assist and guide subjects to participate in the "Automated Telephone Calls from Pharmacies" survey. The keywords are listed in Table 2.

Table 2. Keywords to recruit subjects.

Keywords (Alphabetical Order):			
Behaviors	Customers	Medicines	Prescriptions
Capsules	Healthcare	Pharmacies	Interactions
Communications	Medications	Pills	Tablets

To aid in the recruitment of subjects, potential subjects were given the following short description concerning the study:

> This is a research study that directly addresses automated pharmacy telephone calls and pharmacy customers' interactions. The purpose of this study is to examine the communication behaviors between pharmacy customers in receipt of automated telephone calls.

After subjects committed to completing the survey, they were directed to complete Section 1. Subjects who met the screening criteria were then directed to Section 2, and then they were directed to indicate their responses and preferences on the validated construct scales. Finally, subjects were directed to Section 3 to report their demographic information. The third section of the survey utilized identical socio-demographic ranges as reported in the United States census. Human subjects 18 years of age or older were eligible participants. The survey was administered using stratified sampling, in six intervals based on age to ensure representation over a continuum, see Table 3 for interval ranges. All subjects were paid for participation.

Table 3. Intervals of survey administration based on age.

Group	Age Range
1	Ages 18 years < 25 years
2	Ages 25 years < 30 years
3	Ages 30 years < 35 years
4	Ages 35 years < 45 years
5	Ages 45 years < 55 years
6	Ages 55 years or older

Sources of Validated Construct Scales

The first construct scale to be presented is the "Satisfaction (Generalized)" [18], represented by questions 6 through 10. It is a multi-item, seven-point semantic differential summated ratings scale measuring degree of satisfaction with stimuli. Scale reliability for conducted studies, as measured by Cronbach's alpha were reported as 0.96, and in other studies 0.94, 0.91, 0.90, 0.93 and 0.87. The Satisfaction scale examines a subject's degree of satisfaction after receiving automated telephone calls from a pharmacy. High scores indicate greater satisfaction with the automated telephone message, whereas low scores imply that the subjects are not pleased.

The second construct scale to be presented is Information Relevance [19], represented by questions 11 through 15. It is a five-item, seven-point summated rating scale, measuring the level of usefulness a person reports some piece of information to have. Cronbach's alpha for the Information Relevance scale were reported as 0.94, 0.94, and 0.96. The Information Relevance scale examines the level of usefulness subjects report, concerning the information provided in the automated telephone call. High scores indicate that subjects describe information related to automated telephone calls as being very relevant, whereas low scores imply that the subjects found the information less relevant.

The third construct scale to be presented is Communication Quality [20], represented by questions 16 through 20. It is a five-item, five-point semantic differential scale to assess person's perceptions of the quality of communication between them and the information provider. For reliability, Cronbach's alpha for the conducted study was 0.92. The scale examines subjects' perception of the quality of communication between themselves and the automated telephone message. This Communication Quality scale was reversed scaled. Lower scores on the scale indicate that subjects perceived that high-quality communication occurred between themselves and the automated telephone message, whereas high scores imply that the subjects perceived that low-quality communication occurred between themselves and the automated telephone message.

The forth scale to be presented is a measure of Socially Desirable Response Set (SDRS-5) [21], represented by questions 21 through 25. It is a five-item, five-point scale to evaluate susceptibility to response bias by subjects receiving automated telephone calls from pharmacies. Cronbach's alpha for the conducted study was 0.66 and 0.68. The scale evaluates a respondent's tendency to give socially-desirable response[s] [20]. This scale was used to verify that subjects were giving their true response and not giving responses that they thought were socially appropriate.

Finally, the Need for Cognitive Closure scale [22] measured subjects' tolerance or lack of tolerance for uncertainty. The Need for Cognitive Closure scale consists of 15 items, represented by questions 26 through 40. It consists of a six-point rating scale to measure a variable desire for closure along a continuum with a strong need to attain closure on one end and a high need to avoid closure at the other end [22]. Scale reliability, as measured by Cronbach's alpha was 0.79.

3. Results

There were 319 respondents who participated in the survey process. Only 294 of the 319 respondents were selected as subjects. Respondents were eliminated only as a result of the screening process or if they did not provide a response to all the questions. The demographic data collected during the survey process serves to provide characteristics of the study population. A brief overview of subject characteristics follows. The female to male ratio was approximately 2:1 respectively for all subjects. Most respondents reported having attended some college and bachelor's degree for education level. Very few respondents reported education as high school graduate or G.E.D, trade school or other post-secondary education, or associate degree. The majority of the respondents reported being married, followed by single/never married. A preponderance of respondents reported ethnicity or origin as Caucasian/White. Household income ranged from $15K to less than $150K. The interrelationships amongst the subject characteristics and responses were analyzed based on correlations and linear regression. They are not reported here, except for some comparisons, because there were no significant relationships or interaction patterns observed between survey responses and socio-demographic characteristics. None of the 294 subjects scored high on social desirability, which indicates that subjects were giving their true responses, instead of what they think is socially desirable.

To test the hypotheses, we used correlations and linear regression. The results of the analyses are shown in Table 4. The critical relationship correlations are reported in Table 4.

Table 4. Correlations of critical relationships.

	Satisfaction	Relevance	Quality	SDRS	NFC	I (Q × Like)	I (NFC × Not Like)	Contacted
Satisfaction	1							
Relevance	0.8264	1						
Quality	−0.6760	−0.6981	1					
SDRS	0.0526	0.0478	−0.0341	1				
NFC	0.1574	0.1439	−0.1997	−0.1173	1			
I (Q × Like)	0.4751	0.3631	−0.1200	−0.0420	0.0388	1		
I (NFC × not like)	−0.7663	−0.6348	0.4945	0.0089	0.0022	−0.7972	1	
Contacted	−0.0954	−0.0845	0.2210	0.0214	−0.0431	0.1082	0.0298	1

Hypothesis 1 has been confirmed. Satisfaction with the message content of automated telephone calls is negatively correlated to the number of subjects' telephone calls to the pharmacy. Although the correlation is small ($r = -0.0954$), it is significant ($p \leq 0.10$).

Hypothesis 2 has not been confirmed. Relevance of the automated telephone calls is negatively correlated to the number of subject pharmacy telephone calls to the pharmacy; however, this relationship is not significant. However, when we tested just the subjects who liked to receive ATCs, we found that the level of inverse correlation had increased ($r = -0.2030$) and significant ($p \leq 0.01$).

Quality of the automated telephone call message is positively correlated to the number of subjects' telephone calls to the pharmacy. This relationship was both positively correlated ($r = 0.221$) and significant ($p \leq 0.01$). This relationship was further tested by introducing the indicator variable of whether patients liked receiving ATCs as a moderator to quality. This means that subjects who perceive that the quality of the ATC received from a pharmacy is high will seek information. To confirm Hypothesis 3b, we need to add the interaction term and regress both the quality of the automated telephone call (Q) and the interaction of Q and liking (Like) to receive automated telephone calls—I (Q × Like)—on number of subject pharmacy telephone calls to the pharmacy—contacting pharmacies (CP). The linear model is given below.

$$CP = \beta_0 + \beta_1 \cdot Q + \beta_2 \cdot I_{Q \times Like}, \tag{1}$$

As indicated in Table 5, although the explained variance as measured by r^2 only accounts for 26% of the explained variance, the regression coefficients were both positive and significant; with Quality remaining significant to the $p \leq 0.01$ level and interaction of liking to receive automated telephone calls and Quality significant to the $p \leq 0.05$ level. This means that Quality is positively related to the number of phone calls, and that people who like receiving ATCs play an additional role in the quality relationship. Both Hypotheses 3a and 3b have been confirmed.

Table 5. Regression results communication quality.

Variable	β_i	Std. Error	t Stat	p
Intercept	0.8473	0.0637	13.3034	≤0.01
Q	0.0234	0.0056	4.1630	≤0.01
I (Q × Like)	0.0138	0.0057	2.3976	≤0.05

To test Hypotheses 4a and 4b, we regressed NFC, the interaction between Q and Like, and the interaction of need for closure (NFC) and not liking (NLike) to receive phone calls on to contacting the pharmacies (CP). Some of the results described in the correlation matrix (Table 4) are counter intuitive. For example, Q is negatively correlated to satisfaction. These results led us to test the interaction with Q and Like, since the interaction between NFC and NLike was significant and highly negatively correlated to satisfaction, we wanted to see if isolating people who like receiving phone calls responded differently in terms of the expected measures and whether it was significant. Said another way, we can test whether the people who were dissatisfied with receiving ATCs were driving the counter intuitive relationships. This resulted in the following linear model.

$$CP = \beta_0 + \beta_1 \cdot NFC + \beta_2 \cdot I_{Q \times Like} + \beta_3 \cdot I_{NFC \times NLike}, \tag{2}$$

The multiple coefficient of determination (r) for the regression was 0.71, r^2 was 0.50, while the adjusted-r^2 was also 0.50; with a standard error of 2.87 over 294 observations. Given a mean square error residual (MSR) of 8.23 and a mean square error regression (MSE) of 811, this yields an F(3, 293) of 98.45, meaning that the regression was significant to $p \leq 0.01$. The regression yielded the following results, Table 6:

Table 6. Regression results NFC and interaction terms.

Variable	β_i	Std. Error	t Stat	p
Intercept	6.6326	0.9998	6.6336	≤0.01
NFC	−0.0795	0.0142	−5.6087	≤0.01
I (Q × Like)	0.7958	0.0702	11.3405	≤0.01
I (NFC × not like)	0.1636	0.0101	16.2671	≤0.01

Hypothesis 4a has not been confirmed. In general NFC is negatively related to the number of subjects making telephone calls to the pharmacy. This means that people with a high need for closure are generally less likely to contact their pharmacies. This result lends credence to Kruglanski findings [10] that if the subjects' confidences in belief properties rank high, along with a high NFC, the tendency to seek information is decreased. Hypotheses 4b has been confirmed—people who have a high NFC, who do not like receiving telephone calls from their pharmacy also are likely to call their pharmacy.

By splitting the relationships using the interaction terms, we received confirmation that the negative relationship between satisfaction and communication quality was driven by NLike. Since the β_1 coefficient for NFC remained negative, it is consistent with the overall correlations described in Table 4, this indicates that the regression model is correctly specified. A correctly specified model lends credence that the relationships in the linear regression are credible, and not an artifice of multicollinearity. It is interesting that NFC only plays a role in increasing communication with subjects who do not like to receive ATCs from their pharmacy. See Table 7 for a summary of the hypotheses and results.

Table 7. Summary of hypotheses and results for phenomena of behaviors of pharmacy patients in receipt of an automated telephone call (ATC).

Item	Hypothesis	Result	Relationship	Significance
1.	If subjects are dissatisfied with the content of the ATC received from a pharmacy, then they will seek information.	Confirmed	$r = -0.0954$ negative as predicted	$p \leq 0.10$
2.	If subjects feel that the content of the ATC received from a pharmacy is relevant, then they will seek information.	Not confirmed	$r = -0.2030$ predicted positive but negative relationship	$p \leq 0.01$
3a.	If a subject perceives that the quality of the ATC received from a pharmacy is high, the subject will seek information.	Confirmed	$r = 0.221$ positive as predicted	$p \leq 0.01$
3b.	If a subject perceives that the quality of ATC received from a pharmacy is high, and like receiving the ATC, the subject will seek information.	Confirmed	$\beta = 0.0234$ positive as predicted	$p \leq 0.01$
4a.	If subjects, NFC are high after receipt of the ATC from a pharmacy, the subjects will seek information.	Not confirmed	$\beta = -0.0795$ predicted positive but negative relationship	$p \leq 0.01$
4b.	If a subject perceives that the quality of the ATC received from a pharmacy is low, and has a high NFC, the subject will seek information.	Confirmed	$\beta = 0.1636$ positive as predicted	$p \leq 0.01$

4. Discussion

We asked how many times have pharmacy personnel answered a telephone, to respond to communications from an automated system received by a subject? We were not able to answer that question, but we were able to survey subjects and determine their motivation for wishing to communicate with their pharmacy.

Some of the results revealed the situational impact of information seeking. For example, although subjects who like to receive ATCs find the information significantly relevant ($p \leq 0.01$), the relationship between contacting pharmacies and relevance was inversely correlated. This could be interpreted to mean that since the information is relevant, subjects have no reason to contact the pharmacy after receiving an ATC. This has no bearing on whether patients would contact their pharmacies if they needed information.

We found that NFC played a role only for patients who least liked receiving ATCs. Since we defined a high call volume, as being an individual who makes twelve or more calls to a pharmacy per year, this would mean that a large number of people make these calls based upon not liking to receive automated messages. Although some portion of the calls may be related to therapeutic questions, we suspect a great many are related to either patients' confusion about why they received the ATC, or a desire to express their displeasure. These incidences of communication would be less productive than addressing patient care needs.

We are less certain about the alternative—the patients who call as a result of having an affinity to receive ATCs. Since there is an interaction between liking the ATC and Quality, there is a need to address why these patients like receiving ATCs. Do these patients just like the aspect of communicating, or do they appreciate the information and seek further guidance and clarity? If it is the later condition of seeking guidance or clarity, then either the message needs to be refined or this follow-up call provided the opportunity to engage in meaningful communication that contributes to better patient care.

What we have found is consistent with other work in human communication research. Kellermann and Reynolds [23] found that while a low tolerance for uncertainty motivates greater information seeking, it is in the negative context. If there is a high level of affinity, then people find it easier to conduct communication. This affinity is a form of attractiveness. Only in the case where there is a high incentive or importance will there be communication under all conditions. This means that patients do not necessarily contact pharmacies based upon whether they are uncertain about the information. Rather, they will contact the pharmacy if they already have a positive relationship or they have a low tolerance for uncertainty. This in-turns means that information sharing will not occur; unless patients are comfortable with the pharmacy, or they have a clear understanding of the need or importance of sharing information.

Readers should notice that both interaction terms are positive and significant. In one case, subjects who like to receive ATCs from pharmacies and who have an affinity for receiving telephone calls were more likely to seek further information. In the other case, people who have a high need for closure, who do not like receiving telephone calls from their pharmacy also were likely to call their pharmacy. This is most interesting, since it indicates that communication is a complex multidimensional concept. Further these findings could possibly be explained by Webster and Kruglanski experimental situation model [18]. If the attribute of attractiveness to the task in the model decreased, subjects reflected a high NFC. We saw that the subjects who did not like receiving ATCs from pharmacies, or found ATCs from pharmacies unattractive possessed a high NFC, and called the pharmacy.

Although there needs to be further study and refinement on patient communication, one thing our study makes clear is that interpersonal communication is a complex process. The present results open new challenges for this research area. Our findings are consistent with what Kellermann and Reynolds [23] found. By extension, people are more likely to share information if they are comfortable with their provider, or if they already are aware of the importance of the message. This means that ATCs can only serve a limited role. Sending patients a reminder message to pick-up medication or get a flu vaccine via an ATC only works, if they already like the pharmacy or feel that these things are important to them. Otherwise, patients will only contact their pharmacy if they have a low tolerance for uncertainty. They do not contact their pharmacy to avoid uncertainty.

5. Conclusions

We were able to identify sub-sets within the study population where either communications and/or interpersonal communication occurred. The contributing factors differed for both groups. The less satisfied subjects—who scored high on the NFC scale—were with the ATC medium, the more likely they were to contact the pharmacy. On the other end of the spectrum, subjects that liked receiving ATCs and perceive the quality of the ATC as high were more likely to contact the pharmacy. Both of these groups of subjects sought to further engage in the interpersonal communication process.

We do not know how often subjects specifically call pharmacies after receiving ATC. We were unable to determine the degree to which subjects responded to telephone calls because of the limited response options. Question #4 of the survey asked subjects how many times they received calls from pharmacies, while question #5 asked subjects how many times subjects contacted the pharmacy. These scales were less refined. Only three response options were provided for both questions #4 and #5. We recommend refining the number of response options within these questions in future studies, specifically at the lower range. A more refined scale providing seven anchors would yield more precise results. We can only generalize how subjects with a high propensity to contact their pharmacies after receiving an ATC from pharmacies respond. No further interpretation can be made from the study design. Specifically, a more refined scale is important in the formation of a nuanced understanding of the interpersonal communication process.

We believe that by having a better understanding of patients' communication traits or beliefs and their receptivity to communication will allow senders to design better mechanisms to interact with patients. To arrive at better mechanisms, further study is needed on why some people (a) do not like receiving ATCs, or (b) what attributes of the ATC interact with some peoples' innate need for closure. Minor changes to the form or substance of the communication may make an impact on how pharmacies can better utilize forms of communication. Having an understanding of how and when patients wish to receive communication is critical to designing better communication mechanisms. Accordingly, Sileo and Kayson [24] found that the time of day can affect responsiveness to messaging. Care must be taken to insure that healthcare providers consider patients' receptivity to communication, not just the message itself. As illustrated by Xu, Bates and Schweitzer [25]—when examining telephone messaging in facilitating communications, they were unable to find a significant difference among specific message types. Extensions to this research will allow practitioners to improve the communication process, by either changing ATC messages or segmenting patients, or some combination of changing ATC messages and segmenting patients and then tailoring the message according to patient segments.

Supplementary Materials: The following are available online at http://www.mdpi.com/2226-4787/6/2/47/s1, Table S1: survey, "Automated Telephone Calls from Pharmacies", S2: spread sheet, data set.

Author Contributions: M.B. and M.N. conceived and designed the study; M.B. performed the administration of the survey for the study; M.N. analyzed the data; M.B. and M.N. wrote the paper.

Acknowledgments: Funding for the survey administration was provided by Delaware State University, College of Business, Department of Business Administration, Principle Investigator Account for Martin Nunlee.

Conflicts of Interest: The authors declare no conflict of interest. The founding sponsors had no role in the design of the study; in the collection, analyses, or interpretation of data; in the writing of the manuscript, and in the decision to publish the results.

References

1. Popular Mechanics Phone Calls Are Answered by Machine. Available online: http://blog.modernmechanix.com/phone-calls-are-answered-by-machine/ (accessed on 8 October 2017).

2. Seelhorst, M. Think it's New? Think Again! After the Beep, Leave a Message. *Pop. Mech.* **1998**, *175*, 48.

3. Lapham, L.H.; Mcluhan, M. *Understanding Media (Reprint): The Extensions of Man*; MIT Press Edition; Massachusetts Institute of Technology: Cambridge, MA, USA, 1964; Volume 1, p. 365.

4. Thompson, S. What Did Marshall Mcluhan Mean by Hot and Cool Media? Available online: https://www.quora.com/What-did-Marshall-McLuhan-mean-by-hot-and-cool-media (accessed on 2 January 2018).

5. Worsely, A. Perceived reliability of sources of health information. *Health Educ. Res.* **1989**, *4*, 367–376. [CrossRef]

6. Brasher, D.E.; Goldsmith, D.J.; Hsieh, E. Information Seeking and Avoidance in Health Contexts. *Hum. Commun. Res.* **2002**, *28*, 258–271. [CrossRef]

7. Trenholm, S.; Jensen, A. *Interpersonal Communication*; International; Oxford Univ. Press: New York, NY, USA, 2009; Volume 1, p. 4.

8. Charles, W.L.; Joseph, F.H. *Carl McDaniel, Essentials of Marketing*, 4th ed.; Cengage Learning: Boston, MA, USA, 2004; p. 409.

9. Brashers, D.E. Communication and Uncertainty Management. *J. Commun.* **2001**, *51*, 477–497. [CrossRef]

10. Kruglanski, A.W. Motivation for Judging and Knowing: & nbsp; Implications for Causal Attribution. In *Handbook of Motivation and Cognition Foundations of Social Behavior*; The Guilford Press: New York, NY, USA, 1990; Volume 2, pp. 336–368.

11. Afifi, W.A.; Weiner, J.L. Toward a Theory of Motivated Information Management. *Commun. Theory* **2004**, *14*, 167–190. [CrossRef]

12. Kunda, Z. Motivated Inference: Self-serving Generation and Evaluation of Causal Theories. *J. Personal. Soc. Psychol.* **1987**, *53*, 636–647. [CrossRef]

13. Richard, L. Oliver Cognitive, Affective, and Attribute Bases of the Satisfaction Response. *J. Consum. Res.* **1993**, *20*, 418–430.

14. Crosby, L.A. Effects of Relationship Marketing on Satisfaction, Retention, and Prices in the Life Insurance Industry. *J. Mark. Res.* **1987**, *24*, 404–411. [CrossRef]

15. Pyszczynski, T.A.; Greenberg, J. Role of Disconfirmed Expectancies in the Instigation of Attributional Processing. *J. Personal. Soc. Psychol.* **1981**, *40*, 31–38. [CrossRef]

16. Webster, D.M.; Kruglanski, A.W. Individual Differences in Need for Cognitive Closure. *J. Personal. Soc. Psychol.* **1994**, *67*, 1049–1062. [CrossRef]

17. Peri, N.; Kruglanski, A.; Zakai, D. Interactive Effects of Initial Confidence and Epistemic Motivations on the Extent of Informational Search. Tel-Aviv University, Tel-Aviv, Israel, Unpublished work. 1986.

18. Crosby, L.A.; Stephens, N. Marketing Scales Handbook, A Compilation of Multi-Item Measures. In *Satisfaction (Generalized)*; Bruner, G.C., Hensel, P.J., Eds.; American Marketing Association: Chicago, IL, USA, 1998; Volume 2, pp. 550–552.

19. Mishra, S.; Umesh, U.N.; Stem, D. Marketing Scales Handbook A Compilation of Multi-Item Measures. In *Information Relevance*; Bruner, G.C., Hensel, P.J., Eds.; American Marketing Association: Chicago, IL, USA, 1998; Volume 2, pp. 337–338.

20. Mohr, J.J.; Sohi, R.S. Marketing Scales Handbook, a Compilation of Multi-Item Measures. In *Communication Quality*; Bruner, G.C., James, K.E., Hensel, P.J., Eds.; American Marketing Association: Chicago, IL, USA, 2001; Volume 3, pp. 885–886.

21. Hays, R.D.; Hayashi, T.; Stewart, A.L. A Five-item Measure of Socially Desirable Response Set. *Educ. Psychol. Meas.* **1989**, *49*, 629. [CrossRef]

22. Roets, A.; Van Hiel, A. Item Selection and Validation of a Brief, 15-item Version of the Need for Closure Scale. *Personal. Individ. Differ.* **2011**, *50*, 90–94. [CrossRef]

23. Kellermann, K.; Reynolds, R. When Ignorance Is Bliss The Role of Motivation to Reduce Uncertainty in Uncertainty Reduction Theory. *Hum. Commun. Res.* **1990**, *17*, 5–75. [CrossRef]

24. Sileo, F.J.; Kayson, W.A. When Will Annoying Phone Calls Be Listened to? Effects of Sex, Tone of Voice, and Time of Day. *Psychol. Rep.* **1988**, *62*, 351–355. [CrossRef]

25. Xu, M.; Bates, B.J.; Schweitzer, J.C. The Impact of Messages on Survey Participation in Answering Machine Households. *Public Opin. Q.* **1993**, *57*, 232–237. [CrossRef]

pharmacy

MDPI

Article

The Use of Video Instructions in Patient Education Promoting Correct Technique for Dry Powder Inhalers: An Investigation on Inhaler-Naïve Individuals

Sofia von Schantz [1,*], Nina Katajavuori [2] and Anne M. Juppo [1]

[1] Faculty of Pharmacy, Department of Pharmaceutical Chemistry and Technology, University of Helsinki, P.O. Box 56, 00014 Helsinki, Finland; anne.juppo@helsinki.fi
[2] The Centre for University Teaching and Learning (HYPE), University of Helsinki, Siltavuorenpenger 1 A P.O. Box 9, 00014 Helsinki, Finland; nina.katajavuori@helsinki.fi
* Correspondence: sofia.schantzvon@helsinki.fi

Received: 25 July 2018; Accepted: 20 September 2018; Published: 29 September 2018

Abstract: Introduction: The correct use of a prescribed inhaler device is crucial for achieving successful disease management in asthma. This study investigates non-verbal, demonstrational videos as a method of teaching inhaler naïve individuals how to use a dry powder inhaler (DPI). **Methods:** Video instructions for four DPIs were examined using a mixed methodology; 31 inhaler-naïve individuals participated in the study. Participants were each shown a demonstrational video of one the four inhalers, after each video the participant demonstrated how they would use the inhaler. After demonstrating the use, participants crossed over to the next inhaler. The demonstrations were videotaped. A common questionnaire was filled at the beginning of the study and four inhaler-specific questionnaires which were filled out by the participant after each inhaler demonstration. **Results:** The frequency of participant error varied between inhalers. When asked about how they perceived the video instructions, participants often stated they would have liked to receive feedback on their performance. The importance of feedback was further highlighted by the fact that participants tended to overestimate their own inhaler technique. **Conclusion:** Non-verbal videos may be more efficient for some DPIs than for others as a method for providing inhaler instructions. Lack of feedback on the participants' inhaler performance emerged as a clear shortcoming of this educational method. Some steps in the inhalation process may be harder for individuals to remember and therefore require extra emphasis in order to achieve correct inhaler technique.

Keywords: dry powder inhaler; inhaler technique; inhaler education; asthma

1. Introduction

Asthma is a chronic respiratory disease that may affect as many as 334 million people worldwide [1]. Asthma has become the most prevalent chronic disease in developed countries and affects over 10% of the adult population [2]. The disease is most often treated with inhaled therapies [3], and today dry powder inhalers (DPIs) represent the most rapid-expanding type of device in the treatment of asthma. [4,5]. As such, the correct use of DPIs is important in order for patients to receive the benefits of a proper treatment.

Patient education plays one of the most important roles in the patients' use and misuse of asthma inhalers [6]. Incorrect inhaler use is common and the cost implications are many and appear in such areas as additional doctor visits, hospitalizations and increased use of prescribed inhaler medication. Research suggests that costs can be reduced by spending more time on teaching patients how to correctly use their prescribed inhaler device of inhaler use [7,8]. To counteract for the increasing costs, new and efficient ways of enhancing inhaler technique and safe use of asthma inhalers are needed. Current approaches for providing inhaler training include written instructions, illustrations, audiovisual demonstrations, interactive computer programs, as well as personal and small group demonstrations [9,10], but not all forms of instructions are not equal. Roberts et al. [11] suggested that provision of the manufacturer's instruction sheet alone was ineffective as a method of providing inhaler instructions, partially because patients tended to overlook this information.

Traditionally, healthcare professionals (HCPs) have played an important role in achieving correct inhaler technique and maintaining it over time. Personal instructions provided by a pharmacist have been found more effective than written instructions, and the inclusion of a physical demonstration was found to improve the instructed patient's inhaler technique [12]. Personal and small group demonstrations by trained professionals can be considered adequate possibilities for providing inhaler education, but these alternatives are also often costly [13,14]. Many HCPs, however, exhibit difficulties when asked to demonstrate the correct technique for asthma inhalers [6,15]. Research suggests that 39–67% of nurses, respiratory therapists and doctors are unable to sufficiently describe, or perform, critical steps for inhaler use [6]. Pharmacists have also been found to exhibit insufficient inhaler technique [15]. This may point to a lack of training provided to these groups. Clinicians' ability to use inhalers is typically 5–8 years behind the introduction of new devices [16]. When having received training, HCPs such as pharmacists have been found to be well suited to improve inhalation technique [17]. Nevertheless, problems experienced by HCPs points to the usefulness of standardized teaching methods, such as video education.

Video education and its use among HCPs has become increasingly used in recent years [18]. The videos used in this study are available and used as educational tools in pharmacies across Finland. Video-based education has been used as a tool for providing patients with health education and correct treatment guidelines for individuals with or belonging to risk groups of heart failure and asthma among others [19,20]. Inhaler instructions via video have been suggested as an affordable way to provide easily accessible and standardized inhaler instructions at any time anywhere, and video demonstrations have been found to promote recall on inhaler use in asthma patients [18].

Even though several factors indicate the usefulness of video education and video instructions are becoming an increasingly common ways of providing inhaler education, little research regarding the efficiency of this educational method exists. This study aims to evaluate the use of non-verbal, inhaler specific educational videos as a method of providing inhaler education to inhaler naïve participants with the objective of teaching them how use an inhaler correctly. The study also focuses on identifying areas in which video instructions can be developed in order to fit the needs of individuals without prior inhaler experience.

2. Materials and Methods

The data was collected using a mixed methods study design [21]. The four inhalers used in this study were Diskus, Easyhaler, Ellipta and Turbuhaler. Observational and quantitative data was collected through videotaping of the participants' inhaler performances after having received video education on correct inhaler use. Additionally, qualitative data was collected through semi-structured interviews, after each inhaler performance. All additional comments made about the inhalers and inhalation videos during the data collection process were written down.

2.1. Recruitment

Non-asthmatic, inhaler-naïve, individuals within the age range of 25–34 years were recruited from the general public through flyers posted in several public locations, such as libraries, super markets, cafés, universities and vocational schools in the Helsinki-metropolitan area in Finland.

Participants were considered inhaler-naïve if they did not have asthma or any experience working with, using or helping others to use inhalation devices. A prerequisite for participation was that participants had to be entirely inexperienced regarding inhaler use. Participants who had family members who had asthma were also excluded. The requirement of inhaler naivety was to reduce potential bias against any of the inhalers used in the study.

2.2. Pilot

Before beginning the data collection, the process and the questionnaires were piloted on one individual. Based on the feedback from this individual, the process was standardized. A process chart for how the conduct data collection process was established and the information that was to be provided to the participants was written down and standardized. During the interview it emerged that the pilot had previous experience of inhalers that was not disclosed prior to the study. In order to reduce potential biases towards any of the inhalers the pilot individual was excluded. Due to difficulty finding participants no further pilot study was conducted.

2.3. Study Population and Sample

The primary reason for choosing individuals aged 25–34 was that statistics from the Finnish National Institute for Health and Welfare (THL) suggested that asthma had most frequently been diagnosed in this age group in the adult population in Finland [22]. Additionally, previous research suggests that elderly individuals may find it difficult to operate inhalers, since poor manual dexterity, weakness, and visual limitations present potential problems affecting inhaler use among the elderly [23]. As such, a deliberately young study population was chosen in order to reduce age-related inhalation errors and, as such, focus on the evaluation of video instructions as a method of providing inhaler education.

In total, 31 individuals (excluding the pilot) completed the study. Another two individuals had announced their willingness to participate, but were excluded due to prior inhaler use. The mean age of the participants was 28 years and the distribution of men and women was 17:14 (55%:45%). A clear majority of participants had an academic education (74%, 23/31), another 5 (16%) participants had attended a university for applied sciences and 3 (10%) participants had completed secondary education. All participants lived or worked in the Helsinki Metropolitan Area.

2.4. Data Collection

The data was collected over the span of 1.5 months (04/2015–05/2015). Data collection was carried out in quiet rooms at the University of Helsinki and Hanken School of Economics and all data collection sessions were carried out without interruptions. Each participant had been asked to reserve approximately hour for participation. The approximate length of participation time was 45 to 60 min. The length of the videotaped demonstrations varied from person to person (interval 13–53 s and mean: 30 s). The length of the educational videos varied between 1:30 min and 1:50 min. The rest of the time was spent filling in the questionnaires and talking to the participants.

The data gathering process included the participants watching educational videos of four inhalers and demonstrating the use of these inhalers, filling in five questionnaires as well as freely interacting with the participants and taking notes of additional comments made about the inhalers as well as the instructional videos. In an attempt to increase the reliability of the analysis, each participant was given an identification code and their questionnaire responses were linked to their inhaler scores and treated as anonymous. The material analyzed for this study included 155 questionnaires and 124 videotaped inhaler demonstrations. A flow chart of the data collection process is presented in Figure 1.

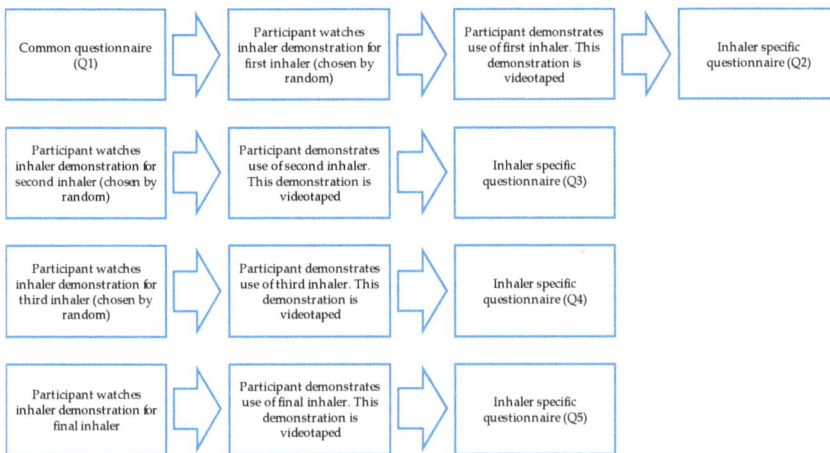

Figure 1. Flow chart depicting the different steps for data collection.

The questionnaires were developed by the authors based on key areas that were identified after a literature review on inhaler use, inhaler errors and inhaler education. The inhaler-specific questionnaires (Q2–Q5) were identical and contained both open-ended and closed questions. The main purpose of the closed questions was to collect data in which characteristics of the different inhalers and the videos could be easily compared to each other. In the closed questions, participant responses to questions assessing their perception of different aspects of the devices were elicited using a five-point Likert scale (strongly disagree, disagree, neutral, agree and strongly agree). The open questions were designed to give participants an opportunity to freely express their opinions and thoughts on the inhalers, as well as the educational material shown to them. Examples of the open-ended questions from the inhaler specific questionnaires can be observed in Table 1.

Table 1. Examples of open ended questions in questionnaires (translated from Finnish).

Example of Ended Questions in Q2–Q5
• What kind of instructions would you need on inhaler technique on order to learn how to use the inhaler?
• How did you feel about the ease of use of the inhaler?
• Did you learn how to use the inhaler based on the video instructions you received?
○ Please motivate why? Please motivate why not.

First, the participants filled in a common questionnaire (Q1) with questions regarding demographics, such as gender, educational background, and home town. In addition, the questionnaire contained questions designed to make sure the participants had no prior inhaler experience. After watching the educational video for a specific inhaler, the participants were asked to demonstrate their first attempt at using the inhaler correctly. This demonstration was videotaped. No additional verbal or demonstrative instructions were given. Participants then moved on to the other inhalers in a random order. The order was determined by lottery and drawn before the participant started watching the first demonstrational video. A random order was chosen with the purpose of minimizing the effect that ordered demonstrations would have on the results. The participants' personal opinions of the inhalers, the video material and self-evaluation of their inhaler performance were assessed using a self-completed questionnaire. Participants' additional spontaneous comments relating to the inhalers or the video material were written down and used to complement the answers in the open-ended questions. The participants' inhaler demonstrations were videotaped and analyzed by the researcher both during and after the demonstration, using an inhaler-specific checklist.

2.5. Educational Videos

The non-verbal demonstrational videos were produced by the Association of Finnish Pharmacies [24] and developed as a collaboration between the association and representatives from the pharmaceutical companies representing each device. The videos are used as training tools by pharmacies across Finland and are publicly available. The videos build on the information provided in the patient information leaflets (PILs), which have been approved by regulatory authorities. The videos can be divided into four sections that are common for all videos: introduction of the device; inhalation instructions' description on how to read the dose counter; as well as instructions on how to clean the device. The videos for Diskus and Ellipta also contain information regarding rinsing of the mouth after use. Participants were asked not to demonstrate mouth rinse.

During the instruction phase, written instructions for every step appeared on the bottom of the video screen. The steps were performed in chronological order and the entire inhalation process was demonstrated. As the written instructions appear, each correct step of the inhalation process is demonstrated by a trained individual. The trained individuals demonstrating the device are different in each video. The phase which describes how to read the dose counter follows the same format. Information regarding the dose counter is written below a still image of the device. The dose counter is highlighted using a red arrow or a red circle. The videos use standardized terminology that can be found in the PIL.

2.6. Analysis of Data

2.6.1. Frequency and Characterization of Errors

The videotaped inhaler demonstrations were checked against a predetermined checklist. This was repeated twice by the first author. As a control measure, the second author made random controls. When determining the frequency of error for each inhaler, only errors that could influence the efficacy of treatment were noted. For example, not closing the cap of the inhaler properly was not noted as a critical error. This error could potentially affect the stability of the product long term, but does not directly affect the measured inhalation. As such this error was not noted.

Errors were defined as: displays of flawed technique or lack of knowledge regarding usage of the inhaler device that conflicted with the inhaler instructions provided by the manufacturers or were causing non-optimal inhaler effect. The errors measured from previous studies were used when compiling the checklist [25]. The errors measured can be observed in Figure 2. Table A1 shows the inhaler instructions participants received for each inhaler in the educational videos, as well as the errors deemed critical for each inhaler. The error assessments for each inhaler type vary somewhat depending on the instructions given to participants. For example, "Holding one's breath after the inhalation" was assessed for Diskus, Easyhaler and Ellipta, but not for Turbuhaler, because this step was not included in the video instructions.

In the context of this study a faulty inhaler performance was defined as one where participants made at least one error. A correct inhaler performance was defined as an inhaler performance where the participant made zero critical errors. The self-evaluated correct use was measured by asking the participants whether they believed they had used the inhalers correctly.

2.6.2. Analysis of Semi-Structured Questionnaires

Participant comments and answers to open questions were analyzed using *qualitative content analysis* [26]. First, all comments and answers to questionnaire questions were gathered into one Word document and read several times without applying any specific framework. After this, sentences that were relevant for the objective of this study were separated out and condensed, still bearing in mind the context in which they were said. Thereafter, the condensed units were grouped into categories. Finally, the categories were processed in order to find underlying themes belonging to each of the categories. In the results section, all participants are given an identification number. All quotes were translated from Finnish to English by the authors.

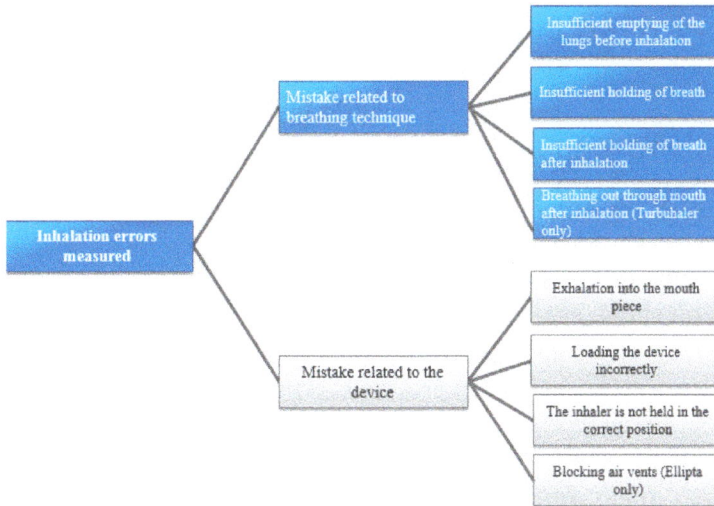

Figure 2. The errors measured throughout the study.

2.7. Ethics

Approval for the materials distributed and the methodology used was obtained by the Ethical Review Board in the Humanities, Social and Behavioral Sciences at the University of Helsinki (statement 4/2015). All participants signed consent forms and were informed how the data would be gathered and stored. Participants were informed about the study and informed of who would have access to the data and assured of their anonymity. Participants were told that they could stop the process at any time without consequences. Participants all gave written informed consent to participate in the study, and their data were anonymized.

3. Results

3.1. Frequency and Characterization of Errors

Inhaler error frequency varied between the four DPIs. Participants' self-evaluated correct use and actual correct use varied greatly (Table 2) and they tended to overestimate their own inhaler technique. Many participants believed they were exhibiting correct inhaler technique when they, in fact, exhibited at least one inhalation error. As seen in Table 2, this phenomenon could be observed for all four inhalers.

Table 2. The self-evaluated correct use and actual correct use for each inhaler type.

	Diskus	Easyhaler [1]	Ellipta	Turbuhaler
Number of participants who believed they had used inhaler without making a single inhalation error	84% 26/31	77% 24/31	84% 26/31	61% 19/31
Number of participants who actually used the inhaler without making a single inhalation error	48% 15/31	19% 6/31	55% 16/31	16% 5/31

[1] After the completion of the data collection for this study, the inhaler instructions for Easyhaler were updated by Orion. The update was independent from this study.

The participants' personal perception of which inhalers were easy to use, and which were difficult, seemed to relate to the actual results for correct use. Upon self-evaluation, participants most often perceived that they had used Diskus and Ellipta correctly. These were also the inhalers for which participants exhibited the fewest number of errors during handling. In contrast, Turbuhaler was the inhaler for which participants appeared to be the most unsure about their inhaler technique. This was also the inhaler for which participants exhibited the highest frequency of error.

When comparing the most common inhalation errors, insufficient emptying of the lungs emerged as the most frequently occurring inhalation error for all inhalers. For Turbuhaler, failure to load the device was as common as insufficient emptying of the lungs. The total number of inhaler related and breathing related errors for each device type can be found in Figure 3.

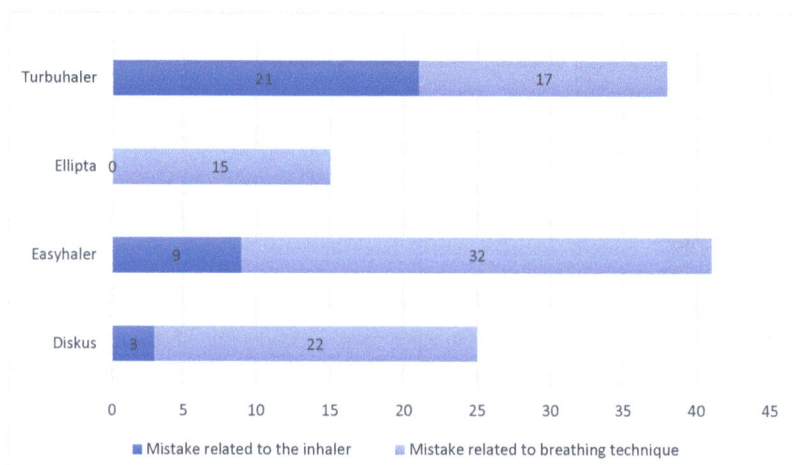

Figure 3. Inhaler-related and breathing-related inhalation errors made by participants.

3.2. Results from Semi Structured Interviews

Three major categories were identified when analyzing the semi-structured interviews. For the first category, three themes were identified, for the second category another three themes were identified and in the final category six themes were identified. The themes for each category, as well as examples, can be seen in Table 3.

Table 3. Three major categories emerged in the semi structured interviews. This table shows the categories and subcategories identified and an explanatory quote from each sub-category.

Category	Sub-Category	Explanatory Quote
Factors enhancing performance	Visual instructions	*"I like visual material, so videos worked well for me. This video was short, concise and easy to understand." PN9*
	Step-by-step instructions	*"In order to learn, I would need clear instructions of each step of the inhaler use. This video was enough." PN2*
	Type of inhaler	*"The video was good and the inhaler was fairly easy to use. I don't think you need any other instructions (than the video)." PN31*
Ideas on improving video education	Spoken track	*"I think the video was good and the tempo was fast enough. I think spoken instructions would have been a good addition to the video instructions." PN21*
	Close-up pictures	*"I think the video could have been improved by adding close-up pictures of the stages, a spoken track or background music." PN27*

Table 3. *Cont.*

Category	Sub-Category	Explanatory Quote
Factors that were perceived as difficult	Complementary material	*"A checklist on the steps to go with the inhaler would probably be good." PN18*
	Uncertainty of own technique	*"I do think that I used the inhaler correctly but I still feel a little uncertain. I think I would feel better if I could check my technique." PN10 "I do think that I used the inhaler correctly but I still feel a little uncertain. I think I would feel better if I could check my technique."*
	Unanswered questions	*"I would have liked to know why I had to shake this inhaler but not the others. PN7*
	Inhaler	*"I don't think I learned how to use this inhaler, at least not very well. The video was good, but using the inhaler was too hard." PN22*
	Unclear instructions	*"The video started out simple but became confusing as it progressed. I don't remember what should be done and in which order." PN28*
	Lack of feedback	*"I think video instructions are much better than text instructions alone. Still, I would like to receive feedback from a pharmacist or someone else who knows how to use it." PN20*
	Tempo of videos	*"The tempo of the videos was quite fast and I did not have time to read all of the instructions on the screen." PN19*

Step-by-step explanations, as well the visual aspect of the educational material, were described as positive and learning-enhancing factors. Factors contributing to a negative perception of a video included comments on the tempo of the videos as well as the medium's lack of interaction. Recurring feedback from participants for all four videos was that the tempo was too fast. The educational video for Ellipta received the most negative comments with many participants stating that the fast tempo made it difficult to follow the instructions properly. The instructions for the Easyhaler video were also criticized for being difficult to understand and having a fast tempo. Some participants (5/31) also commented that they thought a video was a better way of teaching the use of an inhaler than just providing them with written instructions. Participants mentioned unanswered questions, unclear instructions and the lack of feedback as factors they perceived to be difficult with the video instructions. Uncertainty regarding their own technique was also mentioned as a problem related to the video instructions. The addition of a spoken track, music or close-up captures were suggested as ways of enhancing the function of the video training.

When asked what kind of inhaler education would need to be provided for them to best understand inhaler instructions, participants stated that the instructions should be clear and show the inhalation process step-by-step, focusing on loading the device as well as proper breathing technique. The videos used in this study all contained the above-mentioned steps. It was also suggested that combining the video education with written instructions, or a checklist of the different steps, might have been a good reminder of how to use the inhaler. Another frequently reoccurring theme was feedback, and participants also commented that they would have liked to receive feedback on their inhaler performance. The general perception was that face-to-face instructions would be good in the beginning to assure that the inhalation is done correctly. One participant explained:

"I think it would be good if someone checked whether the inhaler is used correctly. After this, the video could work as a great supplement. Overall, I think the video was clear and the tempo was slow enough." Participant nr 1 (PN1).

Similar statements occurred among other participants as well. Some participants explicitly stated that they thought videos were a good or adequate way of providing inhaler instructions (6/31). Others disagreed and highlighted that watching an instructional video once was not enough when teaching correct inhaler technique (5/31). This is an interesting observation, since most participants still answered that they believed they had used the inhalers correctly. The lack of feedback and opportunity to ask questions also led individuals to misunderstand the function of the inhalers. These misunderstandings emerged from the comments made during and after the inhalation process. In addition, participants frequently asked questions after the inhalation process or highlighted questions that they wished the videos would have answered. The type of questions and misunderstandings varied greatly among participants. For example, one participant (PN7) stated that he would have liked more information on the dosage and how it could be adjusted on the inhaler. In fact, none of the inhalers provided the option to adjust the dosage for one single inhalation. Another participant highlighted the issue of storing the product, wondering if it mattered where the product was stored (PN18), and others discussed shaking one of the inhalers and wondered why this was necessary (PN7 and PN6).

In each of the videos shown to participants, written instructions for every step appeared on the bottom of the video screen during the inhalation process. In addition to comments regarding the fast tempo of some of the videos, participants also commented that the text flashed by very fast and that it was hard to simultaneously concentrate on reading the text in the video, look at the visual instructions and let the instructions sink in. It was suggested that verbal instructions in the video may be more favorable compared to written, as this would allow the participant to concentrate on the person showing the correct technique instead of concentrating on reading the instructions.

4. Discussion and Conclusions

4.1. Discussion

The high frequency of error for the four inhalers observed in the results seem to indicate that the non-verbal videos used for this study were an inadequate way of providing inhaler education for first time users of inhalers. The perceived and actual level of difficulty varied between the inhalers, and some inhalers proved to be either harder to use or harder to teach through non-verbal video instructions. (Table 2). As such, one could argue that non-verbal, PIL based educational videos as a method of providing inhaler education may be more efficient for some DPIs than for others. Alternatively, the difference could be explained minor by differences in the instructions provided or differences between the videos. The differences between the videos were consciously minimized by choosing videos with the same format and structure. Based on comments from participants, the pace appeared to be slightly different.

Video education could potentially be considered a cost-effective way of providing inhaler education, at least for some DPIs. The use of video education is supported by previous research suggesting that patient knowledge and understanding can be improved by combining visual images and words using video technology [27]. A long-term comparison of small group demonstrations and video-demonstrations and found small group demonstrations of an interactive nature to be the slightly more effective alternative for providing inhaler individual education through video [13]. Van der Palen et al. [13] also found that the improvements achieved both through video education and through group education showed a significant increase from the baseline. In a study comparing written, video and personal instructions for metered-dose inhalers, no significant distinction in inhaler techniques found between patients instructed in person or by videotape [18]. Interventions using a combination of educational videos, checklists, leaflets and verbal instructions found that this type of education significantly improved inhaler technique in patients with COPD, additionally it was found to decrease attack frequency and dyspnea, and improved quality of life [28]. There is clearly potential for the development of easily accessible educational methods of providing video instructions, but more work needs to be done to understand how the needs of patients can be met using video instructions.

Inhaler technique has been found to deteriorate over time (potentially after as little as 2–3 months) [29]. As such, inhaler handling training must occur regularly in order to achieve and maintain the correct technique [30,31]. Based on the rather high frequency of participant error in this study, it could be proposed that providing inhaler education via video would be more suitable as a means of promoting recall in current inhaler patients than when teaching individuals how to use an inhaler for the first time. This is supported by Wilson et al. [19] who suggests that the use of video and print interventions can promote recall on inhaler use in asthma patients. A study examining personal demonstrations by pharmacists as a learning tool concluded that at least three repetitions of device instructions were needed in order to achieve errorless technique, or less than 10% errors in total [32]. As such, it would be interesting to investigate how repeated video trainings may have affected the participants' inhaler technique. Educational videos distributed online allow for the patients to access the videos at any time in order practice their inhaler technique. There may however be a significant threshold for patients to go looking for these videos on their own initiative, as real-world patients have been known to overlook other easily available educational sources such as leaflets [11].

An interesting observation in this study was that participants tended to overestimate their own inhaler technique. This was apparent for all four inhalers. This is supported by previous research in patient populations suggesting that patients are often not aware of the fact that they use their inhalers inadequately, and they often overestimate their own abilities [33]. The observation is problematic given the concept of video instructions, since the participants are not able to receive feedback on their inhaler technique and may therefore continue making mistakes. The results suggested that the participants would have needed feedback on their own performance, and personal demonstrations with an HCP was often suggested. Correct face-to-face training with feedback supports the patients' treatment by making them aware of their inhalation errors, thereby providing clear guidelines on required technique. The high costs of these types of sessions, however, limit their use in real-life situations and new alternatives are still needed to assure easy and cost-efficient access to inhaler education. Despite the participants' apparent preference for face-to-face demonstrations, many questions regarding this still remain open, as forms of video education have been found to be equal or superior to personal inhaler demonstrations [13,18]. Another argument presenting the potentially problematic side of real world one on one training is that HCPs such as doctors, nurses, respiratory therapists and pharmacists have been shown to exhibited difficulties when asked to demonstrate the correct technique for inhalers [6,15]. As such, it is important to emphasize, that in order for one on one training to be efficient the HPC must have sufficient understanding and training of the use of these devices.

4.1.1. Potential Areas for Development in Educational Videos for Asthma

When developing video instructions and educational material instructing on the use of inhalers, focusing on developing means for providing feedback and interaction would be essential. Results indicated that participants were often left with unanswered questions regarding the inhalers after watching the video instructions. Clear misconceptions about information provided in the videos also emerged. These varied greatly between individuals, which was interesting given that all participants had received identical instructions. Still, they seemed to interpret and focus on different parts of the information. In order for some inhaler-naïve individuals to achieve correct technique, it would be important to provide mechanisms for feedback and correcting misconceptions and flawed inhaler technique.

One option would be developing interactive videos or mobile applications, since educational research appears to suggest that interactive educational videos achieved significantly better learning performance than non-interactive videos [34]. The importance of providing feedback could also be incorporated into the inhaler devices themselves in the future. Furthermore, interactive chats with HCPs could be considered a way of allowing individuals to ask questions and clear up misunderstandings that arise while learning inhaler technique through video. The combination of video and written instructions was also suggested by some of the participants in this study. Orion Pharma has recently included a QR code in the updated patient leaflets for Easyhaler, from which patients can scan and access video instructions directly on their phones. This represents an interesting and innovative way of combining written and visual instructions, as well as making these instructions easily available for the patients [35].

4.1.2. Limitations to This Study

The first limitation of this study was the fact that respiratory flow rate was not measured amongst participants. Slow inhalation has been described as an inhaler mishandling in several studies [36,37]. Since the participants of this study were non-asthmatic, the assumption is that they have inspiratory flow rates typical for a healthy individual. As such their results would not be comparable to those of asthma patients if these measurements had been made.

Secondly, it is important to note that the participants in this study were non-asthmatic and inhaler naïve. Although this was an attempt to eliminate a bias towards any specific inhaler, it is important to note that as these individuals did not need the inhalers and as such, may have been less motivation to learn their use them. This may ultimately have impacted their inhaler technique.

Additionally, the videos used for this study were videos already in use as educational tools for pharmacists and patients alike. While this allowed for a situation closely simulating the current real world scenario of already available videos it was also accompanied by problems. The videos used in this study were all non-verbal, non-interactive of nature. As such the results cannot be extrapolated to all education videos in asthma.

4.2. Conclusions

Since a majority of the participant inhaler demonstrations exhibited incorrect inhaler technique, it could be argued that these non-verbal non-interactive video instructions alone are not enough when teaching technique to inhaler-naïve individuals. The most prominent problem with video instructions is the lack of feedback to the user regarding their inhaler performance. This may present a genuine problem, since the results of this study indicated that people tend to overestimate their own technique.

Breathing technique, especially failure to empty the lungs before the inhalation, was the most common inhalation error among participants. Since the most commonly exhibited error was the same for all four inhalers, it may be fair to conclude that some steps in the inhalation process may be harder for individuals to remember and therefore require extra emphasis in order to achieve correct inhaler technique, especially when teaching individuals how to use an inhaler for the first time. The results may also be indicating that there is considerable room for improvement in video instructions for the purpose of teaching individuals how to use a DPI. Another problem with video education arises from the fact that the users are unable to ask questions and clear up misunderstandings, as expressed by the participants of this study. E-learning and video education could play a part in providing successful inhaler instructions in the future, but if so, more interactive approaches providing patients with the ability to ask questions and receive feedback should be developed.

4.3. Practical Implications

The video instructions in this study were basic, non-interactive, instructional videos that described each step that should be performed during inhalation. Research on instructional videos in e-learning has established that students provided with interactive educational videos achieved significantly better learning performance and a higher level of learner satisfaction than those who were provided with a non-interactive video, or no video at all [34]. These findings indicated that it may be important to integrate interactive instructional video into e-learning systems. If video instructions were to be more widely used as a method of providing instructions on inhaler technique for inhaler-naïve individuals, it would be interesting to consider the possibility of developing interactive videos. Future research should contemplate whether these types of videos would be suitable for providing inhaler education to patients, and how different types of interactive videos could assist in the goal of achieving and maintaining correct inhaler technique. This study was performed on a young population, an interesting subject for future research would be to investigate this phenomenon on an older population. Investigation on how repeated video training affects inhaler technique would also be of interest. Furthermore, instead of looking at video as a tool for providing inhaler education to inhaler-naïve individuals, future research could investigate video education as an educational tool for maintaining correct inhaler technique in asthma patients on a long-term basis.

Author Contributions: S.v.S., N.K. and A.M.J. designed the study together. S.v.S. gathered and analyzed the data, N.K. and A.M.J. were involved in parts of the data analysis. S.v.S. drafted the article with the assistance of N.K. and A.M.J., S.v.S., N.K. and A.M.J. revised as well as approved the submitted version of the manuscript.

Funding: This research was in part funded by Victoria Foundation [12/2016].

Acknowledgments: The authors wish to thank AstraZeneca, GSK and Orion Pharma for providing the empty inhalers used in this study.

Conflicts of Interest: The authors declare no conflict of interest.

Appendix A

Table A1. The inhaler instructions patients received for each inhaler in the educational videos, and the errors deemed critical for each inhaler.

Inhaler	Instructions	Errors measured
Diskus	1. Open your Diskus: Hold it in the palm of your hand, put the thumb of your other hand on the thumb grip and push the thumb grip until it "clicks" into place. 2. Load the Diskus by holding the device with the mouthpiece toward you. Slide the lever away from you as far as it will go to get your medication ready. 3. Adjust your posture. Keep your shoulders down and head held high. 4. Breathe out away from the device for as long as you feel comfortable. 5. Place the mouthpiece gently in your mouth and close your lips around it. 6. Breathe in deeply and evenly though the Diskus. 7. Remove the device from your mouth. 8. Hold your breath for 5-10 seconds. 9. Calmly breath out through your nose. 10. Close the Diskus by sliding the thumb grip toward you until you hear a "click."	1. Failure to open device 2. Failure to hold device in right position 3. Failure to empty lungs before inhalation 4. Failure to load device 5. Failure to hold breath at least 5-10 seconds after inhalation 6. Exhalation into the mouthpiece
Easy-haler	1. Open the protective cover. 2. Insert the inhaler in a protective case. Make sure that the cover is on the mouthpiece. 3. Remove the mouthpiece cover. 4. Shake the inhaler vigorously up and down 3-5 times. Do not trigger the inhaler when shaking it! 5. Hold the inhaler upright. 6. Trigger the inhaler once until you hear a "click" and let the inhaler return to its original position. 7. Keep holding the inhaler in an upright position. 8. Breathe out normally. 9. Place the mouthpiece in your mouth between your teeth and close your lips tightly around the mouthpiece. 10. Breathe in through your mouth forcefully and deeply. Take the mouthpiece out of your mouth. 11. Hold your breath for at least 5 seconds and then breathe out through your nose. 12. Close the protective cover.	1. Failure to open device 2. Failure to hold device in right position 3. Failure to empty lungs before inhalation 4. Failure to load device - Failure to shake device - Failure to press button - Loading in wrong order - Triggering inhaler when shaking it 5. Failure to hold breath at least 5 seconds after inhalation 6. Exhalation into the mouthpiece

Table A1. *Cont.*

Inhaler		Instructions		Errors measured
Ellipta	1.	Wait to open the cover until you are ready to take your dose. Do not shake the inhaler.		
	2.	Slide the cover down to expose the mouthpiece. You should hear a "click."		
	3.	Breathe out away from the device for as long as you feel comfortable. Hold the inhaler away from your mouth - do not breathe out into the mouthpiece.	1.	Failure to open/load device
			2.	Failure to hold device in right position
			3.	Failure to empty lungs before inhalation
	4.	Put the mouthpiece between your lips, and close your lips firmly around it. Do not block the air vent with your fingers.	4.	Failure to hold breath at least 3-4 seconds after inhalation
	5.	Take one long, steady, deep breath in through your mouth.	5.	Holding fingers on air vents
	6.	Hold your breath for at least 3-4 seconds.	7.	Exhalation into the mouthpiece
	7.	Remove the inhaler from your mouth. Breathe out slowly and gently.		
	13.	Slide the cover upward as far as it will go, to cover the mouthpiece.		
Turbu-haler	1.	Unscrew the cap and take it off. Hold the inhaler upright.		
	2.	Twist the grip of your Turbuhaler as far as it will go. Then twist it all the way back. When twisting you will hear a "click."	1.	Failure to open device
			2.	Failure to hold device in right position
	3.	Breathe out deeply away from the device.	3.	Failure to empty lungs before inhalation
	4.	Put the mouthpiece between your teeth, and close your lips around it.	4.	Failure to load device
	5.	Breathe in forcefully and deeply through your mouth.	5.	Failure to breathe out through the nose after inhalation
	6.	Remove the Turbuhaler from your mouth and calmly breathe out through the nose.	6.	Exhalation into the mouthpiece
	7.	Replace the cap.		

Source: [13,25,36,38–40].

References

1. Global Asthma Network. The Global Asthma Report 2014. Available online: http://www.globalasthmarepo rt.org/ (accessed on 3 June 2017).

2. Barnes, P.J. Cellular and molecular mechanisms of asthma and COPD. *Clin. Sci.* **2017**, *131*, 1541–1558. [CrossRef] [PubMed]

3. Svedsater, H.; Dale, P.; Garrill, K.; Walker, R.; Woepse, M.W. Qualitative assessment of attributes and ease of use of the ELLIPTA™ dry powder inhaler for delivery of maintenance therapy for asthma and COPD. *BMC Pulm. Med.* **2013**, *13*, 1–14. [CrossRef] [PubMed]

4. Islam, N.; Gladki, E. Dry powder inhalers (DPIs)—A review of device reliability and innovation. *Int. J. Pharm.* **2008**, *360*, 1–11. [CrossRef] [PubMed]

5. Crompton, G.K. How to achieve good compliance with inhaled asthma therapy. *Respir. Med.* **2004**, *98*, 35–40. [CrossRef]

6. Fink, J.B.; Rubin, B.K. Problems with inhaler use: A call for improved clinician and patient education. *Respir. Care* **2005**, *50*, 1360–1375. [PubMed]

7. Lenney, J.; Innes, J.A.; Crompton, G.K. Inappropriate inhaler use: Assessment of use and patient preference of seven inhalation devices. EDICI. *Respir. Med.* **2000**, *94*, 496–500. [CrossRef] [PubMed]

8. King, D.; Earnshaw, S.M.; Delaney, J.C. Pressurized aerosol inhalers: The cost of misuse. *Br. J. Clin. Pract.* **1991**, *45*, 48–49. [PubMed]

9. Lavorini, F. The Challenge of Delivering Therapeutic Aerosols to Asthma Patients. *ISRN Allergy* **2013**, *2013*, 1–17. [CrossRef] [PubMed]

10. Sanchis, J.; Corrigan, C.; Levy, M.L.; Viejo, J.L. Inhaler devices-from theory to practice. *Respir. Med.* **2013**, *107*, 495–502. [CrossRef] [PubMed]

11. Roberts, R.J.; Robinson, J.D.; Doering, P.L.; Dallman, J.J.; Steeves, R.A. A comparison of various types of patient instruction in the proper administration of metered inhalers. *Drug Intell. Clin. Pharm.* **1982**, *16*, 53–55. [CrossRef] [PubMed]

12. Basheti, I.A.; Reddel, H.K.; Armour, C.L.; Bosnic-Anticevich, S.Z. Counseling about turbuhaler technique: Needs assessment and effective strategies for community pharmacist Counseling about turbuhaler technique:

Needs assessment and effective strategies for community pharmacists. *Respir. Care* **2005**, *50*, 617–623. [PubMed]

13. van der Palen, J.; Klein, J.J.; Kerkhoff, A.H.; van Herwaarden, C.L.; Seydel, E.R. Evaluation of the long-term effectiveness of three instruction modes for inhaling medicines. *Patient Educ. Couns.* **1997**, *32*, 87–95. [CrossRef]

14. De Blaquiere, P.; Christensen, D.B.; Carter, W.B.; Martin, T.R. Use and misuse of metered-dose inhalers by patients with chronic lung disease. a controlled, randomized trial of two instruction methods. *Am. Rev. Respir. Dis.* **1989**, *140*, 910–916. [CrossRef] [PubMed]

15. Kesten, S.; Zive, K.; Chapman, K.R. Pharmacist knowledge and ability to use inhaled medication delivery systems. *Chest* **1993**, *104*, 1737–1742. [CrossRef] [PubMed]

16. Lewis, R.M.; Fink, J.B. Promoting adherence to inhaled therapy. Respir. *Care Clin. N. Am.* **2001**, *7*, 277–301. [CrossRef]

17. Hämmerlein, A.; Müller, U.; Schulz, M. Pharmacist-led intervention study to improve inhalation technique in asthma and COPD patients. *J. Eval. Clin. Pract.* **2011**, *17*, 61–70. [CrossRef] [PubMed]

18. Self, T.H.; Brooks, J.B.; Lieberman, P.; Ryan, M.R. The value of demonstration and role of pharmacist in teaching the correct use of pressurized bronchodilators. *Can. Med. Assoc. J.* **1983**, *128*, 129–131. [PubMed]

19. Wilson, E.A.H.; Park, D.C.; Curtis, L.M.; Cameron, K.A.; Clayman, M.L.; Makoul, G.; Eigen, K.V.; Wolf, M.S. Media and memory: The efficacy of video and print materials for promoting patient education about asthma. *Patient Educ. Couns.* **2010**, *80*, 393–398. [CrossRef] [PubMed]

20. Albert, N.M.; Buchsbaum, T.; Li, J. Randomized study of the effect of video education on heart failure healthcare utilization, symptoms, and self-care behaviors. *Patient Educ. Couns.* **2007**, *69*, 129–139. [CrossRef] [PubMed]

21. Tashakori, M.; Teddlie, C.B. (Eds.) *Sage Handbook of Mixed Methods in Social & Behavioral Research*, 2nd ed.; SAGE: Washington, DC, USA, 2010.

22. Borodulin, K.; Levälahti, E.; Saarikoski, L.; Lund, L.; Juolevi, A.; Grönholm, M.; Jula, A.; Laatikainen, T.; Männistö, S.; Peltonen, M.; et al. *National FINRISKI 2012-Health Study-Part 2: Study Table Annex, National Institute for Health and Welfare*; THL: Helsinki, Finland, 2013; pp. 136–137.

23. Jarvis, S.; Ind, P.W.; Shiner, R.J. Inhaled therapy in elderly COPD patients; time for re-evaluation? *Age Ageing* **2007**, *36*, 213–218. [CrossRef] [PubMed]

24. Finnish Association of Pharmacists Dosing Videos. Available online: https://www.apteekki.fi/apteekin-n euvot/annosteluvideot.html (accessed on 1 March 2017).

25. Melani, A.S.; Bonavia, M.; Cilenti, V.; Cinti, C.; Lodi, M.; Martucci, P.; Serra, M.; Scichilone, N.; Sestini, P.; Aliani, M.; et al. Inhaler mishandling remains common in real life and is associated with reduced disease control. *Resp. Med.* **2011**, *105*, 930–938. [CrossRef] [PubMed]

26. Graneheim, U.H.; Lundman, B. Qualitative content analysis in nursing research: Concepts, procedures and measures to achieve trustworthiness. *Nurse Educ. Today* **2004**, *24*, 105–112. [CrossRef] [PubMed]

27. Ferguson, A.L. Implementing a Video Education Program to Improve Health Literacy. *J. Nurse Pract.* **2012**, *8*, 17–22. [CrossRef]

28. Göriş, S.; Taşci, S.; Elmali, F. The effects of training on inhaler technique and quality of life in patients with COPD. *J. Aerosol Med. Pulm. Drug Deliv.* **2013**, *26*, 336–344. [CrossRef] [PubMed]

29. Ovchinikova, L.; Smith, L.; Bosnic-Anticevich, S. Inhaler technique maintenance: Gaining an understanding from the patient's perspective. *J. Asthma* **2011**, *48*, 616–624. [CrossRef] [PubMed]

30. Takemura, M.; Kobayashi, M.; Kimura, K.; Mitsui, K.; Masui, H.; Koyama, M.; Itotani, R.; Ishitoko, M.; Suzuki, S.; Aihara, K. Repeated instruction on inhalation technique improves adherence to the therapeutic regimen in asthma. *J. Asthma* **2010**, *47*, 202–208. [CrossRef] [PubMed]

31. O'Bey, K.A.; Jim, L.K.; Gee, J.P.; Cowen, M.E.; Quigley, A.E. An education program that improves the psychomotor skills needed for metaproterenol inhaler use. *Drug Intell. Clin. Pharm.* **1982**, *16*, 945–948. [CrossRef] [PubMed]

32. Takaku, Y.; Kurashima, K.; Ohta, C.; Ishiguro, T.; Kagiyama, N.; Yanagisawa, T.; Takayanagi, N. How many instructions are required to correct inhalation errors in patients with asthma and chronic obstructive pulmonary disease? *Resp. Med.* **2017**, *123*, 110–115. [CrossRef] [PubMed]

33. Erickson, S.R.; Horton, A.; Kirking, D.M. Assessing metered-dose inhaler technique: Comparison of observation vs. patient self-report. *J. Asthma* **1998**, *35*, 575–583. [CrossRef] [PubMed]

34. Zhang, D.; Zhou, L.; Briggs, R.O.; Nunamaker, J.F. Instructional video in e-learning: Assessing the impact of interactive video on learning effectiveness. *Inf. Manag.* **2006**, *43*, 15–27. [CrossRef]

35. Orion Corporation. *Easyhaler Budesonide Patient Information Leaflet*; Orion Corporation: Espoo, Finland, 2016.

36. Melani, A.S.; Zanchetta, D.; Barbato, N.; Sestini, P.; Cinti, C.; Canessa, P.A.; Aiolfi, S.; Neri, M.; for the Associazione Italiana Pneumologi Ospedalieri Educational Group. Inhalation technique and variables associated with misuse of conventional metered-dose inhalers and newer dry powder inhalers in experienced adults. *Ann. Allergy Asthma Immunol.* **2004**, *93*, 439–446. [CrossRef]

37. Melani, A.S.; Bracci, L.S.; Rossi, M. Reduced peak inspiratory effort through the Diskus® and the Turbuhaler® due to mishandling is common in clinical practice. *Clin. Drug Investig.* **2006**, *25*, 543–549. [CrossRef]

38. Price, D.; Bosnic-Anticevich, S.; Briggs, A.; Chrystyn, H.; Rand, C.; Scheuch, G.; Bousquet, J. Inhaler competence in asthma: Common errors, barriers to use and recommended solutions. *Respir. Med.* **2012**, *107*, 37–46. [CrossRef] [PubMed]

39. van der Palen, J.; Klein, J.J.; Kerkhoff, A.H.M.; Van Herwaarden, C.L. Evaluation of the effectiveness of four different inhalers in patients with chronic obstructive pulmonary disease. *Thorax* **1995**, *50*, 1183–1187. [CrossRef] [PubMed]

40. Khassawneh, B.; Al-Ali, M.; Alzoubi, K.H.; Batarseh, M.Z.; Al-Safi, S.A.; Sharara, A.M.; Alnasr, H.M. Handling of Inhaler Devices in Actual Pulmonary Practice: Metered-Dose Inhaler Versus Dry Powder Inhalers. *Respir. Care* **2008**, *53*, 324–328. [PubMed]

pharmacy

MDPI

Article

The Introduction of a Full Medication Review Process in a Local Hospital: Successes and Barriers of a Pilot Project in the Geriatric Ward

Lies De Bock [1], Eline Tommelein [2,*], Hans Baekelandt [1], Wim Maes [3], Koen Boussery [2] and Annemie Somers [2,4]

[1] AZ Oudenaarde, Pharmacy, Minderbroedersstraat 3, 9700 Oudenaarde, Belgium; lies.debock@azglorieux.be (L.D.B.); hans.baekelandt@azoudenaarde.be (H.B.)
[2] Pharmaceutical Care Unit, Faculty of Pharmaceutical Sciences, Ghent University, Ottergemsesteenweg 460, 9000 Gent, Belgium; koen.boussery@UGent.be (K.B.); annemie.somer@uzgent.be (A.S.)
[3] AZ Oudenaarde, Geriatrics Department, Minderbroedersstraat 3, 9700 Oudenaarde, Belgium; wim.maes@azoudenaarde.be
[4] Department of Clinical Pharmacy, Ghent University Hospital, Corneel Heymanslaan 10, 9000 Gent, Belgium
* Correspondence: eline.tommelein@ugent.be; Tel.: +32-9-264-80-73

Received: 29 December 2017; Accepted: 27 February 2018; Published: 28 February 2018

Abstract: For the majority of Belgian hospitals, a pharmacist-led full medication review process is not standard care and, therefore, challenging to introduce. With this study, we aimed to evaluate the successes and barriers of the implementation of a pharmacist-led full medication review process in the geriatric ward at a local Belgian hospital. To this end, we carried out an interventional study, performing a full medication review on older patients ($\geq$70 years) with polypharmacy ($\geq$5 drugs) who had an unplanned admission to the geriatric ward. The process consisted of 3 steps: (1) medication reconciliation upon admission; (2) medication review using an explicit reviewing tool (STOPP/START criteria or GheOP^{3}S tool), followed by a discussion between the pharmacist and the geriatrician; and (3) medication reconciliation upon discharge. Ethical approval was obtained from the Ethical Commission of the Ghent University Hospital. Outcomes included objective data on the interventions (e.g., number of drug discrepancies; number of potentially inappropriate prescriptions (PIP)); as well as subjective experiences (e.g., satisfaction with service; opinion on inter-professional communication). There was a special focus on communication aspects within the introduction of this process. In total, 52 patients were included in the study, taking a median of 10 drugs (IQR 8–12). Upon admission, 122 drug discrepancies were detected. During medication review, 254 PIPs were detected and discussed, leading to an improvement in the appropriateness of medication use. The satisfaction of community pharmacists concerning additional communication and the satisfaction of the patients after counselling at discharge were positive. However, several barriers were encountered, such as the time-consuming process to gather necessary information from different sources, the non-continuity of the service due to the lack of trained personnel or the lack of safe, electronic platforms to share information. The communicative and non-communicative successes and hurdles encountered during this project need to be addressed in order to improve the full medication review process and to strengthen the role of the clinical pharmacist.

Keywords: medication review; medication reconciliation; inter-professional communication; clinical pharmacy; elderly

1. Introduction

Transitions of care are defined as the movement of a patient from one healthcare provider or setting to another [1]. Subsequent coordination and continuity of care require timely and accurate communication between the different care providers [1,2]. There are many barriers to effective communication, such as the lack of experience, the complexity of healthcare, the distracting nature of healthcare settings, and the lack of standardization [3].

A lack of communication between caregivers during these transfers of care has been shown to be linked to poor patient outcome [3] as well as to medication errors [4]. The process of medication reconciliation guarantees that the medicines the patient should be prescribed match those that are prescribed. By performing reconciliation at each transfer of care, a comprehensive medication list is continuously available and adapted to the current clinical situation [4–9]. The comprehensive medication list is not only important to reduce the risk of medication errors but also serves as the starting point for medication review [5].

By performing a medication review, potentially inappropriate medication (PIM) use can be detected. PIMs consist of over-, under-, and misprescribing of drugs [10–12]. Inappropriateness can occur on several levels: wrong dose, frequency, modality of administration or duration of therapy, potential drug–drug or drug–disease interaction, no clear evidence-based clinical indication, or the omission of a clinically indicated treatment or prevention [13]. A screening of the medication by the clinical pharmacist using a screening tool can be a valuable aid to routine pharmacotherapy and pharmaceutical care and can be part of a shared decision-making process between physicians and pharmacists [14]. Several explicit (criteria-based) and implicit (judgement-based) methods to screen for inappropriate prescribing in older patients have been published including the Medication Appropriateness Index (MAI) [15,16], the Screening Tool for Older Persons potentially inappropriate Prescriptions/Screening Tool to Alert for Right Treatment (STOPP/START) [14,17], and the Ghent Older People's Prescriptions community Pharmacy Screening (GheOP^{3}S) tool [18].

The complete process of medication reconciliation and review is a good example of a clinical pharmacy service, as it can be performed at an unplanned hospital admission. Clinical pharmacy services, in general, aim to provide patient care that optimizes medication therapy and promotes health, well-being, and disease prevention [19]. However, the introduction of clinical pharmacy services both in primary, secondary, or tertiary care has known some difficulties [20].

To support all Belgian hospitals to introduce or expand clinical pharmacy services, the government implemented supplementary financing (0.25 full-time equivalents (FTE) per 200 beds with a maximum of 2 FTE) [21]. Moreover, the government wrote an implementation plan focusing on four domains with specific subjects or goals for each year (see Supplementary Table S1) [22]. Besides this (financial) encouragement, the implementation of clinical pharmacy is necessary for the hospital to obtain a quality accreditation label. This accreditation is not mandatory but it is an unbiased proof of the process quality in the hospital [23]. Several standards are relevant for clinical pharmacy services in order to improve patient and medication safety.

The new resources provided by the government has enabled the hospital described in this study to supplement the team with a clinical pharmacist (0.5 FTE). This study was conducted to explore the possibilities, the difficulties, and the stakeholders' views on implementing a full medication review process in the hospital setting. We also aim to provide an overview of the communicative contacts during the process.

2. Methods

2.1. Study Design and Participants

This manuscript reports on the (communicative) successes and barriers that were perceived during a prospective interventional study that was carried out from March to September 2016. Patients were eligible if they (1) had an unplanned admission to the geriatric ward; (2) were at least 70 years old; (3) took at least five drugs chronically at the time of admission; (4) were not hospitalized in the preceding 3 months; and (5) did not have any form of cognitive impairment (mini-mental state examination (MMSE) <21/30 or documented confusion as determined by the clinical judgement of the physician or nurse). The study received ethical approval from the Ethical Commission of Ghent University Hospital. All patients provided an informed consent.

2.2. Study Setting

The study was carried out in the General Hospital in Oudenaarde (Belgium), a local hospital with 235 beds and 3 hospital pharmacists. Prior to the study, a number of changes were introduced to enable the minimal conditions to perform clinical pharmacy. A vision on clinical pharmacy was outlined in cooperation with the Pharmacy and Therapeutics Committee. This included access to the full electronic patient file, granted to the pharmacists after approval by the medical board. In 2016, the main focus was shifted to medication reconciliation at the time of admission and discharge. Before the intervention described below, a hospital-wide basic protocol to improve medication reconciliation was developed and implemented in cooperation with the hospital pharmacy.

2.3. Intervention

The intervention consisted of an extended medication reconciliation at the time of admission and a medication review by the clinical pharmacist. Both were completed within 72 h of admission. Additionally, a medication reconciliation was performed at the time of discharge. A summary of the methods of communication is shown in Table 1.

Table 1. Summary of the actions and corresponding methods of communication within each step of the intervention.

Source of Information	Action	Means of Communication
Medication reconciliation upon admission		
Patient file	Obtain initial list of medication	Electronic consultation
Patient	Structured interview	Face-to-face
Community pharmacist	Request dispensing history	Phone
GP (if needed)	Request medication history, clarification	Phone
Treating physician	Report and discuss discrepancies	Phone, internal e-mail
Medication review		
Patient file	Obtain data needed for screening	Electronic consultation
Treating physician	Discuss results of the medication review	Internal e-mail within 72 h upon admission and weekly face-to-face discussion
Medication reconciliation upon discharge		
Patient file	Review of the discharge medication list	Electronic consultation
Treating physician	Discuss discrepancies	Face-to-face, phone, internal e-mail
Patient	Discuss discharge medication list	Face-to-face
GP	Provide pharmaceutical discharge letter	Mail
Community pharmacist	Provide pharmaceutical discharge letter	Mail
Follow-up		
GP	Discuss pharmaceutical discharge letter	Phone
Community pharmacist	Discuss pharmaceutical discharge letter	Phone

2.3.1. Medication Reconciliation upon Admission

For patients included in the study, the clinical pharmacist obtained the best possible medication history, starting with the initial medication list that was used by the ward upon admission. This initial list was composed by the treating physician with the support of a nurse, following the standard hospital procedure, making use of one or more extra sources including (1) the electronic prescription file if the patient was previously admitted; (2) the shared medical record from the collaborative care platform; (3) the referral letter of the GP, if applicable, and (4) the patient interview at admission. Subsequently, the full electronic patient file was consulted by the clinical pharmacist and discrepancies were noted. A structured interview with the patient or caregiver was performed in order to clarify the current drug use. For each drug included in the medication list, the current use, dosage, and time of administration were checked. Additionally, the limited questions list—which was proven they could reveal omissions [24]—and questions on previous adverse drug events or allergies were discussed. Subsequently, a telephone interview was performed with the community pharmacist in order to obtain the full dispensing record for the preceding 6 months. In Belgium, for chronic patients it is advised that besides all prescribed medications, all dispensed over-the-counter (OTC) medications are registered. As well, dispensing records are shared among all community pharmacies. No OTC medication is dispensed outside of community pharmacies. In some cases, it was necessary to contact the general practitioner (GP) to obtain information from his personal medical record (Figure 1).

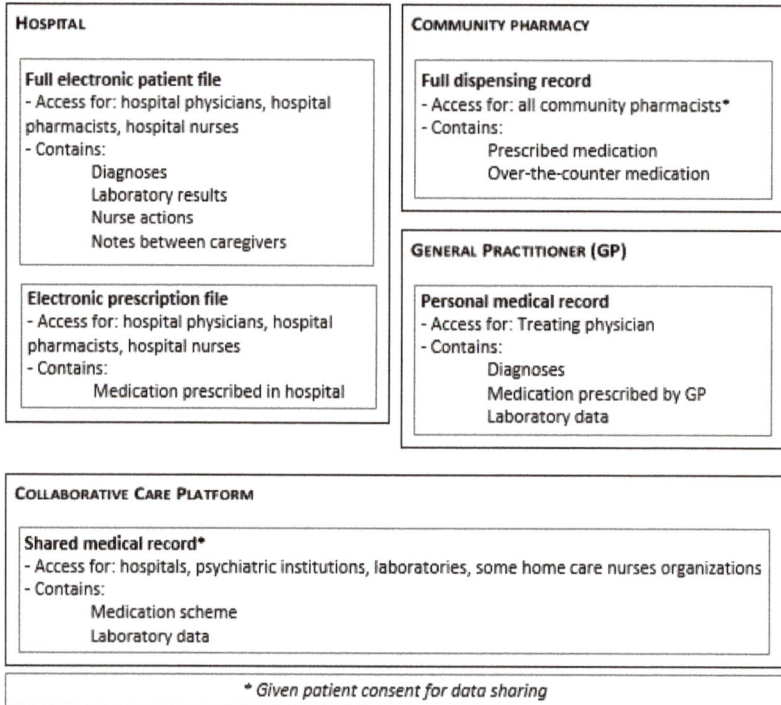

HOSPITAL	COMMUNITY PHARMACY

Full electronic patient file
- Access for: hospital physicians, hospital pharmacists, hospital nurses
- Contains:
    Diagnoses
    Laboratory results
    Nurse actions
    Notes between caregivers
	Full dispensing record
	- Access for: all community pharmacists*
	- Contains:
	    Prescribed medication
	    Over-the-counter medication

	GENERAL PRACTITIONER (GP)

Electronic prescription file
- Access for: hospital physicians, hospital pharmacists, hospital nurses
- Contains:
    Medication prescribed in hospital
	Personal medical record
	- Access for: Treating physician
	- Contains:
	    Diagnoses
	    Medication prescribed by GP
	    Laboratory data

COLLABORATIVE CARE PLATFORM

Shared medical record*
- Access for: hospitals, psychiatric institutions, laboratories, some home care nurses organizations
- Contains:
    Medication scheme
    Laboratory data

* Given patient consent for data sharing

Figure 1. The different patient records consulted during the reconciliation process.

The treating physician was informed of every discrepancy between the initial medication list and the best possible medication list. Based on the current status of the patient, the treating physician adjusted the electronic prescription in order to provide optimal therapy. The detected discrepancies were classified as follows: (a) omission on initial list; (b) patient does not take this drug; (c) wrong dose; (d) wrong modality of administration (route/time of administration); (e) wrong formulation; (f) relevant information on duration of therapy; and (g) allergy previously not registered in file.

Additionally, the contacted community pharmacists were questioned about (1) the presence of a medication list; and (2) their opinion on this inter-professional communication between pharmacists in primary and secondary care.

2.3.2. The Medication Review Process

For the medication review process, patients were allocated to three different groups based on ward and treating physician. The first group consisted of patients treated by a geriatrician on one ward and these patients' medication lists were screened with the STOPP/START criteria [14,17]. The patients in the second group were treated by the same geriatrician but on the other ward and were screened with the GheOP^{3}S tool [18]. Patients who were treated by another internal medicines physician were allocated to the third group, the control group, in which no screening was performed. The medication screening was performed by the clinical pharmacist (LDB) and was based on a pharmaceutical patient file specifically drawn up for the study. This file included (a) the best possible medication history; (b) the current and previous prescriptions in the electronic prescriptions program; (c) relevant adverse drug reactions that occurred in the past; (d) relevant medical history and diagnosis; and (e) information on the current admission, including diagnosis and laboratory results. Although most information was present in the full electronic patient file, it was unstructured. Information could be added to the electronic record, could be in 'free-text notes', or in separate pdf documents (i.e., reports from previous admissions or consults within the hospital). We measured the time needed to compose this file. Detected items were first clinically judged by the clinical pharmacist (e.g., check serum potassium when an ACE inhibitor and a potassium-sparing agent were combined), and recommendations for relevant items were sent to the geriatrician by internal e-mail. The geriatrician adjusted prescriptions when needed and an additional meeting between the geriatrician and the pharmacist was set up once a week to discuss recommendations and acceptance.

In order to estimate the impact of the screening, the adapted MAI (aMAI) [15,16] was calculated by the clinical pharmacist (LDB) and an independent reviewer (ET) in a post-hoc analysis. Medication use at both admission and at discharge were evaluated. A low or high aMAI score suggests appropriate or inappropriate use of the medication, respectively.

2.3.3. Medication Reconciliation upon Discharge

Upon discharge, the clinical pharmacist reviewed the discharge medication list by comparing it with the medications upon admission, changes during hospital stay, and instructions mentioned in the discharge letter. Unintended discrepancies between the different sources were discussed with the geriatrician and incorrect sources were adjusted in order to avoid confusion in the future. Immediately before discharge, the clinical pharmacists discussed the discharge medication with the patient or caregiver. Changes were emphasized, such as starting, changing, or ceasing medication. The necessary counselling was provided for new drugs, such as administration instructions (with/without meal, time of administration), alarm symptoms of frequent adverse drug reactions, or possible important interactions with food or other drugs. At the end of this counselling, the patients or caregivers were asked if this extensive information session was helpful in understanding the discharge medication list. Moreover, to evaluate the effect on transfer between settings, a pharmaceutical discharge letter was sent to half of the general physicians and community pharmacies of the included patients. This letter contained the discharge medication list, as well as details on the changes compared to the prior medication list. During a follow-up phone call to the receiving general physicians (GP) and community pharmacists, the added value of the pharmaceutical discharge letter was discussed. Three questions were asked: (1) Do you think this letter is useful? (2) What actions do you undertake upon receiving the letter (read, read and file, don't read)? (3) Do you have suggestions to improve this clinical pharmacy activity?

2.4. Experiences

A special focus was placed on the different needs for communication within every step of the process. Upon initiation of the pilot project, all internal stakeholders (pharmacist, physician, nurses, etc.) were asked to gather their impressions and experiences (both positive and negative) during the process. These experiences were shared during the other contacts with the clinical pharmacist. Moreover, the professionals were asked to provide ideas on how the performed clinical pharmacy activities could be improved. A short report was written by the clinical pharmacist after every contact that contained relevant information on the process and the impressions of the people involved.

2.5. Analysis and Outcomes

This project aimed to identify the successes and barriers encountered during the implementation of a full medication review process as an example of a clinical pharmacy service in a hospital. The primary outcomes were number and type of medication discrepancies at admission and the improvement of prescribing appropriateness. All other outcomes were considered secondary. Both were evaluated and analyzed by the pharmacist in a descriptive way. Descriptive statistics are displayed as counts with percentages, median with interquartile ranges (IQR), and means with standard deviations (SD) as appropriate. Information about experiences is reported qualitatively.

The combination of the results of the interventions and the experience of all participants, both patients and healthcare workers, resulted in a summarizing box for each step of the project, divided into three parts: (1) successes; (2) barriers; and (3) recommendations for the different involved partners.

3. Results

3.1. General

In total, 52 out of 261 (20%) admitted patients were included in this study. The other 80% of patients were excluded based on the first exclusion criteria following this cascade: (1) age < 70 ($n = 20$); (2) taking <5 drugs at home ($n = 38$); (3) admission to a geriatric ward less than 3 months ago ($n = 40$); (4) cognitive impairment ($n = 94$), or (5) absence of the clinical pharmacist or no consent ($n = 17$), and received standard care.

3.2. Medication Reconciliation at Time of Admission

Fifty-two medication reconciliations were performed. The final medication lists totaled 529 drug or food supplements (median of 10 per patient (IQR 8–12)). In total, 122 discrepancies (122/529; 23%) were detected; 58 (11%) were obtained or altered after the structured interview with the patient or caregiver (median of 1 per patient (IQR 0–2)) and 64 (12%) after consultation with the community pharmacist (median of 1 per patient (IQR 0–2)). For 10 patients (19%), no community pharmacy could, however, be consulted (patients living in a nursing home, family member chooses community pharmacist, or patient did not have a regular community pharmacist). For some patients, the general physician (GP) was contacted when relevant information was missing. These communications often required multiple attempts due to inaccessibility of the GP or patient file while the GP was performing home visits.

The types of discrepancies are depicted in Table 2. Supplementary Table S2 shows the anatomical and therapeutic classes of the drugs that were involved in the 122 items recovered or altered after patient/caregiver or community pharmacist interview, as well as some examples.

Table 2. Types of detected discrepancies during medication reconciliation upon admission.

Types of Discrepancy	*n* (%)
Total	122
Omission on initial list	83 (70%)
Patient does not take drug	19 (16%)
Wrong dose	14 (12%)
Wrong modality (route/time of administration)	2 (2%)
Allergy previously not registered in file	2 (2%)
Wrong formulation	1 (0.5%)
Information on duration of therapy	1 (0.5%)

Every contacted community pharmacist ($n = 20$, some patients visited the same community pharmacy) was positively surprised with the request for additional information and considered this contact positive. For only two patients, the community pharmacist said a medication list was available.

One pharmacist mentioned that she asks patients with complex schemes whether they desire one and often (9/10) patients say they do not want or need one.

The process to obtain the best possible medication history was time consuming with patient interviews sometimes taking over 20 min, or due to the need for multiple attempts to contact the pharmacists or GPs.

3.3. The Medication Review Process

The creation of a useful and clear pharmaceutical patient file took an average (±SD) of 23.5 (±10.5) min. The subsequent mean (±SD) time needed to perform the medication review using the GheOP^{3}S tool and the STOPP/START criteria was 12.0 (±4.3) and 15.2 (±4.9) min, respectively. A total of 254 PIMs were detected, resulting in 195 therapeutic recommendations for the treating geriatrician after clinical judging by the pharmacist (see Supplementary Table S3). Thirteen percent of the recommendations was fully accepted and 6% was partially accepted (e.g., different dose, different alternative drug). Incorrect screening by the pharmacist was observed due to incompleteness of the patient file at the time of consultation by the clinical pharmacist or due to misinterpretation or mistakes by the pharmacist. There was an improvement in the aMAI scores for 75% and 88.2% of the patients after screening with the GheoP^{3}S tool (n =20) or STOPP/START criteria (n = 17), respectively. In the control group (n = 9), this improvement was seen in only 55.6% of patients (Table 3). Due to the small sample size of this study, it was not possible to perform statistical analysis on the results. However, a clear trend towards an improvement of prescribing appropriateness, as expressed by a decrease in aMAI, was observed with both the GheOP^{3}S tool and the STOPP/START criteria.

Table 3. Changes in MAI scores from admission to discharge.

		GheOP^{3}S	STOPP/START	Control
Number of patients upon discharge		20	17	9
Patients with improvement in MAI score	n (%)	15 (75%)	15 (88.2%)	5 (55.6%)
Patients in whom MAI score stayed equal	n (%)	4 (20%)	1 (5.9%)	3 (33.3%)
Patients with deterioration in MAI score	n (%)	1 (5%)	1 (5.9%)	1 (11.1%)

GheOP^{3}S: Ghent Older People's Prescriptions community Pharmacy Screening; STOPP/START: Screening Tool for Older Persons potentially inappropriate Prescriptions/Screening Tool to Alert for Right Treatment.

3.4. Medication List at Discharge and Pharmaceutical Discharge Letter

A total of 46 of the included patients were discharged within the study period. Six patients were lost in follow-up due to death during admission or discharge beyond the study period. Forty-one medication lists were evaluated by the pharmacist upon discharge, as 5 patients were discharged during the absence of the participating pharmacist. Overall, there was a good agreement between the medication list and the information in the discharge letter from the physician. The most important detected non-agreements were the omission of warfarin on a scheme and the wrong dose of pantoprazole. Other interventions by the pharmacist were the substitution to the brand or generic drug used at home from a different brand or generic drug during hospitalization or the adjustment of modalities of administration (e.g., time of administration, need to be sober). Every patient with whom the medication list was discussed evaluated this intervention positively.

For 24 patients, a pharmaceutical discharge letter was sent to the general physician and community pharmacist. Seventeen of the 18 pharmacists thought the information in this letter was useful and saved the information in the pharmacy software or patient file. Only 7 of the 16 general physicians were positive. Main reasons to not support this were (a) information is already available in the discharge letter; (b) unnecessary with the anticipation of an upcoming shared electronic patient file; (c) additional administrative burden (another letter to read and file).

4. Discussion

We performed a prospective interventional study, implementing a full clinical pharmacy service in a local Belgian hospital. The service consisted of medication reconciliation at the time of admission, a medication review, and a medication reconciliation at the time of discharge. Fifty-two patients were included. A discrepancy was detected for about one in four drugs. Medication review with a validated tool improved medication appropriateness according to the MAI score. A discharge consultation with the clinical pharmacist was positively evaluated by the patients.

4.1. Medication Reconciliation at Time of Admission

The results show a positive influence of a pharmacist-led medication reconciliation upon admission, which is in line with many previous studies [7,8,25]. It also reflects the importance to consult more than one source to obtain information on the patient's medication history [5]. The number of detected discrepancies in this study through the communication with the community pharmacist is probably an underestimation of the actual possible gain of information, as the community pharmacist could not be contacted for about one-in-five patients. Difficulties to obtain the best possible medication history following this protocol are expected when patients with cognitive impairment are admitted, as they most likely will lack knowledge on their current and previous drug use, as well as on their community pharmacy.

Many of the detected discrepancies led to changes in the prescriptions during the first days of admission and thus decreased the risk of therapeutic failure or medication errors. Some of the omissions concerning (non-)prescription drugs provided valuable information on additional symptoms experienced by the patient, as these symptoms could be signs for adverse drug reactions (e.g., fall incident with head wound after recent initiation of tramadol/paracetamol; or the need for chronic laxatives or artificial tears due to long term combination of drugs with anticholinergic properties). Additionally, the use of, for example, calcium supplements at home is relevant due to the possible influence on the absorption of several drugs. In contrast, some of the discrepancies were not taken into account by the physician in his evaluation of the prescriptions, such as the omission of multivitamins or homeopathic preparations.

As communication between the pharmacist and geriatrician was performed by telephone call or by e-mail, the only trace was the adjustments by the geriatrician in the electronic prescriptions. In order to improve traceability of the activities and interventions, as well as to provide all known information to every healthcare provider of the patient, future projects would benefit from registration in the electronic patient file. Ideally, this should be done in a section specifically designated for pharmacotherapeutic information.

The request for information on the medication dispensing history was positively experienced by the community pharmacists. Community pharmacists have a strong therapeutic relationship with patients and have access to the full dispensing records. Community pharmacists should use this important qualification in, for example, providing medication lists to patients. They should also inform patients on the helpfulness of an updated medication list in (often unexpected) transitions of care. This key role of the community pharmacist has been recently confirmed by the approval of a multiannual framework in Belgium [26]. Patients with chronic conditions will be able to choose a family pharmacist to help them in the follow-up of their treatment. The family pharmacist can help by providing the patient with an up-to-date medication list and supporting the patient in obtaining maximal therapeutic adherence. Compared to the easy and fast communication with the community pharmacists, contact with the general physicians was more difficult. We often needed multiple attempts; however, the required information was always obtained within a reasonable period.

An important barrier to implement a thorough medication reconciliation as standard care is the time to perform this task. Obtaining the best possible medication history through the above described procedure requires staff who are sufficiently trained to perform this task, possibly a pharmacy technician. Moreover, it is a time-consuming process and staffing is not equal 24/7, making it difficult to provide this service on a regular basis. However, the process of medication reconciliation could be facilitated through a centralized (pharmaceutical) patient file, which creates the possibility to share information between healthcare providers and settings. The Virtual Integrated Drug Information System (VIDIS) platform is being developed by the Belgian government for this purpose but is not yet implemented in every hospital or pharmacy and is, therefore, not yet usable. Until the implementation of this platform, the need for an extensive process of medication reconciliation remains. A summary of the successes, barriers and recommendations concerning medication reconciliation upon admission can be found in Table 4.

Table 4. Box 1: Medication Reconciliation upon Admission.

Successes	Barriers
• Identification of a high number of discrepancies after the consultation of multiple sources • Identification of additional symptoms or adverse reactions through medication use • Communication with community pharmacy was appreciated by both parties	• Lack of patient knowledge (whether or not due to cognitive impairment) • Confusion due to discrepancies between sources • No registration of medication reconciliation in patient file, no separate pharmaceutical section • Accessibility of general physician • Time consuming, 24/7 serviceLack of an integrated (pharmaceutical) centralized patient file

Recommendations for

- Patients: always bring an up-to-date medication list, including non-prescription medication
- Hospitals: provide a protocolled medication reconciliation procedure, including registration in patient file and train healthcare providers to perform them
- Community pharmacists: provide a clear medication list for the patient, including OTC drugs; encourage patients to keep medication list up to date
- Software: develop/provide a section for pharmaceutical interventions in patient file
- Government: facilitate transfer of information (centralized patient file), fund community and clinical pharmacists to improve and expand seamless communication of drug use

4.2. The Medication Review Process

The current software system used in the hospital is not sufficiently integrated to facilitate the creation of a useful pharmaceutical file consisting of crucial patient diagnostic, laboratory, and prescribing (history) information. The need to consult many different sources increases the risk of missing relevant items. Moreover, gathering the information takes a lot of time and decreases the number of patients for whom a medication review can be executed. A clear, uncomplicated patient file is again a must-have in order to perform medication reviews in a timely manner. This integrated patient file should be available for every professional with a therapeutic relationship with the patient. Also, physicians and other healthcare workers should be motivated to keep the file up to date and to make sure that everyone who is involved in the treatment of the patient is sufficiently informed.

The time needed to perform a medication review and to formulate the recommendation was comparable for both tools. This shows that when a clear patient file is present, medication review can be performed within a reasonable amount of time. The adjustment of about 20% of the potential inappropriate prescriptions depicts the potential role a clinical pharmacist can play in the optimization of the medication list.

In most cases, the geriatrician read the internal e-mail containing the recommendations; however, some were missed and recommendations were only evaluated during the weekly meeting. In the case of acceptance of the recommendation, this could lead to a delay in therapeutic change of up to 7 days. To avoid these unnecessary and potentially harmful delays, adjustments in communication strategy are necessary. For example, when recommendations are communicated through e-mail, reading confirmations should be asked for. Moreover, everything should be registered in the patient file, readily available for the physician, and a system should be set up to notify the physician that recommendations are present. A more intense follow-up with a reminder for the physician after a certain amount of time could also be beneficial.

Another way to improve communication is the presence of the clinical pharmacist during multidisciplinary meetings. As such, medication-related issues could be addressed on a regular basis. The pharmacists can also be present on the ward or participate in ward rounds in order to provide immediate pharmacological support, a strategy that has been proven to be successful [27–29]. Table 5 summarizes the successes and barriers encountered during this part of the project, as well as shows the recommendations to the different involved partners.

Table 5. Box 2: Medication Review and Therapeutic Recommendations.

Successes	Barriers
• Full access to patient file	• Scattered information across different programs: risk of incomplete pharmaceutical file + time consuming
• Relatively fast screening with the tools	
• Identification of a significant amount of PIMs	• Continuity of presence of pharmacist(s) and participating physician(s)
• Improvement in prescribing appropriateness (MAI scores)	• Incorrect screening by the pharmacist
	• Inefficient communication
• 20% of therapeutic recommendations were accepted	• Agreements prior to interventions on what to recommend (service level agreement)

Recommendations for:

- Patients: empower patients: they should be involved in decisions
- Hospitals: provide access to complete files for clinical pharmacist; integrate the presence of pharmacists in multidisciplinary meetings/ward rounds (in order to increase insight into patient condition); encourage and support multidisciplinary meetings
- Government: financing of sharing files and the execution of medication reviews
- Training: improve training of physicians and pharmacists to perform medication reviews and to improve communication
- ICT + research: improve electronic patient file management, create automatization of screening, develop clinical decision support systems

4.3. Medication List at Discharge and Pharmaceutical Discharge Letter

Discharge is another important transfer of care that requires specific attention. The patient or caregiver should be informed on the correct therapeutic plan to follow after the hospitalization, which starts with a correct medication list. Evaluation of the scheme by the clinical pharmacist showed that the majority of the schemes were concordant with the actual therapeutic plan of the physician, as noted in the patient file and the discharge letter. However, the detection of some errors confirmed the usefulness of a review, as in rare cases important drugs were omitted or the dosage was incorrect. Additionally, the frequent need to substitute some drugs to the brand the patient was using prior to hospitalization is an important intervention as this could lead to confusion or even double intake of the same drug. The preparation of the medication list prior to discharge is a condition to be able to perform this clinical pharmacy activity. During the study, the participating geriatrician always provided the scheme on time. The software supporting this activity was, however, evaluated to not be user friendly, keeping other physicians from preparing a medication list. The participation of only one clinical pharmacist in the project caused the service of the evaluation of the discharge medication list to not be continuous.

Due to the lack of a safe electronic system used by every healthcare provider to share patient information, the pharmaceutical discharge letters were sent by conventional mail. Community pharmacists reacted overall very positively to the pharmaceutical discharge letter. They believed they could provide better pharmaceutical care for their patient as they could inform the patient on the changes. The therapeutic plan was also clearer for the pharmacist him/herself, which made them more confident they were dispensing the correct drugs. General physicians' opinions on the pharmaceutical discharge letter were divided. The reason to support the use of this letter was the elimination of the need to search the entire discharge letter for scattered information on pharmacotherapeutic information. A summary of the experiences and recommendations on medication reconciliation upon discharge is provided in Table 6.

Table 6. Box 3: Medication Reconciliation upon Discharge.

Successes	Barriers
• Informing patients on medication list upon discharge (pharmaceutical care!) • Pharmaceutical discharge letter • Extra information for community pharmacist	• Software not user friendly to prepare scheme • Time-consuming process • Communication with other healthcare providers: mail versus safe electronic system

Recommendations for:
- Patients: inform them about the possibilities
- Hospitals: implement structural discharge consultation with clinical pharmacist; increase awareness of physicians for the importance of a medication list
- Government: support development of safe ways for communication (VIDIS); increase funding for clinical pharmacy activities
- ICT: facilitate the preparation of the medication list upon discharge

5. Strengths and Limitations

To our knowledge, this is the first study to provide an overview of the communicative contacts during a full medication review process by a clinical pharmacist. The successes and barriers were analyzed from both a quantitative and qualitative perspective, taking into account the opinions of every involved participator in the process. Additionally, the large amount of information and experiences were used to formulate recommendations, which could support the short- or long-term improvement of the implementation or expansion of a full medication review process.

The recommendations described in the study could apply to different patient populations, as medication reconciliation or medication review are important processes for every patient undergoing a transition of care, taking multiple drugs, or with a complex pathology. Moreover, the results from the study could be beneficial for other types of institutions, such as nursing homes, as they also often struggle with the same barriers.

Nevertheless, this study has some limitations. The small number of included patients precluded the statistical comparison of the groups, resulting in only descriptive statistics. This project shows there is a need to include patients with cognitive impairment in studies evaluating the effect of medication screening tools, as they represent a major part of geriatric patients requiring hospitalization. Moreover, the positive effect of screening on medication appropriateness, as reflected in improvement of outcome parameters such as MAI score, cannot be extrapolated to a positive effect on other outcomes, such as drug reactions, drug-related hospital admissions, healthcare use, patient reported outcomes, and mortality [30,31]. These parameters are affected by many interventions and not only by the medication review by the pharmacist. There is, however, not yet a consensus on how to evaluate the effect of a medication review as the outcome reporting from published trials is heterogeneous [30]. Therefore, future trials evaluating the effects of pharmacist-led medication reviews should use a core outcome set (i.e., an agreed standardized collection of outcome variables that should be measured and reported in all trials for a specific clinical area [30]).

Another limitation was the participation of only one clinical pharmacist and one geriatrician, compromising the continuity of this clinical pharmaceutical service. For the pharmacists, the problem is dual: (1) a shortage of staff to provide continuous service; and (2) the lack of training of the hospital pharmacists to perform this task. Shortage of staff is, however, being partially addressed by the Belgian government through structural financing. Nevertheless, the level of knowledge of this subject in Belgian hospital pharmacists should improve in the upcoming years as the training of hospital pharmacists has been prolonged (from 1 to 3 years), with additional focus on clinical pharmacy (theoretical course + training program), and hospital pharmacists could further specialize in clinical pharmacy by following additional courses [23,32]. Informing physicians (in training) on the positive influence of a clinical pharmaceutical intervention could increase their enthusiasm to collaborate.

The experiences of the involved healthcare workers were collected by the same clinical pharmacist who was involved in the execution of the clinical pharmacy service, in reports of the often verbal inter-professional contacts. As this could possibly introduce bias in the obtained results, future studies could benefit from written questions or independent interviewers. Additionally, a formal analysis with focus groups is needed; however, this was beyond the scope of this implementation study.

6. Future Perspectives

Clinical pharmacy services can only be effective if the treating physician uses the results to optimize patient treatment. Therefore, the results from the pilot project will be reported to the medical staff of the hospital in order to create awareness on the potential role of clinical pharmacy for their patients and to stimulate their enthusiasm. After performing and evaluating this pilot project, we are ready to introduce front-office clinical pharmacy at our local hospital. Every project should be preceded by adequate training of the involved pharmacists and other healthcare workers, as well as by the definition of a clear communication plan.

The differences in expectations on inter-professional communication between pharmacists and GPs have been recently described for the German situation by Weissenborn et al. [33]. A similar study, performed on a local or national level in Belgium, could be helpful in the development of means of communication, including standardized recommendations, suitable for every professional.

As demonstrated in the analysis of our pilot project, further extension of clinical pharmacy, in general, will need optimization on different levels. Healthcare providers should receive intensive training and should recognize each others' roles in the optimization of medication and patient safety. Interdisciplinary and seamless healthcare can be facilitated by the creation of structured patient files that are easily and securely accessible by every professional and with the possibility to communicate. This should be developed both locally (within the hospital) and externally through the VIDIS platform currently under development.

7. Conclusions

The introduction of clinical pharmacy should be considered in every hospital as this has a significant impact on patient safety and patient care. The importance of a prominent role of the clinical pharmacist in the optimization of drug use in older people through the implementation of a full medication review process has been shown in this study. However, opposite every success, several barriers were detected or perceived, showing the difficulties in setting up a structure to be able to perform clinical pharmaceutical activities. Clear inter-professional communication has been shown to be essential during every step in order to obtain positive results and to facilitate the process. The identification and analysis of the communicative and non-communicative successes and hurdles encountered during this project need to be addressed in order to improve the full medication review process.

Supplementary Materials: The following are available online at http://www.mdpi.com/2226-4787/6/1/21/s1, Table S1: Domains and themes in the action plan of the Belgian Government (2015–2020); Table S2: Anatomical and therapeutic classes of the drugs involved in the discrepancies detected after medication reconciliation; Table S3: Detected PIMs with the GheoP^{3}S tool (a) and the STOPP/START tool (b).

Acknowledgments: The authors want to thank the participating nurses and patients in this project. No funds were received for this publication.

Author Contributions: L.D.B. and E.T. conceived and designed the study, analyzed the data, and wrote the paper; L.D.B. and W.M. performed the study with support from E.T. and H.B.; A.S. wrote the paper; W.M., A.S. and K.B. reviewed the protocols and the paper.

Conflicts of Interest: The authors declare no conflict of interest.

References

1. Shamji, H.; Baier, R.R.; Gravenstein, S.; Gardner, R.L. Improving the quality of care and communication during patient transitions: Best practices for urgent care centers. *Jonit Comm. J. Qual. Patient Saf.* **2014**, *40*, 319–324. [CrossRef]

2. Luu, N.P.; Pitts, S.; Petty, B.; Sawyer, M.D.; Dennison-Himmelfarb, C.; Boonyasai, R.T.; Maruthur, N.M. Provider-to-Provider Communication during Transitions of Care from Outpatient to Acute Care: A Systematic Review. *J. Gen. Intern. Med.* **2016**, *31*, 417–425. [CrossRef] [PubMed]

3. Foronda, C.; MacWilliams, B.; McArthur, E. Interprofessional communication in healthcare: An integrative review. *Nurse Educ. Pract.* **2016**, *19*, 36–40. [CrossRef] [PubMed]

4. Rodriguez Vargas, B.; Delgado Silveira, E.; Iglesias Peinado, I.; Bermejo Vicedo, T. Prevalence and risk factors for medication reconciliation errors during hospital admission in elderly patients. *Int. J. Clin. Pharm.* **2016**, *38*, 1164–1171. [CrossRef] [PubMed]

5. Almanasreh, E.; Moles, R.; Chen, T.F. The medication reconciliation process and classification of discrepancies: A systematic review. *Br. J. Clin. Pharmacol.* **2016**, *82*, 645–658. [CrossRef] [PubMed]

6. Contreras Rey, M.B.; Arco Prados, Y.; Sanchez Gomez, E. Analysis of the medication reconciliation process conducted at hospital admission. *Farm. Hosp.* **2016**, *40*, 246–259. [PubMed]

7. Mekonnen, A.B.; McLachlan, A.J.; Brien, J.A. Effectiveness of pharmacist-led medication reconciliation programmes on clinical outcomes at hospital transitions: A systematic review and meta-analysis. *BMJ Open* **2016**, *6*, e010003. [CrossRef] [PubMed]

8. Mekonnen, A.B.; McLachlan, A.J.; Brien, J.A. Pharmacy-led medication reconciliation programmes at hospital transitions: A systematic review and meta-analysis. *J. Clin. Pharm. Ther.* **2016**, *41*, 128–144. [CrossRef] [PubMed]

9. Tam, V.C.; Knowles, S.R.; Cornish, P.L.; Fine, N.; Marchesano, R.; Etchells, E.E. Frequency, type and clinical importance of medication history errors at admission to hospital: A systematic review. *CMAJ* **2005**, *173*, 510–515. [CrossRef] [PubMed]

10. Spinewine, A.; Schmader, K.E.; Barber, N.; Hughes, C.; Lapane, K.L.; Swine, C.; Hanlon, J.T. Appropriate prescribing in elderly people: How well can it be measured and optimised? *Lancet* **2007**, *370*, 173–184. [CrossRef]

11. Opondo, D.; Eslami, S.; Visscher, S.; de Rooij, S.E.; Verheij, R.; Korevaar, J.C.; Abu-Hanna, A. Inappropriateness of medication prescriptions to elderly patients in the primary care setting: A systematic review. *PLoS ONE* **2012**, *7*, e43617. [CrossRef] [PubMed]

12. Fick, D.M.; Cooper, J.W.; Wade, W.E.; Waller, J.L.; Maclean, J.R.; Beers, M.H. Updating the Beers criteria for potentially inappropriate medication use in older adults: Results of a US consensus panel of experts. *Arch. Intern. Med.* **2003**, *163*, 2716–2724. [CrossRef] [PubMed]

13. O'Connor, M.N.; Gallagher, P.; O'Mahony, D. Inappropriate Prescribing Criteria, Detection and Prevention. *Drugs Aging* **2012**, *29*, 437–452. [CrossRef] [PubMed]

14. O'Mahony, D.; Gallagher, P.; Ryan, C.; Byrne, S.; Hamilton, H.; O'Connor, M.N.; Kennedy, J. STOPP & START criteria: A new approach to detecting potentially inappropriate prescribing in old age. *Eur. Geriatr. Med.* **2010**, *1*, 45–51.

15. Hanlon, J.; Schmader, K. The Medication Appropriateness Index at 20: Where It Started, Where It Has Been, and Where It May Be Going. *Drugs Aging* **2013**, *30*, 893–900. [CrossRef] [PubMed]

16. Somers, A.; Mallet, L.; van der Cammen, T.; Robays, H.; Petrovic, M. Applicability of an Adapted Medication Appropriateness Index for Detection of Drug-Related Problems in Geriatric Inpatients. *Am. J. Geriatr. Pharm.* **2012**, *10*, 101–109. [CrossRef] [PubMed]

17. O'Mahony, D.; O'Sullivan, D.; Byrne, S.; O'Connor, M.N.; Ryan, C.; Gallagher, P. STOPP/START criteria for potentially inappropriate prescribing in older people: Version 2. *Age Ageing* **2015**, *44*, 213–218. [CrossRef] [PubMed]

18. Tommelein, E.; Petrovic, M.; Somers, A.; Mehuys, E.; van der Cammen, T.J.M.; Boussery, K. Older patients' prescriptions screening in the community pharmacy: Development of the Ghent Older People's Prescriptions community Pharmacy Screening (GheOP^{3}S) tool. *J. Public Health* **2015**, *38*, e158–e170. [CrossRef] [PubMed]

19. American Geriatrics Society updated Beers Criteria for potentially inappropriate medication use in older adults. *J. Am. Geriatr. Soc.* **2012**, *60*, 616–631.

20. Berenguer, B.; La Casa, C.; de la Matta, M.J.; Martin-Calero, M.J. Pharmaceutical care: Past, present and future. *Curr. Pharm. Des.* **2004**, *10*, 3931–3946. [CrossRef] [PubMed]

21. Royal Decree Relating to the Determination and Payment of the Budget of Financial Resources of the Hospitals. Available online: http://www.ejustice.just.fgov.be/cgi_loi/change_lg.pl?language=nl&la=N&table_name=wet&cn=2015010811 (accessed on 20 December 2017).

22. Clinical Pharmacy in Belgian Hospitals: Policy Paper 2015–2020. 2015. Available online: https://www.health.belgium.be/sites/default/files/uploads/fields/fpshealth_theme_file/beleidsnota_kf_2015-2020-juni2015.pdf (accessed on 20 December 2017).

23. Somers, A.; Claus, B.; Vandewoude, K.; Petrovic, M. Experience with the Implementation of Clinical Pharmacy Services and Processes in a University Hospital in Belgium. *Drugs Aging* **2016**, *33*, 189–197. [CrossRef] [PubMed]

24. De Winter, S.; Vanbrabant, P.; Spriet, I.; Desruelles, D.; Indevuyst, C.; Knockaert, D.; Gillet, J.B.; Willems, L. A simple tool to improve medication reconciliation at the emergency department. *Eur. J. Intern. Med.* **2011**, *22*, 382–385. [CrossRef] [PubMed]

25. Cadman, B.; Wright, D.; Bale, A.; Barton, G.; Desborough, J.; Hammad, E.A.; Holland, R.; Howe, H.; Nunney, I.; Irvine, L. Pharmacist provided medicines reconciliation within 24 hours of admission and on discharge: A randomised controlled pilot study. *BMJ Open* **2017**, *7*, e013647. [CrossRef] [PubMed]

26. Multiannual Framework for the Patient with the Community Pharmacist. Available online: http://www.deblock.belgium.be/sites/default/files/articles/2017_03_15%20Meerjarenkader%20apothekers_web.pdf (accessed on 15 December 2017).

27. Miller, G.; Franklin, B.D.; Jacklin, A. Including pharmacists on consultant-led ward rounds: A prospective non-randomised controlled trial. *Clin. Med.* **2011**, *11*, 312–316. [CrossRef]

28. Gillespie, U.; Morlin, C.; Hammarlund-Udenaes, M.; Hedstrom, M. Perceived value of ward-based pharmacists from the perspective of physicians and nurses. *Int. J. Clin. Pharm.* **2012**, *34*, 127–135. [CrossRef] [PubMed]

29. Klopotowska, J.E.; Kuiper, R.; van Kan, H.J.; de Pont, A.C.; Dijkgraaf, M.G.; Lie, A.H.L.; Vroom, M.B.; Smorenburg, S.M. On-ward participation of a hospital pharmacist in a Dutch intensive care unit reduces prescribing errors and related patient harm: An intervention study. *Crit. Care* **2010**, *14*, R174. [CrossRef] [PubMed]

30. Beuscart, J.B.; Pont, L.G.; Thevelin, S.; Boland, B.; Dalleur, O.; Rutjes, A.W.S.; Westbrook, J.I.; Spinewine, A. A systematic review of the outcomes reported in trials of medication review in older patients: The need for a core outcome set. *Br. J. Clin. Pharmacol.* **2017**, *83*, 942–952. [CrossRef] [PubMed]

31. Hill-Taylor, B.; Walsh, K.A.; Stewart, S.; Hayden, J.; Byrne, S.; Sketris, I.S. Effectiveness of the STOPP/START (Screening Tool of Older Persons' potentially inappropriate Prescriptions/Screening Tool to Alert doctors to the Right Treatment) criteria: Systematic review and meta-analysis of randomized controlled studies. *J. Clin. Pharm. Ther.* **2016**, *41*, 158–169. [CrossRef] [PubMed]

32. De Rijdt, T.; Willems, L.; Simoens, S. Economic effects of clinical pharmacy interventions: A literature review. *Am. J. Health Syst. Pharm.* **2008**, *65*, 1161–1172. [CrossRef] [PubMed]

33. Weissenborn, M.; Haefeli, W.E.; Peters-Klimm, F.; Seidling, H.M. Interprofessional communication between community pharmacists and general practitioners: A qualitative study. *Int. J. Clin. Pharm.* **2017**, *39*, 495–506. [CrossRef] [PubMed]

pharmacy

MDPI

Article

Assessment of Prescribing and Monitoring Habits for Patients Taking an Antiarrhythmic and Concomitant QTc-Prolonging Antibiotic

Kelsey Noss, Sandra M. Aguero and Travis Reinaker *

Einstein Medical Center-Philadelphia, 5501 Old York Road, Philadelphia, PA 19141, USA;
kelsey.noss12@gmail.com (K.N.); aguersan@einstein.edu (S.M.A.)
* Correspondence: reinaket@einstein.edu; Tel.: +1-570-881-0432

Received: 26 September 2017; Accepted: 30 October 2017; Published: 1 November 2017

Abstract: Patients may intermittently require antimicrobial therapy with a QTc-prolonging antibiotic, which presents a challenge for prescribers of patients already taking a QTc-prolonging antiarrhythmic. Manufacturers recommend close monitoring for evidence of QTc-prolongation with the concomitant use of QTc-prolonging medications, but the monitoring parameters are not well-defined. Previous studies recommend a surveillance electrocardiogram (EKG) be completed both before and after the initiation of QTc-prolonging medications, but it is unknown to what degree EKGs displaying the QTc-interval are used to alter physician order entry and pharmacist order verification during concomitant therapy. A retrospective chart review was conducted between October 2015–September 2016 to assess prescribing and monitoring habits for patients taking an antiarrhythmic and a concomitant QTc-prolonging antibiotic. Of the 42 patients who received at least one dose of two QTc-prolonging agents, 36 (85.7%) received a baseline EKG, and 23 (63.8%) received a follow-up EKG. Pharmacists intervened on this drug–drug interaction and recommended follow-up EKGs only three times (8.3%) and offered alternative therapy recommendations once (2.8%). The QTc-interval was not optimally monitored in some instances for patients concomitantly receiving two QTc-prolonging agents. These results stress the importance of inter-professional communication to place an emphasis on follow-up monitoring or use of alternative therapy agents to avoid the drug–drug interaction altogether.

Keywords: QTc-prolongation; electrocardiogram; antiarrhythmic; macrolide; fluoroquinolone; drug-interaction

1. Introduction

The QT-interval on an electrocardiogram (EKG) represents the depolarization and repolarization of cardiac ventricles. On a 12-lead EKG, the QT-interval is measured from the beginning of the QRS complex to the end of the T wave as it returns to baseline. Several factors such as gender, heart rate, underlying arrhythmias, and conduction defects influence the QT-interval. The QT-interval will vary depending on heart rate. To standardize the measurement to a heart rate of 60 beats per minute, the QT-interval is corrected and referred to as the QTc [1]. The QTc allows for comparison of the QT-interval across a range of heart rates. The most universally adopted method for correcting QT-intervals for heart rate is the Bazett's formula (Corrected QT-interval (QTc): $QT/\sqrt{RR}$ in seconds; RR is the interval from the peak of one QRS complex to the peak of the next as shown on an electrocardiogram) [1]. QTc-prolongation is defined as a QTc-interval of >450 milliseconds (ms) in males, and >470 ms in females, and can predispose patients to life-threatening ventricular arrhythmias. Several medications have been implicated in the prolongation of the QTc-interval. A complete resource of medications, stratified according to QTc-prolonging risk, can be found at crediblemeds.com.

QTc-prolongation can occur in up to 10% of patients taking QTc-prolonging antiarrhythmics (including amiodarone), and <1% of patients taking macrolide or fluoroquinolone antibiotics. The concomitant use of two QTc-prolonging medications increases this risk [1]. Manufacturers recommend close monitoring for evidence of QTc-prolongation with the concomitant use of QTc-prolonging medications, while previous studies recommend that offending drugs should be discontinued in patients who develop a prolonged QTc-interval >500 ms, or an increase in QTc-interval of >60 ms on follow-up EKG [2–8]. However, it is unknown whether EKGs are used to alter prescribing and monitoring habits when these medications are combined. This is the first study to observe the real-life prescribing and monitoring habits for patients taking an antiarrhythmic and a concomitant QTc-prolonging antibiotic at a large, academic medical center.

2. Materials and Methods

A retrospective chart review, exempt from IRB-approval, was completed to observe the prescribing and monitoring habits for patients taking an antiarrhythmic and a concomitant QTc-prolonging antibiotic. This study included patients admitted to Einstein Medical Center-Philadelphia from 1 October 2015 to 30 September 2016. Patients were identified with an electronic report of drug interaction alerts that had advised pharmacists during order verification of the increased risk of a QTc-prolonging effect between two medications. Patients taking amiodarone upon admission who also received at least one concomitant dose of ciprofloxacin, moxifloxacin, or azithromycin during admission were included. Gender, QTc-prolonging medication, medication dose, pharmacist interventions, presence or absence of a baseline (while on amiodarone only) and follow-up (while on amiodarone and a QTc-prolonging antibiotic), QTc-interval, change in QTc-interval, and therapy modification and justification were collected. The formula used to calculate the corrected QT-interval was Bazett's formula. Descriptive statistics, including the median and range, were used to analyze patient demographics, prescriptions, and monitoring data.

3. Results

A total of 78 patients were assessed, and 42 patients received concomitant QTc-prolonging agents. The most commonly prescribed medication regimen was azithromycin added to home amiodarone therapy in 23 patients (54.5%). Thirty-six out of 42 patients (85.7%) previously taking amiodarone received a baseline EKG (Table 1). The median male QTc-interval was 473 ms (range: 405–602 ms), and the median female QTc-interval was 470 ms (range: 435–599 ms) (Table 1). Of the male patients who received a baseline EKG, nine out of 14 (64.2%) had a prolonged QTc-interval (>450 ms). Of the female patients who received a baseline EKG, 12 out of 22 (54.5%) had a prolonged QTc-interval (>470 ms) (Table 1). Of the 36 patients who received a baseline EKG, a pharmacist recommended a follow-up EKG on three occasions (8.3%) (Table 1). Twenty-three out of 36 patients (63.8%) received a follow-up EKG. The median male QTc-interval was 481 ms (range: 440–628 ms), and the median female QTc-interval was 484 ms (range: 384–645 ms) (Table 1). Of the male patients who received a follow-up EKG, two out of eight (25%) had a prolonged QTc-interval (>450 ms). Of the female patients who received a follow-up EKG, 11 out of 15 (73.3%) had a prolonged QTc-interval (>470 ms) (Table 1). Ten out of 23 patients (43.5%) had a QTc-interval >500 ms or an increase in QTc-interval of >60ms on follow-up EKG, but in only three out of 23 instances (13%), therapy was either discontinued or a different antimicrobial was utilized (Table 1). Of these three patients, two (66.7%) experienced a QTc-interval increase to >600 ms without arrhythmia, and one (33.3%) developed torsades de pointes before alternative therapy was utilized. (Table 1).

Table 1. Electrocardiogram (EKG) results and subsequent therapy modifications. QTc: corrected QT-interval.

Baseline EKG obtained (%)	36/42 (85.7)
Median male QTc, ms (range)	473 (405–602)
Male QTc >450 ms (%)	9/14 (62.4%)
Median female QTc, ms (range)	470 (435–599)
Female QTc >470 ms (%)	12/22 (54.5%)
Follow-up EKG recommended by pharmacist (%)	3/36 (8.3)
Follow-up EKG obtained (%)	23/36 (63.8)
Median male QTc, ms (range)	481 (440–628)
Male QTc >450 ms (%)	2/8 (25)
Median female QTc, ms (range)	484 (384–645)
Female QTc >470 ms (%)	11/15 (73.3)
Follow-up EKG QTc-interval >500 ms, or QTc-interval increase of >60 ms (%)	10/23 (43.5)
Therapy changed based on follow-up EKG (%)	3/23 (13)
Patient developed torsades de pointes (%)	1/23 (4.3)
Patient QTc-interval increased to >600 ms (%)	2/23 (8.7)

4. Discussion

Manufacturers recommend close monitoring for evidence of QTc-prolongation with the concomitant use of QTc-prolonging medications, but the monitoring parameters are not well-defined [2–5]. Previous studies have recommended that surveillance EKGs be completed before and after initiation of QTc-prolonging medications [1,6–8]. This observational study demonstrated that despite prescribers ordering baseline EKGs on most patients, 36.2% of patients still did not receive a follow-up EKG. In the presence of a follow-up EKG, "The Significance of QT-Interval in Drug Development" published in the British Journal of Clinical Pharmacology states that offending drugs should be discontinued in patients who develop an increase of >60 ms in QTc-interval [7]. Additionally, "Practice Standards for Electrocardiographic Monitoring in Hospital Setting" published by the American Heart Association (AHA) states that offending drugs should be discontinued in patients who develop a prolonged QTc-interval >500 ms [8]. In our study, ten patients demonstrated either a QTc-interval >500 ms, or an increase of >60 ms in QTC-interval on follow-up EKG. Prescribers infrequently responded with therapy modifications, which may have led to one patient experiencing torsades de pointes. To avoid the potential development of fatal arrhythmias in the setting of a prolonged QTc-interval, alternative antibiotics could be utilized. The Infectious Disease Society of America provides alternative recommendations for specific disease states, and an antibiotic that does not prolong the QTc-interval could be selected. Pharmacists infrequently recommended follow-up monitoring or offered alternative treatment recommendations. Lack of documentation may have led to the perceived small amount of pharmacist interventions. Pharmacists were also not able to view follow-up EKGs, as results are not readily reposted in the electronic medical record. Additional limitations to the study include its small sample size, and other medications or patient-specific characteristics that cause QTc-prolongation were not assessed. Our study showed that the QTc-interval was not optimally monitored in some instances for patients, despite recommendations from manufacturers. For instance, six patients did not receive a baseline EKG, and 13 patients did not receive a follow-up EKG. These results may also be experienced in other institutions, stressing the importance of inter-professional communication to place an emphasis on follow-up monitoring or use of alternative therapy agents to avoid the drug–drug interaction altogether.

Author Contributions: Kelsey Noss, Sandra M. Aguero, and Travis Reinaker conceived and designed the experiments; Experiments were not performed as this was a retrospective chart review; Kelsey Noss and Travis Reinaker analyzed the data; Kelsey Noss and Travis Reinaker contributed reagents/materials/analysis tools; Kelsey Noss and Travis Reinaker wrote the paper.

Conflicts of Interest: Authors report no conflicts of interest.

Pharmacy **2017**, *5*, 61

References

1. Nachimuthu, S.; Schussler, J.M. Drug-induced QT interval prolongation: Mechanisms and clinical management. *Ther. Adv. Drug Saf.* **2012**, *3*, 241–253. [CrossRef] [PubMed]
2. Amiodarone [package insert]. Sagent Pharmaceuticals, Inc.: Schaumbrug, IL, USA, July 2011. Available online: http://www.sagentpharma.com/wp-content/uploads/2014/11/Amiodarone_PI1.pdf (accessed on 15 May 2017).
3. Ciprofloxacin [package insert]. Bayer HealthCare Pharmaceuticals, Inc.: Wayne, NJ, USA, February 2009. Available online: https://www.accessdata.fda.gov/drugsatfda_docs/label/2009/019537s073,020780s030lbl.pdf (accessed on 15 May 2017).
4. Moxifloxacin [package insert]. Bayer Pharmaceuticals, Inc.: West Haven, CT, USA, December 1999. Available online: https://www.accessdata.fda.gov/drugsatfda_docs/label/1999/21085lbl.pdf (accessed on 15 May 2017).
5. Azithromycin [package insert]. Pfizer Labs, Inc.: New York, NY, USA, January 2013. Available online: https://www.accessdata.fda.gov/drugsatfda_docs/label/2013/050710s039,050711s036,050784s023lbl.pdf (accessed on 15 May 2017).
6. Barbara, J.B.; Ackerman, M.J.; Funk, M.; Gibler, B.W.; Kligfield, P.; Menon, V.; Philippides, G.J.; Roden, D.M.; Wojciech, Z. Prevention of torsade de pointes in hospital settings: A scientific statement from the American Heart Association and the American College of Cardiology Foundation. *Circulation* **2010**, *121*, 1047–1060. [CrossRef]
7. Shah, R.R. The significance of QT interval in drug development. *Br. J. Clin. Pharmacol.* **2002**, *54*, 188–202. [CrossRef] [PubMed]
8. Drew, B.J.; Califf, R.M.; Funk, M.; Kaufman, E.S.; Krucoff, M.W.; Laks, M.M.; Macfarlane, P.W.; Sommargren, C.; Swiryn, S.; Van Hare, G.F. Practice standards for electrocardiographic monitoring in hospital settings: An American Heart Association scientific statement from the councils on cardiovascular nursing, clinical cardiology, and cardiovascular disease in the young: Endorsed by the international society of computerized electrocardiology and the American Association of Critical-Care Nurses. *Circulation* **2004**, *110*, 2721–2746. [CrossRef] [PubMed]

pharmacy

MDPI

Article

Development of a Theory-Based Intervention to Enhance Information Exchange during Over-The-Counter Consultations in Community Pharmacy

Liza J. Seubert [1,*]**, Kerry Whitelaw** [1]**, Laetitia Hattingh** [2]**, Margaret C. Watson** [3] **and Rhonda M. Clifford** [1]

[1]   Division of Pharmacy, The University of Western Australia, M315, 35 Stirling Highway,
       Crawley, WA 6009, Australia; kerry.whitelaw@uwa.edu.au (K.W.); rhonda.clifford@uwa.edu.au (R.M.C.)
[2]   School of Pharmacy and Pharmacology, Griffith University, Gold Coast Campus,
       Queensland 4222, Australia; l.hattingh@griffith.edu.au
[3]   Department of Pharmacy and Pharmacology, University of Bath, 5W 3.33, Claverton Down,
       Bath BA2 7AY, UK; m.c.watson@bath.ac.uk
*   Correspondence: liza.seubert@uwa.edu.au; Tel.: +61-8-6488-7500

Received: 9 October 2018; Accepted: 22 October 2018; Published: 24 October 2018

Abstract: (1) Background: Community pharmacy personnel help mitigate risks of self-care by consumers who seek over-the-counter (OTC) medicines or treatment of symptoms and/or conditions. Exchange of information facilitates the OTC consultation, but pharmacy personnel often report difficulties in engaging consumers in a dialogue. The aim of this study was to describe the development of a behaviour change intervention to enhance information exchange between pharmacy personnel and consumers during OTC consultations in community pharmacies. (2) Methods: The Behaviour Change Wheel methodological framework was used to link factors that influence consumer engagement with information exchange during OTC consultations with intervention functions to change behaviour. Options generated were rationalized and the final intervention strategy was derived. (3) Results: Education, persuasion, environmental restructuring, and modelling were determined to be potential intervention functions. The intervention incorporated placing situational cues in the form of posters in the community pharmacy modelling information exchange behaviour, persuading through highlighting the benefits of exchanging information and educating about its importance. (4) Conclusions: A systematic, theoretically underpinned approach was applied to develop candidate interventions to promote information exchange in OTC consultations. The feasibility and efficacy of the intervention strategy has since been tested and will be reported elsewhere.

Keywords: communication; nonprescription drugs; pharmacists; community pharmacy services; behaviour change; health behaviour

---

1. Introduction

Community pharmacy personnel manage over-the-counter (OTC) enquiries every day [1,2], which include requests for named OTC medicines as well as the treatment of symptoms and/or conditions [3,4]. Consumers are becoming increasingly confident in self-managing minor ailments by using information from a variety of sources, such as the internet, to self-diagnose and select medicines they view to be appropriate [5,6]. This is facilitated by the wide range of OTC medicines available from community pharmacies in many countries, which require varying levels of involvement by pharmacy personnel, depending on the legal classification and regulation [7–9]. Furthermore, community pharmacies are accessible, often with extended opening hours, and without the need to book an appointment to see a pharmacist [10–13].

Benefits of consumers in engaging with self-care for minor ailments include convenience, and time and cost savings [6,14]. However, there is a risk that consumers could misdiagnose their condition(s), resulting in delays in initiating appropriate treatment [6,14]. Consumers may also underestimate the risks of OTC medicines, which could result in adverse effects [15–19]. Pharmacy personnel play an important role in mitigating the risks associated with self-care. Community pharmacists are qualified to manage the complexity of OTC enquiries in the community pharmacy setting by engaging with consumers in a consultation [20–22]. Gathering information from consumers about the symptom or condition, the person's medical history and medicines, and their treatment goals, assists pharmacists in providing appropriate recommendations [2,23]. Many factors influence information exchange during OTC consultations, including the communication skills of pharmacy personnel, consumer expectation to purchase an OTC medicine without needing to answer questions, privacy, and the legal classification of the medicine [24–37].

Pharmacists and pharmacy personnel often report difficulties in engaging consumers in a dialogue, particularly when the request is for a specific medicine by name [25,27,38–40]. OTC consultations ideally should involve two-way communication "between the pharmacist and the patient in which the pharmacist ascertains the needs of the patient and provides them with information required to effectively use medicines and/or therapeutic devices" [20] (p. 50). This interaction requires clinical knowledge and reasoning, as well as effective communication. There is substantial evidence, however, that the management of the diverse range of OTC enquiries encountered in community pharmacies is sub-optimal, and that this is mainly due to inadequate information gathering and/or advice or information provision by pharmacy personnel [1,26–29,31,32,41–46]. While there has been a number of interventions to improve the exchange of information between pharmacy personnel and consumers, with varying levels of success [47], there are also studies which show that pharmacy personnel are not complying with appropriate standards [26,29,41–43,45].

The aim of this study was to describe the development of a behaviour change intervention to enhance information exchange between pharmacy personnel and consumers during OTC enquiries in community pharmacies.

2. Materials and Methods

This study was the third phase of a larger project with the aim of enhancing the quality management of OTC consultations in community pharmacies (Figure 1).

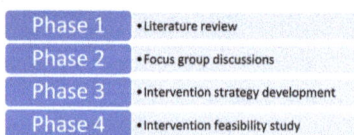

Phase 1	• Literature review
Phase 2	• Focus group discussions
Phase 3	• Intervention strategy development
Phase 4	• Intervention feasibility study

Figure 1. Project phases.

In the first phase, a systematic literature review identified interventions targeted towards improving communication between consumers and pharmacy personnel during OTC consultations in the community pharmacy setting [47]. Focus group discussions were then conducted to determine pharmacist, non-pharmacist pharmacy personnel and consumer perspectives regarding barriers and facilitators for information exchange during OTC consultations in community pharmacies [39]. The results from the first two phases identified that to enhance information exchange between pharmacy personnel and consumers during OTC enquiries, consumers needed to engage with the process. The methodology described in the Behaviour Change Wheel (BCW) [48] was subsequently used to develop an intervention strategy to target this behaviour.

Underpinning Theory

The BCW is a validated methodological framework developed from the synthesis of 19 behaviour change frameworks to assist researchers to apply the COM-B (Capability Opportunity Motivation—Behaviour) model of behaviour in any setting to develop an intervention strategy. The BCW identifies sources of behaviour in terms of the complex interactions between capability, opportunity and motivation.

The Theoretical Domains Framework (TDF) [49] was also applied in this study. The TDF is a validated derivation of the COM-B which identifies 14 domains that determine behaviour. In Table 1, the TDF domains are linked to source behaviours of COM-B. An analysis using TDF provides a more detailed understanding of determinants of behaviour from which an intervention strategy can be developed.

Table 1. Capability, opportunity, motivation–behaviour model (COM-B) linked with the Theoretical Domains Framework (TDF) domains.

COM-B Source Behaviour	TDF Domain
CAPABILITY	Skills (Cognitive and interpersonal; Physical) Knowledge Memory, attention and decision processes Behavioural regulation
OPPORTUNITY	Social influences Environmental context and resources
MOTIVATION	Social and professional role and identity Belief about capabilities Optimism Belief about consequences Intentions Goals Reinforcement Emotion

The BCW describes interventions in terms of nine functions: (i) education, (ii) persuasion, (iii) incentivisation, (iv) coercion, (v) training, (vi) restriction, (vii) environmental restructuring, (viii) modelling and (ix) enablement. A function of an intervention is an aspect of the intervention that influences behaviour. The BCW links intervention functions with behaviour change techniques (BCTs), which are the active components that can be used in the intervention strategy [50]. The BCTs are assessed against the APEASE (Affordability, Practicability, Effectiveness and cost effectiveness, Acceptability, Side-effects/safety, Equity) [51] criteria and to enable decisions on intervention content and delivery that are within the scope of the study.

In Phase 3, a 2-stage process was used to develop the intervention. In Stage 1, to fully understand the target behaviour, an independent duplicate (LS, KW) behavioural 'diagnosis' of consumer engagement with information exchange during OTC consultations was conducted, using themes from the focus groups undertaken in Phase 2 [39]. The researchers coded focus group themes to the COM-B model and TDF. The results were discussed with a psychologist experienced in pharmacy practice (L. Smith, see Acknowledgments) until consensus was reached. Independent duplicate (LS, KW) mapping of the key factors that influenced this behaviour to intervention functions and BCTs [48] was conducted (Stage 2). Disagreements were resolved by consensus and involvement of a third researcher, when required (RC). Options for the intervention were generated by the research team (LS, KW, LH, MW, RC) then rationalised (LS, KW) through assessment against the APEASE criteria [51] and discussion. The final intervention strategy was decided by consensus (LS, KW, LH, MW, RC).

3. Results

3.1. Stage 1: Behavioural Analysis

A behavioural diagnosis on the target behaviour, as described in the BCW and resulting COM-B and TDF coded themes from Phase 2 focus group discussions, was conducted (Table 2).

Table 2. Behavioural diagnosis using themes from focus group meetings.

COM-B and TDF *	Target Behaviour: Consumer Engaging in Information Exchange.		
	Barrier	Is There a Need for Change?	Intervention Function
PSYCHOLOGICAL CAPABILITY			
Knowledge	Consumers did not understand the role and responsibilities of pharmacists.	✓	
(An awareness of the existence of something) [52]	Consumers did not understand the qualifications of pharmacists.	✓	Education
	Consumers did not understand the risks of medicine use.	✓ Consumers do not perceive risks with OTC medicines. Consumers believe medicines available without prescription are safe.	
Cognitive and interpersonal skills	Pharmacy personnel consultation & communication skills	Improving these skills may improve interactions.	Training
(An ability or proficiency acquired through practice) [52]			
PHYSICAL OPPORTUNITY			
Environmental context and resources	Privacy is required for conversations.	✓ Discussing health can be a sensitive issue.	Training
(Any circumstance of a person's situation or environment that discourages or encourages the development of skills and abilities, independence, social competence, and adaptive behaviour) [52]	Pharmacy personnel should have time to engage in interactions	✓	Restriction
	Pharmacists were not always identifiable	✓	Environmental restructuring
	Appropriate remuneration for pharmacist consultations is required	✓	Enablement
	The environment should look like a professional/healthcare setting	Potentially yes. Some community pharmacies are very retail/warehouse/discount oriented.	
	The OTC consultation area is not always clearly identifiable	✓	
REFLECTIVE MOTIVATION			
Social and professional role and identity	Consumers did not trust the person asking questions	✓ Consumers do not know the role of the pharmacist	Education
(A coherent set of behaviours and displayed personal qualities of an individual in a social or work setting) [52]	Service between pharmacies and personnel is not consistent so consumers did not know what to expect	✓	Persuasion
			Modelling
Belief about capabilities	Consumers believed they are able to appropriately self-asses their condition before consultation	✓	Education
(Acceptance of the truth, reality, or validity about an ability, talent, or facility that a person can put to constructive use) [52]	Consumers did not believe pharmacy personnel were able to help with OTC enquiries	✓	Persuasion
			Modelling
			Enablement

Table 2. *Cont.*

Target Behaviour: Consumer Engaging in Information Exchange.

		√ Consumers engage in information exchange if they ask about a symptom but not if they ask for a specific product	√ Consumers do not know that pharmacy personnel are bound by privacy laws	
Belief about consequences (Acceptance of the truth, reality, or validity regarding outcomes of a behaviour in a given situation) [52]	Consumers did not understand the risks of medicine use			Education Persuasion Modelling
	Consumers did not know that being asked questions is for their benefit	√		
	Consumers did not know that their consultation information will be kept confidential		√	
Intentions (A conscious decision to perform a behaviour or a resolve to act in a certain way) [52]	Consumers expected to purchase an OTC product without exchanging information	√		Education Persuasion Incentivisation Coercion Modelling
	Consumers expected to answer questions if asking about a symptom		√	
	Consumers resisted information exchange if repeatedly requesting the same product		√	
AUTOMATIC MOTIVATION		√ If consumers exchange information and have a positive outcome as a result, this will subconsciously encourage information exchange behaviours in future consultations.		
Reinforcement (Increasing the probability of a response by arranging a dependent relationship, or contingency, between the response and a given stimulus) [52]	Consumers did not feel it necessary to be asked questions (not from focus group but an observation of the research group)			Training Incentivisation Coercion Environmental restructuring
Behavioural diagnosis of the relevant COM-B components	Psychological capability, physical opportunity, reflective and automatic motivation need to change in order for the target behaviour "consumer engaging in information exchange" to occur.			

* COM-B: Capability Opportunity Motivation—Behaviour model of behaviour; TDF: Theoretical Domains Framework.

3.2. Stage 2: Identify Intervention Options, Content and Implementation Options

Education, persuasion, environmental restructuring, and modelling were determined to be potential intervention functions (Table 3) that met the APEASE criteria.

Table 3. Linking intervention functions to Behaviour Change Techniques (BCTs).

Intervention Function	BCTs Identified to Enable Delivery of the Intervention Function	BCT Examples
Education	• Information about social and environmental consequences • Information about health consequences • Prompts/cues	Explain the role and responsibilities of the pharmacist. Explain the qualifications of the pharmacist. Explain the risks of OTC medicine use. Explain the confidentiality of personal information.
Persuasion	• Credible source • Information about health consequences	Inform consumers about positive health consequences from information exchange.
Environmental restructuring	• Adding objects to the environment • Prompts/cues	Pharmacy personnel to wear badges identifying their role. Provide cues/prompts for engaging in information exchange.
Modelling	• Demonstration of the behaviour	Demonstrate the type of questions that might be asked.

The BCTs identified to be able to deliver the four intervention functions are listed in Table 3 with examples of BCTs to address identified barriers.

3.3. Intervention Strategy

The research team discussed the results of the analysis and developed the intervention. Situational cues, in the form of a poster displayed in a community pharmacy (**environmental restructuring**), depicting consumers with OTC enquiries engaging in information exchange (**modelling**), highlighting the benefit of this behaviour (**persuasion**) and the reasons why it is important (**education**), were identified as the most appropriate intervention. A second poster depicting a pharmacist and information about the qualifications and role of a pharmacist was developed. An additional situational cue, in the form of a badge, was developed to be worn by pharmacy personnel to identify their position as either pharmacist or pharmacy assistant.

4. Discussion

This study described the development of an intervention strategy to enhance information exchange during OTC consultations. With the growing trend for self-care and the empowerment of consumers to make health decisions, it is essential that their safety is protected through the expertise available from pharmacists and other pharmacy personnel.

A systematic, theory-based approach was undertaken to fully understand the key components impacting information exchange.

The target of most interventions to date has been pharmacy personnel, with varying degrees of success [47]. Interventions targeting consumers have been neglected [47]. Through the systematic process, the behaviour of interest was identified to be information exchange and the consumer's engagement in information exchange was determined to be the target as there was a scarcity of interventions directed at the consumer.

The scope of this study was to derive an intervention to promote information exchange. The strength of this study lies in using a rigorously developed theory-based methodology for the systematic development of an intervention. The steps involved in the intervention development are described in detail, therefore making it reproducible.

Pharmacy **2018**, *6*, 117

5. Conclusions

A systematic, theoretically underpinned approach was applied to candidate interventions to promote information exchange in OTC consultations. The feasibility and efficacy of the intervention has since been tested and will be reported elsewhere.

Author Contributions: Conceptualization: L.J.S., L.H., M.C.W. and R.M.C.; methodology: L.J.S. and K.W.; writing original draft: L.J.S.; review and editing of manuscript: K.W., L.H., M.C.W. and R.M.C.

Funding: This research was funded by the Pharmaceutical Society of Western Australia J.M. O'Hara grant. MW was funded by the Health Foundation Improvement Science Fellowship.

Acknowledgments: The authors would like to thank Lorraine Smith for her assistance with understanding behaviours.

Conflicts of Interest: The authors declare no conflict of interest.

References

1. Collins, J.C.; Schneider, C.R.; Faraj, R.; Wilson, F.; De Almeida Neto, A.C.; Moles, R.J. Management of common ailments requiring referral in the pharmacy: A mystery shopping intervention study. *Int. J. Clin. Pharm.* **2017**, *39*, 697–703. [CrossRef] [PubMed]

2. Blenkinsopp, A.; Paxton, P.; Blenkinsopp, J. *Symptoms in the Pharmacy: A Guide to the Management of Common Illness*, 6th ed.; Blackwell Publishing Ltd.: Oxford, UK, 2009; ISBN 978-1-118-59844-3.

3. Boardman, H.; Lewis, M.; Croft, P.; Trinder, P.; Rajaratnam, G. Use of community pharmacies: A population-based survey. *J. Public Health* **2005**, *27*, 254–262. [CrossRef] [PubMed]

4. Benrimoj, S.I.; Frommer, M.S. Community pharmacy in Australia. *Aust. Health Rev.* **2004**, *28*, 238–246. [CrossRef] [PubMed]

5. Hibbert, D.; Bissell, P.; Ward, P.R. Consumerism and professional work in the community pharmacy. *Sociol. Health Illn.* **2002**, *24*, 46–65. [CrossRef]

6. Hughes, C.M.; McElnay, J.C.; Fleming, G.F. Benefits and risks of self medication. *Drug Saf.* **2001**, *24*, 1027–1037. [CrossRef] [PubMed]

7. Therapeutic Goods Administration Reasons for Scheduling Delegate's Final Decisions, June 2017. Available online: https://www.tga.gov.au/scheduling-decision-final/scheduling-delegates-final-decisions-june-2017 (accessed on 29 August 2017).

8. Association of the European Self-Medication Industry. Available online: http://www.aesgp.eu/facts-figures/otc-ingredients/#undefined (accessed on 24 October 2017).

9. US Food and Drug Administration. What Are Over-the-Counter (OTC) Drugs and How Are They Approved? Available online: https://www.fda.gov/aboutfda/transparency/basics/ucm194951.htm (accessed on 23 October 2017).

10. Khdour, M.R.; Hallak, H.O. Societal perspectives on community pharmacy services in West Bank—Palestine. *Pharm Pract.* **2012**, *10*, 17–24. [CrossRef]

11. Todd, A.; Copeland, A.; Husband, A.; Kasim, A.; Bambra, C. Access all areas? An area-level analysis of accessibility to general practice and community pharmacy services in England by urbanity and social deprivation. *BMJ Open* **2015**, *5*. [CrossRef] [PubMed]

12. Paola, S. "Convenience and Accessibility" An Evaluation of the First Pharmacist-Administered Vaccinations in WA Has Shown Positive Results for Patient and Practitioner. Available online: https://ajp.com.au/news/providing-convenience-accessibility/ (accessed on 24 October 2018).

13. Lam, B. How to Increase the Accessibility of Pharmacists When the Pharmacy Is Open. Available online: http://www.pharmaceutical-journal.com/news-and-analysis/event/how-to-increase-the-accessibility-of-pharmacists-when-the-pharmacy-is-open/20066487.article (accessed on 8 December 2017).

14. Bennadi, D. Self-medication: A current challenge. *J. Basic Clin. Pharm.* **2014**, *5*, 19–23. [CrossRef] [PubMed]

15. Fielding, S.; Slovic, P.; Johnston, M.; Lee Amanda, J.; Bond Christine, M.; Watson Margaret, C. Public risk perception of non-prescription medicines and information disclosure during consultations: A suitable target for intervention? *Int. J. Pharm. Pract.* **2018**. [CrossRef] [PubMed]

16. Roumie, C.; Griffin, M.R. Over-the-counter analgesics in older adults—A call for improved labelling and consumer education. *Drugs Aging* **2004**, *21*, 485–498. [CrossRef] [PubMed]

17. Calamusa, A.; Di Marzio, A.; Cristofani, R.; Arrighetti, P.; Santaniello, V.; Alfani, S.; Carducci, A. Factors that influence Italian consumers' understanding of over-the-counter medicines and risk perception. *Patient Educ. Couns.* **2012**, *87*, 395–401. [CrossRef] [PubMed]

18. Stosic, R.; Dunagan, F.; Palmer, H.; Fowler, T.; Adams, I. Responsible self-medication: Perceived risks and benefits of over-the-counter analgesic use. *Int. J. Pharm. Pract.* **2011**, *19*, 236–245. [CrossRef] [PubMed]

19. Mullan, J.; Weston Kathryn, M.; Bonney, A.; Burns, P.; Mullan, J.; Rudd, R. Consumer knowledge about over-the-counter NSAIDs: They don't know what they don't know. *Aust. N. Z. J. Public Health* **2017**, *41*, 210–214. [CrossRef] [PubMed]

20. Pharmaceutical Society of Australia. *Professional Practice Standards—Version 5—2017*; Pharmaceutical Society of Australia: Deakin West, Australia, 2017; ISBN 978-0-908185-05-4.

21. Pharmaceutical Society of Australia. *National Competency Standards Framework for Pharmacists in Australia 2016*; Pharmaceutical Society of Australia: Deakin West, Australia, 2016; ISBN 978-0-908185-03-0.

22. Bell, J.; Dziekan, G.; Pollack, C.; Mahachai, V. Self-Care in the twenty first century: A vital role for the pharmacist. *Adv. Ther.* **2016**, *33*, 1691–1703. [CrossRef] [PubMed]

23. World Health Organisation. The Role of the Pharmacist in Self-Care and Self-Medication. 4th WHO Consultative Group on the Role of the Pharmacist, Ed. 1998. Available online: http://apps.who.int/medicinedocs/en/d/Jwhozip32e/#Jwhozip32e (accessed on 14 September 2017).

24. Watson, M.C.; Johnston, M.; Entwistle, V.; Lee, A.J.; Bond, C.M.; Fielding, S. Using the theory of planned behaviour to develop targets for interventions to enhance patient communication during pharmacy consultations for non-prescription medicines. *Int. J. Pharm. Pract.* **2014**, *22*, 386–396. [CrossRef] [PubMed]

25. Watson, M.C.; Cleland, J.A.; Bond, C.M. Simulated patient visits with immediate feedback to improve the supply of over-the-counter medicines: A feasibility study. *Fam. Pract.* **2009**, *26*, 532–542. [CrossRef] [PubMed]

26. Watson, M.; Bond, C.; Grimshaw, J.; Johnston, M. Factors predicting the guideline compliant supply (or non-supply) of non-prescription medicines in the community pharmacy setting. *Qual. Saf. Health Care* **2006**, *15*, 53–57. [CrossRef] [PubMed]

27. Berger, K.; Eickhoff, C.; Schulz, M. Counselling quality in community pharmacies: Implementation of the pseudo customer methodology in Germany. *J. Clin. Pharm. Ther.* **2005**, *30*, 45–57. [CrossRef] [PubMed]

28. Rutter, P.M.; Horsley, E.; Brown, D.T. Evaluation of community pharmacists' recommendations to standardized patient scenarios. *Ann. Pharmacother.* **2004**, *38*, 1080–1085. [CrossRef] [PubMed]

29. Watson, M.C.; Hart, J.; Johnston, M.; Bond, C.M. Exploring the supply of non-prescription medicines from community pharmacies in Scotland. *Pharm. World Sci.* **2008**, *30*, 526–535. [CrossRef] [PubMed]

30. Krishnan, H.S.; Schaefer, M. Evaluation of the impact of pharmacist's advice giving on the outcomes of self-medication in patients suffering from dyspepsia. *Pharm. World Sci.* **2000**, *22*, 102–108. [CrossRef] [PubMed]

31. Schneider, C.R.; Everett, A.W.; Geelhoed, E.; Kendall, P.A.; Murray, K.; Garnett, P.; Salama, M.; Clifford, R.M. Provision of primary care to patients with chronic cough in the community pharmacy setting. *Ann. Pharmacother.* **2011**, *45*, 402–408. [CrossRef] [PubMed]

32. Schneider, C.R.; Everett, A.W.; Geelhoed, E.; Padgett, C.; Ripley, S.; Murray, K.; Kendall, P.A.; Clifford, R.M. Intern pharmacists as change agents to improve the practice of nonprescription medication supply: Provision of salbutamol to patients with asthma. *Ann. Pharmacother.* **2010**, *44*, 1319–1326. [CrossRef] [PubMed]

33. Queddeng, K.; Chaar, B.; Williams, K. Emergency contraception in Australian community pharmacies: A simulated patient study. *Contraception* **2011**, *83*, 176–182. [CrossRef] [PubMed]

34. Kippist, C.; Wong, K.; Bartlett, D.; Bandana, S. How do pharmacists respond to complaints of acute insomnia? A simulated patient study. *Int. J. Clin. Pharm.* **2011**, *33*, 237–245. [CrossRef] [PubMed]

35. Kelly, F.S.; Williams, K.A.; Benrimoj, S.I. Does advice from pharmacy staff vary according to the nonprescription medicine requested? *Ann. Pharmacother.* **2009**, *43*, 1877–1886. [CrossRef] [PubMed]

36. Watson, M.C.; Bond, C.M.; Grimshaw, J.M.; Mollison, J.; Ludbrook, A.; Walker, A.E. Educational strategies to promote evidence-based community pharmacy practice: A cluster randomized controlled trial. *Fam. Pract.* **2002**, *19*, 529–536. [CrossRef] [PubMed]

37. Watson, M.C.; Bond, C.M. The evidence-based supply of non-prescription medicines: Barriers and beliefs. *Int. J. Pharm. Pract.* **2004**, *12*, 65–72. [CrossRef]

38. Kaae, S.; Saleem, S.; Kristiansen, M. How do Danish community pharmacies vary in engaging customers in medicine dialogues at the counter—An observational study. *Pharm Pract. (Granada)* **2014**, *12*, 422. [CrossRef] [PubMed]

39. Seubert, L.J.; Whitelaw, K.; Boeni, F.; Hattingh, L.; Watson, M.C.; Clifford, R.M. Barriers and facilitators for information exchange during over-the-counter consultations in community pharmacy: A focus group study. *Pharmacy* **2017**, *5*, 65. [CrossRef] [PubMed]

40. Hanna, L.-A.; Hughes, C. 'First, do no harm': Factors that influence pharmacists making decisions about over-the-counter medication. *Drug Saf.* **2010**, *33*, 245–255. [CrossRef] [PubMed]

41. Watson, M.C.; Bond, C.M.; Johnston, M.; Mearns, K. Using human error theory to explore the supply of nonprescription medicines from community pharmacies. *Qual. Saf. Health Care* **2006**, *15*, 244–250. [CrossRef] [PubMed]

42. Schneider, C.R.; Everett, A.W.; Geelhoed, E.; Kendall, P.A.; Clifford, R.M. Measuring the assessment and counselling provided with the supply of non-prescription asthma reliever medication: A simulated patient study. *Ann. Pharmacother.* **2009**, *43*, 1512–1518. [CrossRef] [PubMed]

43. Schneider, C.R.; Emery, L.; Brostek, R.; Clifford, R.M. Evaluation of the supply of antifungal medication for the treatment of vaginal thrush in the community pharmacy setting: A randomized controlled trial. *Pharm. Pract. (Granada)* **2013**, *11*, 132–137. [CrossRef] [PubMed]

44. Benrimoj, S.I.; Werner, J.B.; Raffaele, C.; Roberts, A.S.; Costa, F.A. Monitoring quality standards in the provision of non-prescription medicines from Australian Community Pharmacies: Results of a national programme. *Qual. Saf. Health Care* **2007**, *16*, 354–358. [CrossRef] [PubMed]

45. Schneider, C.R.; Gudka, S.; Fleischer, L.; Clifford, R.M. The use of a written assessment checklist for the provision of emergency contraception via community pharmacies: A simulated patient study. *Pharm. Pract.* **2013**, *11*, 127–131. [CrossRef]

46. Watson, M.C.; Cleland, J.; Inch, J.; Bond, C.M.; Francis, J. Theory-based communication skills training for medicine counter assistants to improve consultations for non-prescription medicines. *Med. Educ.* **2007**, *41*, 450–459. [CrossRef] [PubMed]

47. Seubert, L.J.; Whitelaw, K.; Hattingh, L.; Watson, M.C.; Clifford, R.M. Interventions to enhance effective communication during over-the-counter consultations in the community pharmacy setting: A systematic review. *Res. Soc. Adm. Pharm.* **2017**. [CrossRef] [PubMed]

48. Michie, S.; Atkins, L.; West, R. *The Behaviour Change Wheel. A Guide to Designing Interventions*, 1st ed.; Silverback Publishing: Great Britain, UK, 2014; ISBN 978-1-291-84605-8.

49. Atkins, L.; Francis, J.; Islam, R.; O'Connor, D.; Patey, A.; Ivers, N.; Foy, R.; Duncan, E.M.; Colquhoun, H.; Grimshaw, J.M.; et al. A guide to using the Theoretical Domains Framework of behaviour change to investigate implementation problems. *Implement. Sci.* **2017**, *12*, 77. [CrossRef] [PubMed]

50. Michie, S.; Johnston, M. Behavior Change Techniques. In *Encyclopedia of Behavioral Medicine*; Gellman, M.D., Turner, J.R., Eds.; Springer: New York, NY, USA, 2013; pp. 182–187. ISBN 978-1-4419-1005-9.

51. Michie, S.; van Stralen, M.; West, R. The behaviour change wheel: A new method for characterising and designing behaviour change interventions. *Implement. Sci.* **2011**, *6*. [CrossRef] [PubMed]

52. Cane, J.; O'Connor, D.; Michie, S. Validation of the theoretical domains framework for use in behaviour change and implementation research. *Implement. Sci.* **2012**, *7*. [CrossRef] [PubMed]

MDPI

St. Alban-Anlage 66

4052 Basel

Switzerland

Tel. +41 61 683 77 34

Fax +41 61 302 89 18

www.mdpi.com

Pharmacy Editorial Office

E-mail: pharmacy@mdpi.com

www.mdpi.com/journal/pharmacy

www.ingramcontent.com/pod-product-compliance
Lightning Source LLC
Chambersburg PA
CBHW051908210326
41597CB00033B/6070